THIN
for
LIFE

THIN
for
LIFE

10 Keys to Success
from people who have
Lost Weight & Kept It Off

~

Anne M. Fletcher, M.S., R.D.

Foreword by Jane Brody

HOUGHTON MIFFLIN COMPANY
Boston   New York

For information about permission to reproduce
selections from this book, write to Permissions,
Houghton Mifflin Company, 215 Park Avenue South,
New York, New York 10003.

Visit our Web site: www.houghtonmifflinbooks.com.

Library of Congress Cataloging-in-Publication Data
Fletcher, Anne M.
Thin for life : 10 keys to success from people who
have lost weight and kept it off / by Anne M. Fletcher;
foreword by Jane Brody.
p. cm.
Includes index.
ISBN 0-618-19543-2
1. Reducing. 2. Reducing—Case studies. I. Title.
RM222.2.F536 1994
613.2'5—dc20 93-40218

Designed by Susan McClellan

Printed in the United States of America

QUM 10 9 8 7 6 5 4 3 2

Questionnaire in "Setting a Comfortable Weight Goal" adapted by permission of Kelly Brownell, Ph.D., from Brownell, K. D. and Wadden, T. A. (1992), Etiology and treatment of obesity: Understanding a serious, prevalent, and refractory disorder. *Journal of Consulting and Clinical Psychology,* 60 (4) p. 509. Copyright © The American Psychological Association, Inc.

Sections of "Are You Read?" adapted from *The Truth About Addiction and Recovery* by Stanton Peele, Ph.D., and Archie Brodsky with Mary Arnold, pages 203–5. Copyright © 1991 by Stanton Peele and Archie Brodsky with Mary Arnold. Reprinted by permission of Simon & Schuster, Inc.

"Reasonable Weight-Control Programs" from "Popular Diets for Weight Loss: From Nutritionally Hazardous to Healthful" by Dwyer, J. T. and Lu, D., in *Obesity: Theory and Therapy,* 2nd ed., edited by A. J. Stunkard and T. A. Wadden, pp. 237–52, Raven Press, Ltd.

"Caloric Values for 10 Minutes of Activity" reproduced with permission from *The LEARN Program for Weight Control,* by Kelly D. Brownell, Ph.D. Dallas: American Health Publishing Company, 1991. All rights reserved.

"Rosy Red Beet Dip," "Snow Peas and Carrots," and "No-Stir Five-Minute Risotto with Salmon" adapted from *Quick Harvest: A Vegetarian's Guide to Microwave Cooking* by Pat Baird, Prentice Hall, 1991.

Food lists and serving sizes in the Jump-Start Diet are based on the "Exchange Lists for Weight Management." Copyright © 1989 The American Diabetes Association and the American Dietetic Association.

For my husband and children,
whose support enabled me to write
Thin for Life

ACKNOWLEDGMENTS

FIRST, I WISH TO THANK THE HUNDREDS OF PEOPLE who shared their time, enthusiasm, recipes and, most important, their inspiring stories. My deep appreciation goes also to friends, relatives, weight-loss organizations and professionals who helped recruit the masters.

I am grateful to the weight-control experts who shared their time, opinions and expertise—notably Drs. Kelly Brownell, Susan Ross, Susan Olson, Daniel Kirschenbaum and John Foreyt. Also, Larry Lindner and Gail Zyla, of the *Tufts University Diet & Nutrition Letter*, were always available to give feedback and thoughtful advice at various stages of *Thin for Life*. Carla Chesley's recipe-testing skills and willingness to be "on call" were invaluable. I also want to thank Don Mauer for his time and contributions.

For her time and expertise, which she gives way beyond the call of duty, I am indebted to my agent, Chris Tomasino, with RLR Associates. And for her fine editing and wise ways, I thank my editor, Rux Martin. In addition, I appreciate editor-in-chief Barry Estabrook's tireless efforts on behalf of *Thin for Life*. Finally, I thank my special husband and sons for their infinite patience and support this past year.

AUTHOR'S NOTE

As with all diets and weight-loss programs, you should obtain your physician's permission and seek his or her supervision before and while following the diet, menu plans, recipes and/or advice in *Thin for Life*. This is particularly important if you have a medical problem, such as diabetes, high blood pressure or heart disease. A registered dietitian's counsel is advised as well. If you have psychological distress, such as serious depression or high stress in your life, you should see a psychologist or psychiatrist before following *Thin for Life*'s recommendations. The author and publisher disclaim any liability arising directly or indirectly from the use of *Thin for Life*.

All masters in *Thin for Life* have given their permission to share information about their weight histories. Some of their names have been changed to protect privacy and anonymity. Sometimes the masters' remarks were edited slightly for clarity.

CONTENTS

FOREWORD

PEOPLE WHO HAVE MET ME WITHIN THE LAST 25 YEARS find it hard to believe that I was once a third bigger than I am now. Like many women in their early 20s, I had become obsessed with weight and quite miserable about the extra pounds that had begun to clutter up my 5-foot frame. So, like millions of others in the same boat, I tried dieting. All kinds of diets. Many commercial programs and gimmicks and a few I made up on my own. And sure, I would lose weight, but then I'd gain it back—and usually some extra pounds to boot—when I got sick and tired of feeling deprived and living on eggs and grapefruit or cottage cheese and carrots or whatever happened to be the popular weight-loss concoction of the day.

Believe me, I tried them all—even the ridiculous drinking man's diet—and all they did was result in an ever-bigger me. As my girth expanded, I got increasingly desperate and tried starving all day and eating only one meal at night. But as soon as I put the first morsel of food in my mouth, I couldn't stop eating. Like the starved person I was, I ate and ate and ate until I would fall asleep, often with unchewed food still in my mouth. And like a starved person, I became increasingly undiscriminating about what I would eat, until I was living on an alternating intake of sweet foods and salty foods, all of questionable nutritional value. I had turned myself into a compulsive eater who knew the locations of every all-night grocery in town.

Then one day I panicked. I was fat. But even more important, I realized, I was probably killing myself with my atrocious eating habits. I vowed to turn over a new leaf. I decided that if I was going to be fat, so be it, but at least I could be healthy and fat.

I gave up diets and gimmicks and cycles of starving and binging, and I started eating: three wholesome meals, with wholesome snacks if I was hungry between meals, and one little "no-no" each day—two cookies, a couple of spoons of ice cream, a thin sliver of cake or pie—something I loved and did not want to miss. No deprivation, no starvation, no binging. Only moderation. And I put myself on a regular exercise program. Every day I would do something physically challenging: walking, cycling, skating, swimming, tennis—something that got me breathing hard (I kept thinking about how all that oxygen was restoring my cells to health) and feeling good about my body.

Losing weight wasn't part of this plan, but lose weight I did. Even though I was eating whenever I was hungry and consuming what felt like mountains of food, I lost weight: about 7 pounds the first month and then about 1 or 2 pounds a month thereafter, until my weight stabilized 2 years later at 35 pounds lighter. And there it has stayed, give or take 5 pounds here or there, for a quarter-century.

Once I dropped to a normal weight for my size, I had to come to terms with another common obsession: wanting to have a perfect body. I had to convince myself that I could be the best possible me without wanting to look like a fashion model (and if you could see what fashion models live on, you wouldn't want to look like one either). Of course, I could be thinner. I could stop snacking on cereal, bread and pretzels. I could refrain from splurging from time to time on ice cream or frozen yogurt. But in doing so, I could also risk the return of my old fixations on unhealthy foods and of the unwanted pounds that used to drag me down mentally and physically. I long ago decided that being perfect simply wasn't worth it. Besides, as I am writing this, I am in the middle of my 53rd year of life, and I know that people looking at my body find it hard to believe I'm a day over 40. That's largely because daily physical activity has remained an essential ingredient in my program, both for reasons of health and looks.

I know I would have been a lot happier had this book existed 28 years ago when I was a chunky 24-year-old. In *Thin for Life*, Anne M. Fletcher has produced a weight-control program that can work for anyone and everyone who is really ready to give up on quick gimmicks and false promises about weight loss, anyone who is at least as serious about health as about weight—in other words, anyone with an ounce of good sense. Anne's program is not a prescription, it's an approach that can be molded to individual lifestyles and temperaments. It promises only that you can lose weight, not how much you will lose or how fast.

In fact, trying to lose weight fast is probably the single biggest mistake dieters make. Weight that comes off quickly nearly always comes back on even faster. You didn't gain those extra pounds in a fortnight, and you shouldn't be trying to take them off in two weeks, or even necessarily in two months or two years. The idea is to adopt an eating and exercise plan that you can go on and can stay on for the rest of your life, a program that will allow you to lose weight slowly, tone up your body gradually and eventually stabilize at a weight and shape that is right for you.

Thin for Life can lead you down the path of sensible weight control. Anyone faced with a weight problem, and especially anyone who has tried and failed one or more times to lose unwanted pounds and keep them off, should read this book, digest its message and start on a new road to a healthy and practical weight.

—Jane Brody
Pesonal Health columnist
The New York Times

INTRODUCTION

I'VE LONG BEEN FOND of a cartoon posted on my office wall of a man, his head in the shape of a book, sitting on a physician's examining table. The physician asks him, "So, how long has this book been in your head?" And so it goes with many authors who toy with an idea for many years before it comes to fruition. Such was the case with *Thin for Life*, which has been in my head for more than 10 years—from the time I counseled overweight patients at an obesity program in Massachusetts. Despite the fact that so many of the people I worked with lost and regained their weight, I knew that success stories had to be out there. Over the years, I collected more and more facts to support my premise.

In *Thin for Life*, I set out to prove that people really can lose weight and keep it off. I'd grown weary of conflicting messages we receive about our society's terrible weight problem (and the constant push for all of us to be slim and fit), yet the hopelessness of trying to lose weight and keep it off. I decided it was time to stop hearing about all the horror stories of people who gain weight back, and instead, to start learning about the many individuals who have found success. In a short time, I located 160 masters at weight control—people who had lost at least 20 pounds and kept the weight off for a minimum of 3 years. Most of them more than met the criteria, and their responses far exceeded my expectations.

They shared inspiring stories that offer a strong message of encouragement, whether you want to lose just a small amount of weight or a lot. (In my experience, some of those who want to lose 10 or 20 pounds suffer just as much as those who struggle with larger amounts of weight.) The principles of *Thin for Life* will help you get a handle on your weight problem regardless of your size.

Thin for Life is the first book to weave together research-based methods of weight maintenance with tried-and-true practices of masters at weight control. The "10 Keys to Success" encapsulate the critical steps that the masters have taken to become thin for life. *Who better to tell you how to lose weight permanently than the very people who have done it?* Many were eager to tell their stories to help others:

• Peppi S., master of 62 pounds: "If I can be of help to someone who was like me before I lost weight, feeling despair and as if I couldn't get through another day, then I have been truly successful."

• Nancy K., master of 60 pounds: "I am open to sharing my story to help other people lose weight. I was heavy during my high school and college years. It affected me greatly, and I feel for anyone who is heavy and unhappy about it."

• Paul A., master of 51 pounds: "I would be happy to be interviewed by you, as I feel there are plenty of men out there who feel that weight loss can be achieved by running around the block after a major feast."

• Holly L., master of 97 pounds: "I sincerely hope that you can use my story to encourage other kindred spirits to live a carefree, healthy lifestyle, away from the burden of being overweight."

It doesn't matter if you've lost weight before and gained it all back, because most of the masters didn't make it the first, second or even the third time around either. You don't have to starve, buy fancy foods or potions or stay away from sweets and so-called "junk" foods. And no, you don't have to turn into an exercise fanatic. *Thin for Life* demonstrates the sensible, livable approaches the masters take to control their weight.

In telling the masters' stories, I am not saying that what any one master does is the "best" way to go about weight control. I'm simply telling you what worked for these people, whose approaches are highly individual. One of the goals of *Thin for Life* is to guide you to find what is right *for you.*

Although *Thin for Life* is based on a survey of masters at weight control, it is not a scientific study. My intent is to prove that the masters do indeed exist and to show you exactly what they have done to win the weight battle.

THIN
for
LIFE

I

Believe That You Can Become Thin for Life

THEY'RE OUT THERE—THE MASTERS AT WEIGHT CONTROL. They're people who have lost a lot of weight and kept it off for a long time. They may be people you've known for years who once had other lives as much heavier people.

Tim H. is one of them. I'd seen him around town—a big guy, but good-looking: muscular-big. I never would have dreamed that 7 years ago, he carried around an extra 40 pounds. Then there's my former neighbor Tami B., a pretty brown-haired slip of a woman who, for 6 years, has kept more than 35 pounds off her tiny 5'1" frame. Doug S. is a master too. Before I met him in person, I often talked to him on the phone when he called to speak with my husband. When I finally came face to face with Doug—the man my husband described as one of the best players in his "A-level" racquetball league—I found it hard to believe that he once weighed more than 300 pounds!

I *knew* the masters were out there; I just didn't know how many of them there really were. In a short period of time, I was able to locate 160 masters at weight control, all of whom have managed to keep off at least 20 pounds for a minimum of 3 years. *The story gets even better:*

- 7 out of 10 of them have lost 40 pounds or more.
- More than half have lost 50 pounds or more; the weight loss for the entire group averaged 63 pounds.

◆ 20 people have lost 100 pounds or more. Not only that, but most masters have been maintaining that loss for more than 3 years.

◆ Well over half have maintained at least a 20-pound loss for 5 or more years.

◆ More than one-third have maintained it for 10-plus years.

◆ 12 people have maintained it for 20 or more years.

Their stories will help you believe in your own power to lose weight and keep it off forever. Permanent weight loss may seem like a long shot, particularly when you hear over and over that just about everyone who loses weight gains it all back—and then some. Indeed, as far back as 1958, renowned obesity expert Albert J. Stunkard, M.D., concluded, "Most obese persons will not stay in treatment . . . Of those who stay in treatment most will not lose weight and of those who do lose weight, most will regain it." And just recently, a journal for physicians stated that even in professionally run research programs for weight loss, participants usually lose just 10 percent of their weight. According to the same article, "One-third to two-thirds of the weight is regained within 1 year, and almost all is regained within 5 years."

As Roseanne Barr Arnold once warned (before her most recent weight-loss attempt), "Do not even try goin' on no diet because you ain't gonna lose no weight and even if you do, you're gonna gain the whole damn thing back!" How can you hope to have any hope with "failure talk" like this?

You *can* have hope because, as obesity expert Daniel S. Kirschenbaum, Ph.D., puts it, "There are many thousands of people who are success stories." As Director of the Center for Behavioral Medicine in Chicago and as an affiliate of Northwestern University School of Medicine, he has worked with hundreds of them. Dr. Kirschenbaum is one of many experts I interviewed who believes the odds against losing weight and keeping it off are *not* so grim.

The 160 masters I found are living proof that it can be done. Theresa D., who is 5'4" tall and has kept off 28 pounds for 5 years, says, "People need to realize that it isn't impossible to lose weight. I am 100 percent behind your efforts to help people realize that they *can* do it."

In talking with masters again and again, I saw connecting threads in the stories of all people who have lost weight and kept it off. *Thin for Life* weaves together these common themes with the findings of scientific studies on weight maintenance and presents them as Keys to Success. Whether you want to lose 10 pounds or 100 pounds, the Keys—presented in the masters' own stories and words—will enable you to master *your* weight problem.

They Break the Rules

A S I READ letter after letter and talked with person after person, it struck me that many of the masters break many of the "rules" or commonly held notions about weight control and maintenance. What are these notions and how do the masters challenge them?

◆ **Myth # 1: If you've been overweight since childhood, it's next to impossible to lose weight and keep it off.**

About 45 percent of the masters I interviewed indicated that they'd been heavy since childhood. Close to another quarter of them gained weight as teenagers. Says master Joe M., "I was always extremely overweight as a child and teenager. I do remember weighing at least 300 pounds as a senior in high school." Joe, whose height is 6'2", now weighs 175 and has for the past 19 years. (For a discussion of genetic and metabolic contributors to a weight problem, see "If You're Fat, It May Not Be Your Fault—But That Doesn't Mean You Can't Do Something About It" on page 29.)

◆ **Myth # 2: If you've dieted and failed many times before, there's little hope of ever licking your weight problem.**

Most masters at weight control didn't make it the first time around. On the contrary, nearly 60 percent of them had tried to lose weight at least five times before they were finally successful; close to another 20 percent had dieted three or four times before they finally got it right. This finding is supported by research studies on successful maintainers. Alyce C. is a good example of someone who tried nearly everything—from Metrecal to Overeaters Anonymous to diet pills. Finally she came up with her own weight-loss plan, one that was right for her. Since then she's maintained a 90-pound loss for 20 years. (She's 5'8" and weighs 130.) (Chapter III, "Do It Your Way," shows how you can learn from your past attempts and use them to launch yourself to long-term success.)

◆ Myth # 3: If you do succeed at losing weight and keeping it off, you'll have to eat like a bird for the rest of your life.

It's quite the opposite: most masters eat several meals a day, often with snacks in between. Many told me they really don't deny themselves any foods—including sweets and snack foods. They eat what they want, but in moderation. In the words of Irene S., who started losing her 77 pounds in 1989 (she's 5'4", weighs 153 and is still dropping), "If I want pie or cake or whatever, I have a controlled amount and that's it!" (Chapter IV, "Accept the Food Facts," tells how masters come to grips with a new way of eating and how they learn to control their craving for foods they don't want to give up.)

◆ Myth # 4: In order to lose weight and keep it off, you have to become an exercise fanatic.

Although most masters at weight control do exercise much more than typical people (North Americans, in general, are quite sedentary), there aren't many who engage in extreme forms. My survey, as well as research studies, suggest that what's most important about exercise is *the consistency with which it's done*—that is, making it a regular part of your life. About 70 percent of the 160 masters told me they exercise three or more times a week. But only about 16 percent of them do so every day. Walking is the most popular form of exercise. Surprisingly, 15 masters (about 9 percent) said they don't exercise at all. Exercise is extremely important for the vast majority of people who want to lose weight and keep it off, but it's encouraging to know that it is possible to be successful if you don't want to or can't exercise. (In Chapter VII, "Move It to Lose It," you'll learn how to customize your own physical-activity program, one you can live with for the rest of your life.)

◆ Myth # 5: It's really hard to lose weight once you pass the age of 40.

I was surprised at the number of masters who lost their weight when they were older than 40. Holly L., for instance, started to lose her 97 pounds at age 69. And Jean B. started losing her 45 pounds in 1985, when she was 52. (Her weight's still going down.) Currently at 164 pounds (she's 5'5"), she lost the weight slowly, so, she says, "I won't wrinkle any faster than I have to—and I'm keeping it off. I'll probably lose another 30 pounds over the next 5 years, but I'll stay healthy so I can be a nice grandma."

◆ Myth # 6: You can't lose weight on your own, let alone maintain weight loss.

Masters are quite evenly split between those who lost weight on their own and those who said they found success with formal weight-loss programs and self-help groups. The vast majority of masters maintain their weight loss without the support of a group. Remember, though, that most masters had made many previous attempts at weight loss, often through structured programs. It's likely that the valuable approaches gleaned from these programs contributed to their eventual success. That's how Suzanne T. lost the 70 pounds that she's kept off for 4 years. (She's 5'3" and weighs 150.) She had been to Weight Watchers in the past, but when she lost weight once and for all, she did it on her own—following the "basic Weight Watchers plan," coupled with exercise. "I did not go to Weight Watchers meetings," she maintains; "I followed their basic ideas." (Chapter III tells how you can find a weight-loss approach that's right for you.)

◆ Myth # 7: If you hit a plateau while losing weight, there's little hope of moving on.

In fact, a good number of masters lost weight in stages, over a period of years rather than weeks or months. More than a quarter took longer than a year; some are still losing. Joy B., who became overweight as a child, lost 20 pounds her junior year in high school and kept it off. (Her peak weight was over 150 pounds; she's 5'1½".) "Then, after 10 more years of struggling," she admits, "I took off another 10-plus pounds." Anna has held her weight at about 115 for the past 4 years. (See page 73 for the discussion "Give Yourself Time.")

• Myth # 8: If you start regaining weight, you're bound to gain it all back.

The most striking finding of my survey is that the masters of weight control have learned to catch themselves when they start to regain weight: 98 percent of them keep their weight within a 10-pound range. Most have a specific plan of action if their weight creeps up. Bonnie R., who's been a weight-control master for 18 years (she's kept 53 pounds off her 5'1" body), maintains her weight within a 1-to-5-pound range. If her weight climbs, she stops snacking, finds healthful substitutes and tries to determine what is causing her to put on the pounds. She says, "I stay conscious of what I gain and never let myself forget my 'being heavy' experience. I refuse to do that to myself again—ever!" (Chapter V, "Nip It in the Bud," helps you design a plan for stopping small weight gains before they get out of hand.)

• Myth # 9: If you don't stay at your original weight goal, then you're a failure.

About one-third of the masters in *Thin for Life* have settled for a maintenance weight that is somewhat higher than their original goal. Chuck F., who stays around 140 to 145, explains, "I realized that my earlier goal of 135 was unrealistically hard to maintain." (He's 5'6" and has kept off 62 pounds for 10 years.) Many masters expressed the same sentiment. Some have regained a portion of the original weight they lost, but they are still significantly thinner than before. I consider them success stories because they're happier and healthier now than they were at their maximum weights. Lisa B. is a good example. She hit 385, her highest weight ever, in 1985. She dropped all the way down to 140—quite low for someone who is 5'8" tall. She's regained about 30 pounds but can now proudly say, "I wanted to get to my lowest low (140 pounds), but it took so much to get to where I am.

And I'm truly happy with my appearance. I'm a size 14. I'm thrilled!" (Chapter II, "Take the Reins," shows how to set your own livable, realistic weight goal and how to accept a less-than-perfect body.)

The list could go on. Masters have overcome other challenges that should put them at odds with becoming thin for life. They've maintained their weight loss through quitting smoking, having babies, losing jobs, dealing with alcohol problems, marital strife and more.

How Did I Know I'd Find the Masters?

M Y OWN INTEREST in weight maintenance began 10 years ago when I was a clinical nutritionist and assistant director of a sophisticated weight-loss program called the New England Institute of Nutrition and Health. I became discouraged, however, because although we employed what were believed to be state-of-the-art techniques for helping people with weight control, more often than not our patients would regain the pounds they'd worked so hard to lose.

Then I came across a 1982 report by veteran obesity expert Stanley Schachter, Ph.D., of Columbia University, arguing that "obesity's reputation for intractability" is grossly exaggerated. After interviewing 161 individuals, Dr. Schachter found that of the 46 people who had a history of obesity (which he defined rather stringently as being 15 percent or more overweight), 25 were no longer fat. On average, they had lost about 35 pounds and had maintained their losses for 11 years. Dr. Schachter also analyzed the heaviest people in the group and found that of those who were once more than 30 percent overweight, about 64 percent were classified as "successful cures." On average, they'd lost around 47 pounds and had remained within a few pounds of their current weight for approximately 8½ years.

Dr. Schachter's findings were soon confirmed by psychologists in the professional journal *Addictive Behaviors*. In just a few months, using advertisements in newspapers and on radio and television in the Phoenix, Arizona, area alone, Robert Colvin, Ph.D., and Susan Olson, Ph.D., tracked down 41 women who had lost and kept off an average of 53 pounds for 6 years. They also located 13 men who had maintained an average 76-pound loss for about the same period of time.

Why the "Failure Talk"?

W HY THE GRIM STATISTICS on weight maintenance? I posed this very question to renowned Yale University obesity expert Kelly Brownell, Ph.D., when I first met him in 1984. Dr. Brownell contends that one reason for the depressing statistics is that they are based on the individuals who are likely to be the "hard-core" over-weight—people with the most to lose who have failed many times over. Because they've had so much trouble with their weight, they may be drawn to university-based research studies. In contrast, people who are successful—particularly those who lose weight on their own—tend not to wind up in research studies from which the statistics are derived.

I don't mean to suggest that there aren't success stories from re-search-based weight-loss programs, because there are. But the problem with scientific studies is that they usually report averages that may blot out the cases of success. Consider a study by Thomas Wadden, Ph.D., of Syracuse University, and Albert Stunkard, M.D., that compared the long-term effect of three different weight-loss approaches in a group of women and men. Regardless of the type of treatment, at the end of 3 years, most of the people had gained back most of their weight. The authors of the study noted, however, that 6 of the 45 individuals in the study showed "perfect maintenance" of weight loss 3 years after treatment. Typically, though, you don't hear about the success sto-ries—what's reported is the discouraging *average* weight loss of a group like this.

Another problem with drawing broad conclusions from research studies is that the weight-loss methods are selected by experimenters and are similar for every participant in any one segment of a study. More often than not, however, the masters lose weight by coming up with their own personal plans, which vary from person to person. The common research approach for weight loss has been to take a group of heavy people (the "hard core") and try various treatments (for exam-ple, very-low-calorie diets, behavior modification and/or exercise) to see how they work. Too little attention is paid to long-term follow-up and support of the successful losers in the critical maintenance phase after they've lost the weight. Then, when most people fail, it's concluded that almost no one succeeds at weight loss.

There is surprisingly little research on weight maintenance, and much of that research is less than a decade old. Hard to believe, in view of the fact that 1 out of 4 Americans is significantly overweight, that obesity is a serious medical problem and that by 1995, Americans will spend $40.7 billion annually on weight-loss products and services. "The demand for long-term studies continues, and the number of published studies declines," state Drs. Brownell and Wadden. Research on long-term weight loss is difficult and frustrating, requiring large numbers of people who must be studied for a long time—not very enticing to a young Ph.D. who lives under the "publish-or-perish" gun and must write multiple research articles in a short time period to keep his or her job.

Switching Gears to Find Success

ALL OF THIS SUGGESTED to me that we've been looking for success in the wrong places and going about research in the wrong way. Why not study the people who are the real experts at weight control—those who have succeeded at losing weight and keeping it off? Why not closely examine what the masters do to keep weight off forever? Not only did I find my own group of masters, but I found even more support—from some little-known studies—for my theory that far more people are successful at weight control than we're led to believe:

• University of Minnesota researcher Robert W. Jeffery, Ph.D., sent me a study for which he and a colleague located 64 people who had lost an average of 51 pounds and kept them off for an average of 30 months.

• In an old file, I came across a mention of an unpublished doctoral dissertation by Susan Ross, Ed.D, R.D., of 23 successful maintainers who had lost at least 20 pounds and kept them off for at least 1 year. Ross discovered that 15 of the people had lost 40 or more pounds and that the same number had maintained that loss for at least 3 years.

• A 1992 study on successful dieters, conducted at the University of Iowa College of Medicine, located 82 people who had kept off a significant amount of weight for an average of 4½ years. On average, the men had lost 53 pounds, and the women had lost 60 pounds.

◆ In a recent nationwide survey of 541 of its leaders, Weight Watchers International found that they had been at or near their goal weights for an average of 6 years. On average, they've lost nearly 50 pounds.

◆ A 1993 *Consumer Reports* survey of some 19,000 readers who had used commercial diet programs revealed that about one-fourth of them kept off more than two-thirds of their weight, on average, 2 years after completing the programs. That's more than 4,700 people.

Like many of the masters I spoke to, master Ann F. refused to let the "failure talk" get in her way. "Don't pay attention to the odds," she advises. "It's a terrible burden on people to hear that you can't do it— if you think you can't, you won't. You have to ignore people who say you can't do it. I had a terrible weight problem. It wasn't easy; I'm not a superwoman. But I did it." What she did was drop from her all-time high of 380 pounds (she's 5'7½") to a weight of about 160 (she fluctuates from 140 to 170), which she has maintained for nearly 10 years.

Who Are the Masters?

THE MASTERS IN *Thin for Life* come from all walks of life. Quite a few are secretaries, teachers and retired people. One is a state senator. They include psychologists, homemakers, lawyers, repairmen, writers, a former showgirl and even a chocolate scientist. How did I find them all? It wasn't hard. Many came my way by word of mouth. In addition, I sent public service announcements to newspapers in many different cities and towns.

Friends and relatives across the country posted flyers about my project in public places like supermarkets and health clubs. Finally, I approached major weight-loss organizations, including Weight Watchers, Health Management Resources (HMR), Nutri/System, Diet Center, Jenny Craig Weight Loss Centres, Take Off Pounds Sensibly (TOPS) and Overeaters Anonymous (OA) for "success" stories. Wherever I turned, I found masters.

What Exactly Is Maintenance?

F OR SOME PEOPLE, maintenance means sticking to a set number on the scale. For others, it's being able to fit in one size of clothing. For the vast majority of masters, however, maintenance means keeping weight within a defined range, most often 1 to 5 pounds.

But maintenance is not just reaching your weight goal. As weight-maintenance expert Michael G. Perri, Ph.D., of the University of Florida, stresses, "Maintenance means much more than *weight* maintenance. It includes the maintenance of other healthy lifestyle behaviors, such as healthy eating patterns, exercise, reducing stress, keeping healthy relationships and more."

I often encountered an all-too-common scenario with my former patients. After weeks or months of dieting, they'd see the scale drop to the number they'd been shooting for. Then, after a few weeks, they would cancel their appointments and tell me that they were fine and "knew what to do." I would call them at several-month intervals to see how they were doing and learn that slowly—but surely—the weight was coming back. Or they wouldn't return my calls, and I'd see them a year later in the supermarket or at a restaurant, just as heavy as before. Why does this happen?

"If you spent six months getting in shape by jogging and lifting weights, how long would you expect the positive effects to last after you'd stopped?" responded Dr. Thomas Wadden, currently director of Syracuse University's Center for Health and Behavior, when I posed the question to him. "Exercise training doesn't last three years later. You have to keep practicing the good habits—or you lose the skills." Master Kerry K. now realizes that. He says that after he lost 100 pounds in 1986 (with the help of Health Management Resources), "I thought I knew it all: exercise, decrease fats, keep food records." But he left the program sooner than was recommended, and over the course of the next 4 years, he gained back half of his weight. "I learned that I didn't learn enough," he says. He went back to HMR and lost weight again, this time staying in the program long enough to learn the critical skills for maintenance. All in all, he's kept 83 pounds off his 5'10" frame for about 5 years.

While you are losing weight, you're in what Dr. Kirschenbaum and his colleagues at Northwestern University Medical School call the "honeymoon stage." You're enthusiastic, optimistic and consistent—a veritable tower of strength. It feels good to take control of a problem, and you delight in seeing the numbers on the scale drop.

But just as in marriage, the honeymoon doesn't last forever. As blues singer B.B. King would say, "The thrill is gone." Often my patients would implore, "If I could just get 'it' back. It was so easy before." This is the frustration stage, a "poor me" frame of mind, when you feel resentful that you have to keep working at it and that you can't go back to your old eating habits. The masters at weight control have accepted this reality and decided it's worth the effort. After maintaining a 32-pound weight loss for 5 years, Liane F. still struggles. She says, "It's the hardest thing I've ever done in my life for myself, but it is also the *very, very* most rewarding thing ever. I love being able to wear so many styles of clothing."

Most masters, however, seem to have moved past the frustration stage into what Dr. Kirschenbaum terms the "tentative acceptance stage." They have a peaceful sense of resolve most of the time: it's not so hard to maintain weight anymore, but there's a tendency to gain some weight in certain situations—say, on vacation, during illness or over the holidays, or after an injury that interferes with exercising. As indicated in Chapter V, however, most masters quickly get a handle on the situation and nip the weight gain in the bud.

Some reach Dr. Kirschenbaum's final stage, "lifestyle change." They are confident they'll never gain the weight back and know what works and what doesn't work for them. Food is less of an emotional issue— they handle life's problems without turning to food, and they even maintain their healthful eating and exercise habits when vacationing. As Kerry K. told me, keeping his weight off does entail a tremendous amount of energy and work. But he insists the effort is minuscule compared with the pain of being at his old, heavy weight of 282.

If You're Fat, It May Not Be Your Fault—

But That Doesn't Mean You Can't Do Something About It,

I T MAKES ME ANGRY when I hear it said that heavy people "just eat too much." It supports the prevailing notion that people become fat from gluttony and lack of willpower; it implies that if you just tried a little harder, it would be so easy to lose weight. It *is* true that if you're overweight, you're eating more calories than your body needs to maintain a healthy weight. But is it really a fact that overweight people eat more than their normal-weight counterparts? In some cases, the answer is yes, but in many cases it's no.

Experts who work with overweight people report that some of their patients eat a great deal, sometimes in private. *But I believe that the majority of overweight people are not gluttonous.* A good number of studies suggest that obese individuals consume no more daily calories than do people of normal weight.

It's important to note, however, that studies cannot detect subtle differences in calorie intake that can really add up. For example, if you were to consume just 30 calories more per day than your body needs to maintain your weight—say, by adding an extra teaspoon of nondiet mayonnaise, salad dressing or margarine to your food—you'd gain about 30 pounds in 10 years' time. But even if there are such subtle differences in calorie intake, they don't seem to be great enough to explain the degree of overweight in many people.

◆ Why are some people fat, but not others?

The answer, according to a recent survey of 50 physicians and scientists involved in obesity research, is, in large part, "genetic factors." In other words, the tendency to become overweight is inherited. How do we know it's genetic? Isn't it just as likely that you become overweight because you learned bad eating habits or a sedentary way of life from your parents?

One way researchers have attempted to answer this "nature-versus-nurture" question is by studying people who were adopted as infants to see if their adult weights are more similar to weights of their adoptive parents or of their biological parents. Several studies of this sort have revealed that the weights of adoptees are far more similar to those of their biological parents than to those of their adoptive parents. One study suggested that you're more likely to inherit obesity than most medical and psychiatric disorders.

Another way to determine whether there's an inherited tendency to become overweight is to compare weights of identical twins (who have the same genes) with nonidentical twins (who share no more genetic heredity than siblings). Again, studies reveal that the genetic influence is powerful: identical twins have been found to be twice as likely to have similar body weights as nonidentical twins. One study showed that weights of identical twins raised apart were essentially the same as those of identical twins raised together, again suggesting that weight is determined more by genetic than environmental factors.

• The genes you inherit appear to determine not only whether you're likely to become overweight but how efficient your body is at processing calories.

Studies suggest that while one person may need 2,300 calories a day to maintain her weight, another of the same weight, height, age and activity level may require just 1,500 calories. As one of my former Cornell professors once said, "Some people seem to have more of an ability to 'waste' calories," while others convert them to body fat.

• Could it be that differences in calorie needs are the result of chronic dieting?

Indeed, it is known that dieting can lower your metabolic rate, at least temporarily. That is, if you cut back on calories, your body protects itself from this state of semi-starvation by slowing down the rate at which it burns food. According to a landmark study published in the *New England Journal of Medicine*, however, many people probably have sluggish metabolism *before* they become heavy. Researchers with the National Institutes of Health kept track of weights and metabolic rates of a group of Pima Indians (a population prone to obesity) over the course of 2 to 4 years and found that people who gained the most weight by the end of the study burned significantly fewer calories at the beginning than did people who gained less or no weight. This study also suggested that slow metabolic rates tend to run in families.

♦ So what if you come from a heavy family— and you're a slow burner who doesn't need many calories? Are you doomed to become heavy and doomed to stay that way?

Not according to Gary D. Foster, M.S., of the University of Pennsylvania School of Medicine's Obesity Research Group. In *The Weight Control Digest,* he points out, "Obesity is *not* a trait like eye color, which is determined at the moment of conception and does not change. A *tendency* for obesity is inherited. This tendency needs to have an environment that will nurture its development *before* it becomes a reality. . . . Remember, your heredity is not your destiny! All of the researchers agree: providing an environment of low-fat foods and increased physical activity can stifle even the most stubborn genes."

Several years ago, I had the opportunity to meet with Arlen Price, Ph.D., a geneticist at the University of Pennsylvania. He did some studies on identical twins confirming that if one twin is overweight, it's highly likely that the other will be. "But," Dr. Price told me, "there is great variation in the degree of overweight of twin siblings. One brother might only be 20 percent overweight, while his identical twin is 40 percent overweight." The implication is that, even if you are genetically "programmed" to be overweight, you have control over how overweight you will become or remain, depending on how you eat and how active you are. Such was the case with master Kevin C. Part of what spurred him to do something about his long-standing weight problem was recognizing that he had become 50 pounds heavier than his identical twin brother who had always been the more physically active of the two. (Kevin managed to lose 45 pounds and has kept it off for 7 years.)

The masters at weight control are living proof that weight destiny need not be controlled by your genes or by the fact that you're a "slow-burner." Yet the studies on genetic and metabolic causes of overweight provide an understanding of why it's harder for some masters to control their weight than others, and they help to explain why many comfortably settle in at weights higher than their original goals. The studies also give insight about why so many people lose weight and gain it back. The masters are those who have learned how to "stifle" their genetic legacy.

What Have You Got to Lose?

LOSING WEIGHT can help you get rid of a lot of health "baggage." In fact, a good number of masters report a health-related reason as the primary motivation for losing weight when they finally did it once and for all. Many of them now report feeling good not only about the way they look but about the way they feel.

You may already know the positive health consequences of losing weight: it can help lower blood pressure, blood cholesterol and blood sugar. One study suggests that for each 10 percent drop in body weight, the incidence of heart disease decreases by 20 percent.

A number of the masters also report relief from the emotional pain of being heavy in a society that, rightly or wrongly, reveres thinness. Master Jeffrey B. (he's kept off 55 pounds for 22 years) reports that when you're overweight, "people you don't even know feel free to comment on your size. Friends want to advise you to lose weight 'for your own good.' " He recalls a friend who, when advising him to lose some weight, said, "You'd look better, you'd feel better." Jeffrey asked her where she "got off" talking to him that way if she was his friend. He said to her, "I'll make you a deal—you get a nose job, and I'll lose 50 pounds." After she expressed her indignation, he replied, "Well, you'd look better, you'd feel better."

But not everyone is as forthright as Jeffrey. A recent report in *The New York Times* describes a heavy woman who has endured strands of spaghetti being thrown in her face, pig sounds and comments like "wide load." Some comedians mercilessly poke fun at heavy people, and certain tabloids have no qualms about making spectacles of celebrities who have lost and regained weight.

When I asked Dr. Susan Olson, currently director of psychological services at the Southwest Bariatric Nutrition Center in Scottsdale, Arizona, why, in our climate of political correctness, overweight people are still fair game, she replied, "People see it as a willpower issue. You can't change the color of your skin, but they think being fat has to do with being lazy and a lack of control."

The Anti-Dieting Movement

THIS DISCRIMINATION AGAINST HEAVY PEOPLE—coupled with the information about the inherited aspect of weight problems—has spurred a strong anti-dieting movement. Even some experts argue that continually pressuring overweight individuals to lose weight does more harm than good. The anti-dieting movement also decries the gain-lose-gain (yo-yo dieting) syndrome and the emphasis our society places on physical appearance.

Certain aspects of the anti-dieting movement are laudable, moving people away from unrealistic body images and getting them off the dieting merry-go-round. It is true that several studies have suggested that people whose weight fluctuates (the experts call this weight cycling) are at greater risk of medical problems, such as heart disease, than are people who hold steady on the scale. It is also commonly said that yo-yo dieting lowers metabolic rate, making it harder to lose weight with each new attempt.

But there have been several studies that have not shown deleterious effects of weight cycling. In a recent review of research on the subject, obesity expert Rena R. Wing, Ph.D., of the University of Pittsburgh School of Medicine, concluded that the majority of studies "do not support the hypothesis that weight cycling makes subsequent efforts at weight loss more difficult."

Chicago's Dr. Kirschenbaum is one of a number of experts who believe that the probable benefits of weight loss outweigh the potential risks of weight cycling for obese people. Note, too, that while most masters at weight control had been on multiple diets, many now maintain their slimmed-down weights without tremendous difficulty. In no way do I mean to suggest that yo-yo dieting is a good thing.

Nor do I feel that anyone should stay on a diet merry-go-round in pursuit of a body weight that can never be or to lose small amounts of weight for cosmetic reasons. The possible negative consequences of yo-yo dieting suggest *not* that you should give up your effort to lose weight, but that *you should take a long, hard look at how serious you are before you make your next attempt at weight loss.* (See "Are You Ready?" on page 57.) The other important message is that *you may need to re-think your weight goal.* In terms of health, you may be better off if you accept a smaller weight loss, one that you can comfortably maintain.

Finally, as much as I applaud individuals who free themselves from the notion that self-worth is determined by physical appearance, the sad truth is that most overweight people are not happy being heavy. One study on people who underwent surgery to lose weight reported that nearly all said they'd rather be a normal weight and have a major handicap, such as deafness, severe acne or legal blindness—or even have a leg amputated—than be fat again. All said they'd prefer to be of normal weight than to be an obese multimillionaire.

Master Jeffrey B. shares his feelings about the anti-dieting movement: "If this were a perfect world, we'd leave fat people alone. But I went through these things. I was the fat man. I think it's impossible to be the happy fat person because of our society. I'd do anything to avoid being fat again."

It's Your Choice

GIVING UP DIETING doesn't have to mean giving up the effort to lose weight. Dr. Susan Olson thinks that people often need permission not to diet. "But," she adds, "the next step is to decide what you *do* want—either love yourself and love your fat or do something about it. It's a choice that you have." And choosing to take control of your weight in a healthful, positive way—as well as developing a more realistic attitude about what you "should" weigh—as the masters have done, can be a freeing experience. It does not mean that you are continuing to be controlled by a world that says everyone should look like a fashion model.

Many of the masters did lose weight with a nondieting approach when they were finally successful. They switched to healthful eating and increased physical activity. There are, however, a number of masters who lost their weight with structured diets. Then, at the maintenance stage, many of them made the shift to the nondieting approach.

Tami B. is a good example of someone who lost weight and keeps it off with a nondieting method. When asked how she finally succeeded, she said, "I had to take control—cleaned up my mac-n-cheese, pizza, ice cream environment. I started eating a balanced diet and exercising." Six years later and 35-plus pounds lighter, she's in control. "I basically eat what I want—I watch the amount and cut back on fat. I eat candy, ice cream and chips on occasion, but it's not on hand at home."

"Learning proper eating habits is not putting someone in a straitjacket," remarks Ronna Kabatznick, Ph.D., a psychological consultant for Weight Watchers International, who also has a private weight-management practice in Berkeley. She adds, "Learning how to eat is an empowering thing."

It's all a matter of choice. It is possible to become thin for life. But it's up to you to decide if you are happy the way you are or if you want to take the reins and make a change.

If You Think You Can, You Will

I F YOU CHOOSE TO BECOME THIN FOR LIFE, one of the most important steps is believing in yourself. In her study on successful maintainers (page 25), Dr. Ross saw in many a "newfound belief in themselves as the ultimate authority." They had come to see themselves as people "capable of maintaining a thin body and having no need to return to a heavy one." Master Mindy B., who's lost 84 pounds and kept it off for 7 years, says it well. "Losing weight is hard, [but] it's always within reach. Take a long look at yourself within and find that inner self-determination. It's there for all of us—use it to your advantage."

You can start to believe in yourself by accepting that your weight condition is not the result of fate: you can control it. Reading about the masters will help you do that. Over and over again, they describe moving from a state of hopelessness to one of self-control and power.

A shining example is Donna C., who says, "When I got to more than 200 pounds, it seemed like so much to lose." But she lost it— 108 pounds to be exact, which she's kept off for 3½ years. Of her final effort, Donna maintains, "This time I felt in control. I knew it was in my hands. It was not an act of fate [that I was heavy], not bad luck. I knew it was up to me, within my control. It's exactly the same for keeping the weight off."

Psychologists call this belief in yourself "self-efficacy." It's the sense of how competent you believe yourself to be in any particular situation. You can have a high sense of self-efficacy in some circumstances, but not in others. You may, for instance, have a strong sense of your abilities when it comes to work or being a parent. If you're like many people who struggle with their weight, you may also have a fairly high sense of self-efficacy about your ability to *lose* weight—you're probably a pro, having done it many times before. But your belief in your ability to *maintain* weight loss is likely quite weak. That's because you have little or no experience with weight maintenance.

When I asked the University of Minnesota's Dr. Robert Jeffery, "Is there any way to increase someone's sense of self-efficacy about weight maintenance?" he replied, "The best way is to show people they can do it." Indeed, Albert Bandura, a well-known psychologist, proposed that one way you can increase self-efficacy is to observe models—individuals who have struggled to master situations that you fear or see as difficult.

All of these observations firmed my conviction that sharing the experiences of the many masters at weight control could help others who want to be thin for life. I wanted to show how many success stories there are in order to fuel your belief that *"If they can do it, so can I."*

II

Take the Reins

H OW DID the masters finally make the choice to do something about their weight? Most of them had tried many times and in many ways before they were finally successful. It struck me that, by virtue of experience, a good number were experts at weight control long before they finally lost weight. "At least half of the people who want to lose weight could write the whole book on dieting! Knowing never equals doing," maintains Mariah Smith, M.S.W., director of obesity treatment for Health Management Resources.

So, for me, the burning question for each master was, "What was different that last time you lost weight? Why, at this one point in time, were you able to change your life forever?" It soon became clear that, when they decided to take action for that final, successful time, there was one common theme: something happened that spurred them to *take the reins*. They stopped looking to others for all the answers and decided to lose weight for no one other than themselves.

Cindy P.'s Story

I 'M AN EX-FATTY," Cindy P. wrote me. "I was heavy all my life, from 6 through 21. I got up to 235 pounds and started losing weight when I was 21. Now, I weigh 155, the same weight I've been for over 10 years." (She's 5'8".) The photo she enclosed revealed a stunning, dark-haired woman who looked like she'd never been heavy.

Cindy took the reins—took responsibility for her weight problem—when someone in her life finally accepted her as she was: heavy.

Up until that time, she had tried any number of ways to lose weight. But she had been doing it for other people, people who let her know that she wasn't quite worthy as a person because she was fat. She spent most of her early years hearing statements like, "If only you lost weight . . ." However, the more people tried to take control *for* her and nag her about her weight, the less she did about it.

Cindy thinks her weight problem started when she was in kindergarten, living temporarily with an aunt because her parents had gone through a divorce. The aunt had been raised during the Depression and was of the school that "you'd better eat now because you don't know if you'll have it later." Cindy recalls that even at this early age, people would comment, "She's so pretty; it's too bad she's fat."

When Cindy was a teenager, her mother told her, "Men don't like fat girls." So Cindy found another reason to be liked: she developed a great sense of humor. "I was the class clown, and everyone always wanted me to come along. I went to a lot of parties. But I didn't date. I think I developed my sense of humor *because* of my weight. I think it bothered my mother more than me that I wasn't going to proms and out on dates. She had been the cheerleader, the skinny girl, the pretty one that the guys liked."

Cindy wanted to get close to boys, but they often made comments about her weight. "I always had a crush on someone," Cindy says, "but as soon as he'd ask, 'How 'bout if you lost some weight?' I'd write him off."

Cindy did try to lose weight many times with over-the-counter diet pills, medically prescribed appetite suppressants and various diets. She thinks that these attempts were for her mother. She always gained the weight back.

Then Cindy went to college and met a guy (on a blind date) who liked her unconditionally—at 235 pounds. For the first time, she was ready to take the reins and lose weight *for herself.* "He never bothered me about my weight. Finally, I had found someone who accepted me *for me.* I didn't need to keep weight on to keep men at a distance anymore." She adds, "I wasn't being bugged. I wasn't doing it for Mom, for Dad, so my brothers wouldn't call me names. I didn't even need a doctor to help me lose weight. I did it because it made me feel good."

Within months, Cindy dropped down to 185 by following the

Weight Watchers food plan. (She was too self-conscious about her weight to go to meetings but got the food plan from her mother.) Cindy liked the plan because "it didn't make you starve, and they didn't say you were a bad person if you ate a chocolate-chip cookie." Then she hit a plateau. "I got stuck at 185 for 3 or 4 months. I never thought I'd get off that." But she didn't give up.

She realized that to lose more weight, she'd have to begin exercising. So she joined an all-women's health club and started doing aerobics. When her mother asked her, "Aren't you too self-conscious to be wearing a leotard?" her determination was fueled. "That's when I really started becoming my own person." From there, Cindy kept on losing, dropping as low as 140 pounds.

Like many masters, she came up with her own plan for weight control, which is pretty much the same now as when she was losing. (She reads a great deal and has taken courses about food and nutrition.) "I eat a healthy breakfast, snack, lunch, snack, dinner, snack. All very light meals. And I drink a lot of water." She still follows the basic Weight Watchers food plan, which emphasizes fruits, vegetables and grains. She doesn't eat much meat and tries to limit fat to no more than 20 grams a day. She does most of her eating between when she gets up and 1:00 in the afternoon. Typically, she has a salad or something light while her husband eats his supper. When it comes to eating, it's her way, on her terms.

Cindy doesn't have many "shoulds" about food. One morning when I spoke with her, she'd had a tuna sandwich for breakfast. "I suppose some people would say I should have a bowl of cereal or something, but *I* wanted a tuna sandwich." She writes down everything she eats, even if she has a candy bar, but doesn't feel bad about it.

Her exercise consists of working out with aerobic videotapes for 45 minutes three to four times a week. She is also active socially, which she feels is a key to her success. Instead of going out to dinner, she encourages friends to go dancing or horseback riding with her. "I also keep my hands busy with crafts. And I try to avoid sitting in front of the TV because it makes me think of food." When her weight creeps up 5 to 10 pounds, Cindy exercises more, goes back to her original Weight Watchers plan and gives up sweets for a week or so. "It's not easy. Yeah, I'd like to be eating hot fudge sundaes or brownies, but for me the weight is more important."

That doesn't mean Cindy deprives herself of sweets. She's always loved to bake. So about once a week, she whips up a "mound of something," like cookie dough or pralines. But she eats a controlled portion—say, ½ cup of cookie dough, savoring every bite. Then she throws or gives the rest away. Sometimes she'll buy a package of doughnuts, but only eat the centers or the toppings. Again, what's left goes in the trash. She says, "A lot of people can't throw food away. My husband has a hard time with it. So I ask him, 'What am I gonna do: stick it on my hips?'" She listens to her stomach, asking herself, "Do I really want that?" She adds, "I eat until I feel comfortable, not full. I used to stuff myself, but I don't do that anymore. I rarely eat a whole anything." She says to herself, "Okay, now I've had that sensation."

To this day, if someone says to Cindy, "You shouldn't eat that cookie," she wants to eat it all the more. On the other hand, if someone pushes food on her, saying, "You know you want it; go ahead and have some," she can refuse it easily. What's the difference? In the first situation, someone is trying to make the choice for her; Cindy wants to be the one who decides what she can and can't have.

She is the first to admit that the reins get a little slack when she feels someone isn't accepting her as she is. Sometimes, for instance, her husband (not the man she met at college) will comment that she's gained a little weight. Then she'll find herself overeating to spite him, blaming him all the while. "He's not letting me notice my weight and do something about it. I want to be the one to make the decision and do something. If only my husband would just accept me the way I am and think I'm sexy. I want to be liked unconditionally." When he remarked on her weight recently, she caught herself turning to food but gained control by recognizing what was going on. She said to herself, "'Wait a minute. *That's* why I'm eating this instead of taking control. *He* has the problem with my weight.' I see that I'm really hurting myself. I can keep blaming my husband. But I stand back and say, 'I'm the one who's getting hurt.'"

Whatever happened to the guy who enabled Cindy to take the reins by not bothering her about her weight? She says that after she lost the 80 pounds, he "dumped" her because he was not comfortable with other men's attraction to her. Now, she says, "I am happily married and really enjoy being thin."

Look Within

I T'S STRIKING. It's consistent. The critical starting point for most masters at weight control is *taking the reins.* Like Cindy, they're on top of making the decision to take action, choosing their own way to lose weight and making day-to-day decisions about food. Researchers have found the same phenomenon. For example, researcher Susan Ross, who studied 23 individuals, most of whom had lost at least 40 pounds and kept weight off for a minimum of 3 years, told me, "They seemed to take responsibility from the beginning; they said, 'This is me, this is my problem, and this is how I'm going to do it.'" In addition, "taking responsibility for one's own behavior" was rated as *the* most important skill for losing weight and successfully keeping it off by the 541 Weight Watchers leaders (page 26), who were themselves long-term maintainers.

Arizona researchers Drs. Susan Olson and Robert Colvin (page 23) found, too, that a critical first step for their 54 success stories was taking responsibility. If their people could only make one point, it would be, "You can't hire someone to do it for you," they note in their book *Keeping It Off.* Dr. Olson told me, "You need to get to where you say, 'No one is going to do it for me; there are no gurus, no magic pills.' Once people are convinced the ball is in their own hands, they can start to do something about their weight."

The masters, like Peppi S., say it best: "I just keep telling myself that no one is going to take care of me except *me.* So I take responsibility for me, which is a far cry from the old days when I would blame everything and everyone for my being overweight." Peppi, who is 5'7", weighed 200 pounds in 1985; she now maintains her weight around 138. She lost her weight with the help of Nutri/System, but realized that, ultimately, weight loss was up to her.

In looking within, you have to accept that you may have been dealt a rotten hand of cards when it comes to metabolism or genes. But like the masters, you can overcome what you've been dealt. I recall one of my favorite patients who, before she accepted responsibility for her weight problem, was one of the angriest people I'd ever come across. She literally pounded her fist on my desk and demanded, "Why do I have this problem? It's not fair! Why me?" I responded, "Pat, if I were to tell you that you have a weight problem because your mother stopped breast-feeding you too early—or because your grandmother overfed you as a toddler—where would that get you? How would that help you lose weight? The real question is, *What are you going to do about it?*"

Do It For You

H OW DO YOU BEGIN to take the reins? Master Lynne C., who has maintained a 77-pound weight loss for 4 years, said it succinctly: "I did it for myself." In other words, start by asking yourself, "Who am I losing weight for?" If the answer isn't, first and foremost, "For me," you may not be ready to lose weight. (See "Are You Ready?" page 57).

Master Jennifer P. describes her old college boyfriend who would tell her she'd be a "10" if only she slimmed down. "I refused to lose weight during the school year, but when I was away from him in the summer, I'd lose and exercise." Eventually, she dropped from 186 to 142, which she's maintained for 7 years. (She's even had two babies in those years.)

Mary Ann K., who's maintained an 84-pound weight loss for 3 years, told me, "Your weight is yours. You have to be responsible for your body. If you are going to lose and keep your weight off, you must be selfish. You do it for you and no one else. [I] realize I am worth it!"

As Cindy P. says, if you really want to be thin, "You have to stop listening to your husband and your mother." As a side benefit, you may make your family, colleagues, friends and physician happy. But ultimately, the message from the masters is that *you have to want to lose weight for you.*

Face the Truth

A S ARIZONA RESEARCHERS Drs. Robert Colvin and Susan Olson stress, before you can take the reins with a weight problem, you first have to *face the truth*. You can't kid yourself about your weight, how you eat or how you look anymore. Master Alisa S. admits she used to rationalize her size by telling herself, "I'm married now, have two kids, am a housewife, and this is all I can expect to be." When she became motivated to lose weight, however, she realized, "It was myself I was unhappy with. I set out to return to the trim, lively person I was." And she did. Alisa has weighed 135 for 7 years, down 66 pounds from her all-time high.

Kathleen H. was forced to face the facts when, at her videotaped 40th birthday party, friends and family goaded her into putting on a T-shirt that said, "This is what 40 looks like." She recalls, "I couldn't stretch it over my (then) 47-inch hips!" As if that weren't bad enough, her children insisted upon watching the tape over and over. "It was different from glancing in a mirror or looking at photos. It was like I really saw myself and how I looked to others. I knew 40 had to look better." Now, at the age of 43, Kathleen weighs 125, very slim for someone who is 5'8" tall.

When you're honest with yourself, Drs. Colvin and Olson believe, you are ready to "own" your weight problem and recognize your responsibility for it. Once the problem belongs to you, you can lose the weight.

The Attitude Shift

I N ASKING EACH MASTER the question "What was different that last time you lost weight?" I had hoped to discover a miracle—some experience shared by all masters that awakened them to take responsibility. But like others who have studied maintainers, I found that there is not a single answer or experience common to all. I did, however, discover an attitude shift that took place in most masters when they decided to lose weight for the last time. They had undergone a critical change in thinking about themselves and their feelings toward weight control. "It's as if a light bulb goes on, and they do it. Sometimes I think it's like a religious conversion!" notes University of Minnesota researcher Dr. Robert Jeffery, who studied successful maintainers. In her study, Dr. Susan Ross observed a similar shift: "The attitude was described in different ways but usually reflected a sense of self-responsibility and determination. Most could not describe how they arrived at the decision or what made them shift their attitude, but all were clear as to when it was the right time or decision for them. It seemed that in some way all of them came to realize a 'truth' that had not been in their awareness in that way before."

Jeffrey B. described a striking attitude shift: "I firmly believe that 90 percent of weight loss is mental. When it finally worked, I knew from day one that I was going to lose weight. I had no choice. My eating habits changed naturally, and the weight melted off." He went on to describe a friend who "starved" himself for 2 years but who couldn't seem to lose weight. "I tried to explain to him the almost audible click in the mind when it decides it is time to lose weight. He didn't understand. Then I lost track of him for about 6 months. When I saw him again, he had lost about 80 pounds. The first thing he said to me was, 'Now, I understand.' "

Not every master could articulate the "click" that spurred weight loss, and a number—including Jeffrey B.—were uncertain about why the change took place at that one point in time. But as I went through the answers to the question "What motivated you to do it—once and for all?" I could see that one of five situations had initiated most of their attitude shifts:

♦ **I saw the light**—a single eye-opening experience. For Jim V., it was dramatic. He says he was never too concerned about his weight of 475 pounds—until he almost drowned and couldn't save himself. That near-fatal event started Jim on the course of losing 250 pounds, which he's kept off for 3 years. (Jim is the profiled master in Chapter VII.) For a number of masters, the critical incident involved seeing a photograph or videotape of themselves. For others, turning a certain age triggered the change. Fern C., who has maintained a 28-pound loss (she's 5'2") for 21 years, says she became motivated when "I saw a snapshot of myself and knew that I would be turning 50 on my next birthday." Cindy P. fell into this category: her critical incident was finding someone to accept her unconditionally, which, in turn, gave her the confidence to lose weight.

* **I was scared to death**—a worrisome health situation. A number of people expressed general concern about how unhealthy their weight had been. For others, like Kelly D., the situation was far more serious. It took a massive heart attack to get him to lose his 55 pounds nearly 5 years ago. Edith S. became motivated to lose 56 pounds after "a severe angina attack and a serious talk with my cardiologist."

* **I couldn't take it anymore**—simply becoming tired of how you look and feel. Bob W., who peaked at 400 pounds in the eighth grade, stated, "I was sick and tired of being sick and tired." He now weighs 150, which he's maintained for 21 years. Says Lou Ann L., "I was tired of being self-destructive and turning my anger inward by eating. I was also tired of being overweight and feeling limited by my weight." That sentiment, 20 years ago, triggered a 43-pound weight loss. Some masters were worn down by their weight-control efforts. Kelly S., who for 6 years has weighed 50 pounds less than her all-time high of 180, responded, "I was tired of having food run my life. I said, 'Enough is enough is enough already.'"

* **I liked the new me.** For some masters, the real attitude shift didn't seem to take place until *after* they had lost some weight: they liked what they saw and how they felt, so they kept going. Joseph M., who has kept off 115 pounds for 19 years, states that what motivated him to lose weight once and for all was "seeing results: clothes beginning to loosen, being noticed by females, feeling better physically and mentally."

* **I wanted to attract the opposite sex.** Not surprisingly, some masters' desire to lose weight was spurred by a wish to find a mate. Eight years ago, Sandy P. was motivated because she wanted to have a boyfriend, like the rest of her friends. "In order to achieve that goal, I had to lose weight." And lose she did—73 pounds to be exact.

It's More Than a Commitment to Lose Weight

I LOOKED BAD and felt fat."

"The scale kept climbing—it was time, and I had had it."

"My mind was made up."

"Wait a minute," I asked the masters, *"Didn't you want to look better and feel better all those other times you lost weight? And wasn't your mind made up with just as much determination? Weren't you sick and tired of being heavy before?"* I was *still* left with that question "Why did you do it—finally?"

When I had the opportunity to speak at length with the masters, as well as interview experts on weight control, I began to realize that much more had taken place in the masters' lives than just making a commitment to lose weight. Other critical changes in their lives had taken place—some deliberate, others incidental—that kept them going after they had made the decision.

Health Management Resources director of obesity treatment Mariah Smith says, "It's not just that something 'clicks.' Several factors take place in the final attempt to lose weight, and it's different for each person. But most people who are successful at keeping weight off have worked at some imperative things that help them live thin in the world. They may have learned how to solve their problems more effectively. If they don't exercise because of hecticness at work, they find a way to do it."

Indeed, the more I talked with the masters and the more I studied other researchers' findings, it became clear that many masters made *multiple* changes in their lives either before or while they were losing the weight. Says Dr. Daniel Kirschenbaum, of Chicago's Center for Behavioral Medicine, "It isn't just 'motivation' that last time that makes the difference, it's making changes in your life to sustain the weight loss. For instance, someone who has worked for years in a candy factory, where he's exposed to constant temptation, finally changes jobs." Along the same lines, Dr. Ross found that readiness to lose weight often relates to changes in life situations, personal maturity or growth, changes in values or some combination of these.

One woman who had a history of dieting on weekdays then binge eating all weekend, told me that she literally woke up one Monday morning and said, "I'm never going on another diet." That was 12 years ago, and she honored her pledge. Taking her comment at face value, it would appear that the change in attitude was like some sort of awakening—the "click" that certain people describe. But when she reflected about what else had gone on in her life, she admitted that many aspects of her life had changed so that she was finally ready to give up her compulsive dieting. "Over the course of many years, I learned to like myself better. I had the confidence to change careers and, therefore, became much happier in my work. I also became involved in a supportive rather than a destructive relationship with a man. Part of it, too, was that I had matured and I could accept imperfections about my body; I realized that *I* was so much more than my weight."

The Keys to Success in subsequent chapters reveal the critical changes made in masters' lives to sustain their weight loss.

Inoculation Concepts

I N ORDER TO BE SUCCESSFUL, the masters first had to figure out or accept some things about themselves. Knowing these "inoculation concepts" in the beginning can give you a shot in the arm to take charge of your weight problem *and* can make things easier down the road. (Not all of them will necessarily apply to you.)

• **Put yourself first.** You need to get stubborn and develop a kind of selfishness about yourself and your weight. In her book *Alyce's Fat Chance*, master Alyce C. says, "Get ornery. Get stubborn. Figure out what it takes to take care of yourself and *do that*. If you have to carry baked potatoes in your flight bag in order to take the weight off, then *do that*." (She does.) "Stop being concerned about what it looks like." (For more on taking care of your own needs, see Chapter IX, "Get More Out of Life.")

• **Get in touch with what your weight is doing for you.** Ask yourself what you're getting out of *not* losing weight. Many people hide behind their weight, allowing it to help them avoid challenges or escape intimacy with the opposite sex. Cindy P. thinks her weight served not only as a statement of anger because boys didn't accept her as she was, but also as a defense to keep them at a distance. "I suppose it had something to do with my parents' divorce. I was afraid of being hurt or left." Being heavy allows some people to put off making decisions or taking action about life. Kelly S. realizes that her weight had something to do with her family's pressure on her to achieve. "It was all assumed. I didn't feel like I had a choice. Food was a coping mechanism to deal with pressure. At some level I must have thought that if I were heavy, maybe people would expect less of me." (You can't always get in touch with what your weight is doing for you. As indicated in Chapter VIII, some people need to work with a professional to uncover what their weight really means to them.)

♦ **Prepare for the hardship of being thin.** As Alyce C. puts it, "The world treats you differently at 210, at 185, at 160 and 135." Some of the changes will be positive, others negative—at least initially. People may have different expectations of you, you'll have to deal with buying new kinds and sizes of clothing, and people of the opposite sex may treat you very differently. The praise you get may start to irritate you after a while. You may have trouble accepting yourself as thin. Heavy friends and relatives may resent your success and try to sabotage your efforts. It's important to realize, too, that after you lose weight, you'll still have problems: you'll probably still argue with your husband, have a rebellious teenager to deal with and worry about money. In fact, for some people, certain problems become more acute, particularly if they were hiding behind their weight. Your relationships may change as well. Recall Cindy P., whose boyfriend left her because he couldn't handle other men's interest in her when she slimmed down. Being aware may help you better handle what's ahead. (Subsequent chapters offer guidelines for dealing with these issues.)

♦ **Look forward to what you'll gain.** Masters report more favorable changes in their lives than negative ones. Says Ann F. of her 220-pound weight loss, "It has really changed my life in a positive direction. It is so wonderful to buy clothes in a 'normal' store and not have to deal with all the discrimination, insensitive comments and other humiliations. I also met my husband right after my weight loss, and we have been happily married for the last 6 years." Donna C. exclaims, "I've enjoyed the compliments (and disbelief) regarding my weight loss and improved appearance. My energy level is better. I'm more active, outgoing and self-assured. I'm attractive to men. And most important, I like myself!" Note, too, that although losing weight will not make your other problems evaporate, you may feel more confident about solving some of them.

◆ **Accept that it's not easy, it's not always fair.** Losing weight and keeping it off is not a piece of cake—it may be one of the hardest things you ever do. But a number of masters told me that it does get easier with time. As Cindy P. told me, "My weight is something I will have to struggle with all my life. But I've accepted it. It's not 'poor me.' It's just something I have to do. And I care enough about myself to do it. It definitely gets easier with time." Dr. Kirschenbaum feels that eventually people get to the point where they say, "Yeah, it's unfair that I have this problem, but I'm tired of it." He himself eats only around 1,500 calories a day—not much for a man. "It's not easy," he admits, "but it beats the alternative. There are a lot of things in life that you have to adjust to. It's a choice that you make—instead of fighting it, I accept it."

◆ **Your motivation for weight control will wax and wane.** Sometimes it's just plain harder than at other times to keep a handle on your weight. It's especially difficult when people stop noticing the "new" you. As Dr. Thomas Wadden, director of Syracuse University's Center for Health and Behavior, points out, "*Losing* weight is exciting: your waist gets smaller, and everyone notices. But maintenance is tough because there's no change. And 'no change' is about as exciting as watching paint dry." Although it's important to be prepared for this, note that the masters have not let it get in their way. I was impressed by the enthusiasm and excitement many of them had about their success—long after they'd lost the weight. They seem to develop their own internal incentives, rather than looking to others for praise. One way that Gretchen G. has maintained her 40-pound weight loss for 3 years is, "I try to think thin and visualize myself in a party dress at a social event. I imagine people noticing me and my feeling good about their reactions. This keeps me from binge eating and helps me stay focused on my weight goals." Although Gretchen may seem to be looking to others, she is really engaging in self-praise.

+ **Give yourself permission to fail.** You *will* make mistakes, and you *will,* from time to time, revert to old habits. But the masters have learned how not to let a "lapse" become a "relapse." (See Chapter V, "Nip It in the Bud: Break the Relapse Cycle.") They've learned how to pick themselves up after a spill, dust their knees off and start again. As Kevin C., who has lost 45 pounds and kept it off for 7 years, advises, "Learn to forgive yourself. If you mess up, start again tomorrow. You're not going to change overnight." In my experience with counseling overweight people, I found that those who were the most rigid— the ones who never made "mistakes" on their diets—were the most likely to gain the weight back (and gain it rapidly) when they finally did deviate. No one can be a tower of strength all the time.

+ **Maintenance is not static.** What works at one point in time may not at another. But you'll find new solutions to your problems. Karen S., who's kept 24 pounds off her 5'4" frame for 15 years, says, "I am always trying to improve my eating habits. Some weeks are better than others. Serious overeating is a problem that is always beneath the surface. I must be aware of it in order to prevent it from resurfacing."

+ **Don't feel you have to rush.** You've probably heard the saying, "You didn't gain it overnight; you won't lose it overnight either." It's true. Besides, what's your hurry? You're on your way to becoming thin for life. Dorothy C. took her time. "I feel strongly that many habits leading to overweight can be changed permanently because I achieved drastic changes, but over a long period of time and *gradually.*" She lost her 32 pounds over the course of 5 to 6 years and has weighed about 123 for the last 8 years. (For more, see "Give Yourself Time," page 73.)

Thin Is Relative

B Y USING THE WORDS "thin for life," I am *not* suggesting that you should pursue the cultural definition of thin or "ideal" body weight. "The prevailing ideal in the United States, particularly for women, is very lean . . . the aesthetic ideal has grown consistently leaner and is now much thinner than the health ideal," Yale University's Dr. Kelly Brownell and Syracuse University's Dr. Thomas Wadden said in a recent review. In other words, American women (and a fair number of men) are obsessed with being *too* thin, thinner than most people—particularly overweight individuals—can ever comfortably be. My definition of "thin" is relative.

A growing number of experts agree that *any* weight loss is likely to be good for an overweight person. Research studies suggest that losing just 10 percent of your body weight (a 20-pound loss for a 200-pound person) can have beneficial effects on high blood pressure, adult diabetes and heart-disease risk factors. Relatively small amounts of weight loss can provide a psychological boost as well. Just the decision to take action can make you feel virtuous and more confident about your body.

Traditionally, overweight people have been encouraged to set a goal based on a desirable or ideal weight according to life-insurance company charts. Not only have questions been raised about whether these targets are, in fact, ideal from a health standpoint, but they may be unrealistically low for many overweight individuals. In my experience, one of the major reasons many of my former patients regained weight was that they had set their sights on unrealistic goals. Frequently, they would lose about half of their weight, then give up, viewing the cup as half-empty rather than half-full. They couldn't see that even though the charts indicated they should lose 100 pounds, a 50-pound weight loss was a major accomplishment. Many times patients who did meet their goals (based on the charts) would quickly regain because it was too difficult for them to maintain their weight at that level.

As noted earlier, many masters at weight control gained back some weight after they hit their lows. "When I weighed 140, I felt like I was in a cage; I had to count everything. I'm definitely not model-thin now, but I figure no matter what you weigh, it could always be another 10 pounds that you want to lose," notes Cindy P. Cindy has found that not resisting where her body seems to "want" to be is another way of holding the reins—it's easier to control your weight when you're not starving all the time.

Setting a Comfortable Weight Goal

B Y SAYING your body "wants" to be at a certain weight, I'm suggesting that I at least partially subscribe to the setpoint theory, which proposes that each person has a preset biological weight—one that may or may not fit societal norms—which the body will fight to maintain. If, say, your setpoint is 160 pounds, and you diet down to 135, your body will fight to get back to 160. It does that by making you feel constantly hungry and by slowing your metabolism down. After you have stabilized at around 160 pounds again, the theory is that you will maintain that weight without a great deal of effort.

Of course, if there is a setpoint, it's not necessarily a hard and fast number; it may be a considerable range. And you have control over which end of that range you maintain. It is also thought that you may be able to lower your setpoint by regular exercise and, possibly, by following a low-fat diet. A good number of masters have switched to a low-fat, high-exercise lifestyle and thus may have lowered their setpoints.

So how do you set a comfortable weight goal—one that you're likely to maintain—low enough that you feel successful, but not so low that you feel like you're suffering? Based on guidelines by weight-control experts Drs. Kelly Brownell, Judith Rodin and Thomas Wadden, I put together the following to help you come up with a *comfortable* weight goal, one you can live with:

1. Were/are either your parents or grandparents considerably overweight? If you have a family history of obesity, it may be harder for you to maintain a low weight. Furthermore, if you are very heavy and have been that way for a long time, it makes sense to start with a higher weight goal.

2. As an adult, what is the least you have weighed—and main-

SAVE
ON EVERYTHING
YOU BUY AT
BARNES&NOBLE

tained—for at least 1 year? It may be difficult to comfortably maintain a weight any lower than that.

3. What weight would you be if you fit in the largest size clothing that you feel comfortable in? At what point can you say, "I look quite good given where I've been?" (Yes, it might be nice to wear a size 10, but aren't size 14's better than the "plus sizes" you're wearing now?)

4. Think of a few friends or family members of your approximate age and body frame—people who look "normal" to you, not like models. Ask what they weigh.

5. At what weight can you live with the required changes in eating and/or exercise? If you feel constantly hungry at your dream weight and/or you have to exercise more than is realistic, your reasonable weight is higher. You really have to ask yourself whether weighing what a chart says you "should" is worth the price you'd have to pay to stay there.

Consider petite Cathy C., who, at her current weight of 117, has kept off 38 pounds for about 11 years. "Although I'm 5'1", I have a sturdy frame. I wear large-size hats, gloves and shoes. I used to compare my weight with a friend's (she is the same height as I), but found she wears small hats, gloves and tiny shoes. It's hardly a reasonable comparison." Similarly, Chuck F., who's 5'6" and once weighed 205, admits his maintenance weight of 140 to 145 is about 10 pounds more than he originally intended. "I realized that my earlier goal was unrealistically hard to maintain."

In short, a reasonable weight is one that you can maintain without undue suffering, at which you feel quite good about the way you look, and at which you have no serious medical problems caused by weight. Dr. Kelly Brownell suggests that after you've lost the first 10 pounds, you ask yourself if you're willing to continue the food and activity changes you've been making. If so, set your goal at another 10-pound loss, and so on. That's how Ann Q. has lost 49 pounds. Starting out at 245, she's been losing in 10-pound increments. Over the course of several years, she's gotten down to 196 and is still losing.

I do feel compelled to say something about a relatively new means of assessing your weight called the waist-to-hip ratio. Apple-shaped people, who have a waist that is bigger around than their hips, are at greater risk for problems like cardiovascular disease and diabetes than are pear-shaped individuals, whose hips are larger than their waists. It's healthiest if men have a waist-to-hip ratio no greater than 1.0; for women, it should be 0.8 or less. (To determine your ratio, measure your waist at the level of your belly button, then measure your hips at the widest part. Divide the waist number by the hip number.)

With weight loss, the waist-to-hip ratio tends to improve. But it's possible to get down to your reasonable weight and find that your ratio is not ideal. If that's the case, it's all the more wise to see your physician regularly and have him or her monitor you for problems like heart disease and diabetes. Women in particular should be checked for ovarian and adrenal abnormalities, according to weight-control expert Wayne Callaway, M.D., at George Washington University in Washington, D.C.

Accepting a Less-Than-Perfect Body

I HAVE TO ADMIT that I've never liked the way I look in a bathing suit. But one summer afternoon, while I was lying on a beach, I took a long, hard look at the bodies around me. Where were all those beautiful women that I see on TV? Instead, I saw one body after another that was far from perfect. My guess is that, at best, 1 in 50 people really look terrific in a bathing suit. Who was I to think that I could—or should—be one of them?

Most people do not have perfect bodies—even after they lose weight. Says dietitian and obesity expert Melanie Polk, M.M.Sc., R.D., "If a person is genetically destined to be shaped like a pear, if she loses weight, she will still be shaped like a pear. She will just be a smaller pear. The same thing is true for a person shaped like an apple."

You can accept your flaws better if you don't focus on your imperfect body parts and instead try to see yourself as a whole. One woman who was obsessed with the "saddle bags" on the outside of her thighs started to see herself differently after her husband told her, "You know, when you walk into a room, people are not staring and thinking, 'Oh my God, look at her thighs.' Instead, they see you as a total person, and the overall impression you give is of a tall, trim woman."

Karen S. told me, "It was important for me to realize that I will never have long, thin legs, nor will I ever look like a fashion model." Karen is one of my dearest friends, and she looks great at 127. (She's kept off 24 pounds for 15 years.) And Linda W., who has been 39 pounds lighter for 6 years, says, "By heritage, I have very heavy calves. For years I tried to diminish their size only to finally find out that all I was doing was building more muscle. I get compliments on my size, so apparently my weight of 126 suits me." (They're both 5'4" tall.)

Male masters had to learn to accept their shortcomings as well. Ernie L., the profiled master in Chapter III, maintains, "We have to face up to what we are. No matter how hard I work out, I will never have a body that looks muscular." He adds, "But it's great to have a healthy cardiovascular system."

Once you lose the weight, you do have to be aware of the possibility of what body-image expert Thomas F. Cash, Ph.D., calls "phantom fat." Cindy P. alludes to this when she says, "I don't know if I'll ever look in the mirror and say, 'Gee, I look good.' " According to Dr. Cash, phantom fat occurs when someone who's lost weight has a sense that his or her body is still unacceptable. More often than not, however, masters are able to rejoice in their new bodies. And, like Cindy, even those with phantom fat are much happier with themselves now.

More Than a Weight Goal

D R. SUSAN ROSS FOUND that many of the successful people in her study lost weight with an attitude of taking one day or one week at a time without an expectation of what the end point would be. Likewise, some masters told me they never set a weight goal. "For me, contentment and normal eating were my goals—not a specific weight," maintains master Claudia B., a philosophy professor who has done research on women's body images. "I'm worried about the amount of attention we give to our bodies. Thus I have *worked* to develop an attitude toward my body that says, 'It's fine just where it wants to be.' " At 5'7½", her body "wants" to be at 135, down 35 pounds for 6½ years.

Some masters had better health and fitness as their goals rather than a set weight. Tom F., profiled in Chapter VIII, said, "My motivation was not to lose weight but to become a runner." So at the age of 28 and at a weight of 230 (he's 6' tall), he quit smoking and started running. Within 2 years, he had lost 80 pounds, which was too thin for comfort. He now weighs 185 and has maintained that weight for many years.

A number of experts agree that it's actually better to set health and improved eating habits as your goals rather than a predetermined number on the scale. John Foreyt, Ph.D., co-author of *Living Without Dieting,* maintains, "The focus should be on healthy lifestyle change. The more you focus on the scale, the worse the outcome." He stresses, "Weight is *part* of one's life; it is *not* one's life."

Indeed, I found that many masters in my survey approached their weight as a symptom of an undesirable lifestyle. Says Irene S., now at a reduced weight of 153 (down from 230), "It's not a matter of dieting. It's a lifetime change. It's a personal change. It's focusing on eating behavior, choices and the rewards of a better quality of life."

Master Becky M. apparently agrees. "When I quit dieting and decided to lead a healthier lifestyle with exercise and good eating, the weight was no longer a struggle. I quit 'living' to eat and hating myself for it." Becky is 5'5" and weighs 120, down 40 pounds from her all-time high. Kelly S. says that what motivated her to lose weight once and for all was the realization that her entire life and self-worth were tied to her weight. "I decided that the weight was not going to be a barrier to feeling good about myself and pursuing my goals." (Be sure to see "You Are Much More Than Your Weight," page 243.)

"You can't just change your lifestyle all at once," points out Weight Watchers psychologist Dr. Ronna Kabatznick. "That would be like trying to get your Ph.D. in a week. People who are successful meet many small, gradual goals that add up to total lifestyle change." In future chapters, you'll see the many strategies the masters used to change their lifestyles.

Remember you don't *have* to do anything. You have a choice. It's up to you to decide if you're ready to become thin for life.

Are You Ready?

ARE YOU READY to take the reins, to make the attitude shift? In their book *The Truth About Addiction and Recovery,* psychologist Stanton Peele, Ph.D., and co-author Archie Brodsky suggest that people trying to overcome weight, alcohol or smoking problems consider the following questions to determine if they're ready to change:

How much do I want to quit the negative behavior— overeating and underexercising?

   __ very much   __ a little

   __ a good deal   __ not at all

   __ somewhat   __ I don't know

Am I ready to change now?

   __ ready to change   __ not ready to change

If you are unresolved about these questions, you are not likely to succeed, at least at this point. (Don't give up, though, because the answers can change with time.) Dr. Peele thinks, too, that you can sometimes "light the right kind of fire under yourself" by reflecting on the information you place on the following two lists (sample responses are included):

Reasons for not changing

I like to eat.

My husband has never known me thin.

I need food when I'm tense.

I hate to exercise.

I'd have to buy all new clothes.

Reasons for changing

I'd have more energy.

My legs and feet would ache less.

I could wear more fashionable clothing.

I'd feel proud of myself.

I'd feel less bloated.

My blood cholesterol would come down.

The book points out, "It doesn't really matter which list is longer—the one on the right just has to be better." Dr. Peele believes that carefully reflecting on these lists and keeping the positive reasons for change in the forefront of consciousness can motivate some people to change. But if your right-hand list includes few "I's" and "my's"—suggesting you want to lose for others—you probably are not losing the weight for yourself and may not be ready to take the reins.

If you *are* ready, you need to be able to endure some discomfort. Indeed, not every master experienced a mystical attitude shift before losing weight that made the process easy. Some had to really work at changing, and the work was hard. To see if you can handle the discomfort, Dr. Peele suggests asking yourself the following:

If quitting or changing my eating and exercise habits is uncomfortable or painful, how prepared am I to endure this discomfort in order to make the change?

__ very   __ somewhat   __ slightly

You also need to accept the fact that you're in it for the long haul—that this will not be just another couple of weeks of dieting. Can you envision yourself continuing to work on your weight 6 months or a year from now? If the answer is no, now may not be the right time for you to do something about your weight.

Another important consideration in assessing your readiness is looking at your life circumstances. If you have a number of problems right now—or if you've experienced or anticipate any major changes in your life—then it may be better to wait until life is less stressful. Ask yourself the following questions:

+ Is my financial situation reasonably stable?
+ Is my (or my spouse's) job likely to stay the same for at least the next year?
+ Is my workload manageable and will it likely stay that way?
+ Am I willing to find time to devote to weight control?
+ Are my family members reasonably healthy from a physical standpoint?

- Are my relationships with my spouse, friends and relatives reasonably healthy?
- Can I find a way to become more physically active?
- Are my family members and friends supportive of my desire to lose weight?
- Overall, am I reasonably happy right now?
- Am I ready to accept the fact that there is no magic answer—that I have to come up with a plan that works for me in order to lose weight?

In general, the more "yeses" you have to the questions above, the closer you are to being ready to do something about your weight. Sometimes people do lose weight in the midst of personal crises—it may be one aspect of their lives they feel they can control. And, as Dr. Brownell points out, for some individuals, "life is *always* complicated." Sometimes complications can be the impetus for losing weight, as was the case for several masters who had ended bad relationships and wanted to start "new" lives.

Only you can decide if the time is right.

III

Do It Your Way

H OW DID THE MASTERS lose their weight? Let me count the ways! The more I looked at their answers to the question "When you were finally successful, how did you do it?" the more I was struck by the diversity of their answers. They lost weight using everything from a macrobiotic diet to a diet high in alcoholic beverages (not recommended!) to a high-fish diet. But it soon became apparent that there was a common theme in how the masters took it off that last time. *Their message—loud and clear—is that if you want to lose weight, you have to find what's best for you. You have to do it your way.*

Ernie L.'s Story

I AM CONVINCED that permanent weight loss is something that each individual must work out for himself," Ernie L. wrote. "For me, it was a combination of exercise, psychological and philosophical enlightenment and healthy diet—low-fat, low-protein, low-alcohol and high-carbohydrate." Ernie came up with this weight-loss plan on his own, but not without years of trial and error. It took him 27 years to find his own way. At a height of 5'11", Ernie weighs 185, down 45 pounds from his all-time high. For the past 12 years or so, his self-styled plan has worked for him.

Until he was 16, Ernie was a skinny kid. That summer, after he started working at a gas station, he explains, "I had money and access to candy and soda machines. I went to drive-ins and loaded up on foods like burgers and shakes. I went from 135 to 180 pounds in one summer."

After high school, he spent 7 years in the Navy, where people always "got on him" because his weight was at the upper limit. (He stayed in the 205 to 215 range; his frame is small, so he can't carry a lot of weight.) "Every diet that came out, I went on. But I'd only lose 4 to 5 pounds." Then, at age 25, Ernie "got very serious" and went on prescription diet pills. "After 6 months on amphetamines, I crashed and ended up in the naval hospital for 2 weeks." He gave up the pills but not the quest to lose weight. Yet he never lost much. In fact, he gained.

After finishing his term in the Navy and completing graduate school, Ernie got a job as a college administrator. With all the sitting around and the two-martini business lunches, his weight soared to 230. Still, Ernie was one of those people who was *always* on a diet. "If anyone asked me, I'd say I'd been on a diet since I was 16 years old." Then, at age 35, Ernie found short-term success by following the Weight Watchers diet and recipes. (He never attended meetings.) He got down to 175 but slowly regained the weight.

The beginnings of what finally did work for Ernie took place about 5 years later. It was his own combination of exercise and a sensible food plan that suited his lifestyle. First, he discovered the value of exercise. He started out with swimming, which did little for his weight but firmed him up. Several years later, he decided to try running. "I hated running, so I started out with one minute a day for the first week. The second week, it was two minutes a day." Within 3 to 4 months, Ernie had worked up to 25 to 30 miles a week. That really slimmed him—all the way down to 175, where he stayed for about 8 years. (Ernie's weight crept up some after he had to give up running because of knee and ankle problems. He now takes a one-hour step aerobics class four times a week as well as doing some long-distance bicycling.)

"When I started running, I became nutritionally aware. I read a lot and discovered that the foods I loved in life might actually be good for me. Over the past 12 years or so, I've structured a diet that works for me. The way I eat now is basically the same way I ate while I was losing weight." When Ernie reflects on his long history of diets, he now sees that they worked for just four or five days. He believes that it was because most of the fad diets at the time were high-protein, low-carbohydrate. "I was raised Italian, or an almost total carbohydrate diet: we had pasta at least two or three times a week, lots of bread, plenty of vegetables, and cereal in the morning. Whenever I went on diets, I went off them because I craved carbohydrates. I realized that the way I ate had to match where I came from culturally.

"So about 10 years ago, when dietitians started talking about increasing carbohydrates, I decided to try it." To this day, Ernie eats lots of pasta and vegetables and views meat more as a condiment or flavoring for foods than as the main part of the meal. He makes an effort to choose chicken or fish, but when he does have meats, they're very lean. He adds, "I had to face up to what I could and couldn't do. I love barbecued spare ribs, so I have them once a month. But there are some things I decided to change for the rest of my life—for instance, I gave up butter on bread because it wasn't a big deal to me. I also pretty much gave up beer: I used to drink maybe a six-pack a week. Now, I might have a six-pack in a year."

Ernie also mapped out a daily food plan that works for him. He eats a large, healthful breakfast—say, juice, cereal, banana and 2 percent milk. He finds no need to eat during the day and often works out during his lunch hour. His supper typically is a small portion of broiled meat, chicken or fish, pasta, salad and lots of vegetables. "Then I hit my danger period—from 8 to 10:00 p.m. It's my grazing time. I take care of it with herbal tea or no-sugar European coffees, maybe some cocoa, a piece of fruit or popcorn."

Ernie adds, "This strictly pertains to me. You have to ask yourself *not* 'What diet can I go on?' but 'How can I change my eating habits permanently?' If you live 30 more years, what can you do for the rest of your life?" For Ernie, it's an ongoing process. He says, "My diet gets better and better; it's changing today."

Ernie also believes there's a strong psychological component to losing weight permanently. He says every heavy person needs to start by asking, "Is there any possibility I'm getting a pay-off for being fat?" For him, there was a positive component to being overweight. "I wouldn't have to mow my lawn on a hot day because I was afraid of having a heart attack. I couldn't do so many things because of my weight. You have to ask yourself if there's a less neurotic way to get what you want. If you don't want to mow the lawn, you don't have to stay heavy to get out of it. Maybe you could hire a kid to do it."

On a deeper level, Ernie feels that his weight shielded him from competition. "There's a whole physical nature in being masculine, and being heavy meant I didn't have to compete in the same way as if I were not heavy. Then, when I realized I could be physical without being competitive, I saw that there were things other than basketball and football. With running, I could compete with myself."

Over and over, Ernie stressed, "I'm convinced that this is my own thing. Of all the issues, weight control ranks as one of the most complex. Of all the things that need absolute, individual attention, it is weight."

Self-Styled vs. Program People

A T TIMES, I was tempted to call this chapter "Get It Off, I Don't Care How." But as I talked with masters like Ernie L., I realized that how you lose weight *is* important. It's a matter of finding a healthful plan or program that's right for you, that's safe to follow, that you can tailor to meet your own needs *and* that prepares you for maintenance. "When it comes to weight-loss success stories, just about any program will work for someone, but no one thing will work for everybody," notes registered dietitian Gail A. Levey.

There were, as always with the masters, common themes. Most of their weight-loss plans fell into one of two categories:

• **The *self-styled* masters**—people who lost weight on their own. Responses from nearly half the masters indicated they lost their weight as Ernie L. did, by following self-styled schemes, commonly consisting of low-fat, low-calorie food plans and increased exercise. It was a rare self-styled master who lost weight by following any sort of stringent diet. In fact, many used a nondieting approach similar to that which starts on page 109. (Chapter IV, "Accept the Food Facts," offers plenty of ideas for becoming a self-styled master.)

• **The *program* people**. Nearly half the masters lost weight with the aid of some sort of structured weight-loss program or self-help group, such as Take Off Pounds Sensibly (TOPS), Weight Watchers, Health Management Resources, Nutri/System, Jenny Craig Weight Loss

Centres or Diet Center. Some of these programs do offer fairly stringent diets on which a number of masters lost weight. (It may be that outside support and/or a more structured program are crucial for a formal diet to work.)

Very few masters lost weight by following fad diets. None attributed their success to diet pills.

When asked how they finally lost weight, *self-styled* masters gave me responses like:

- "I threw out the scale and changed my daily activities and attitudes about food."
- "No fat, no meat, eating tiny meals and lots of willpower."
- "Regular exercise, eating low-fat healthy foods (fruits, vegetables, whole grains) and eating only when hungry."
- "Watched diet closely and exercised. No seconds at meals, no bread, no soft drinks and sweets. Plus, I had a friend to do it with me, and we gave each other encouragement."

There were lots of individual techniques that helped masters lose weight. Some mentioned such simple things as eating smaller portions, counting calories and keeping diet diaries. For one person, the key was eating the majority of calories before 5:00 p.m. Another said her secret was not getting upset if she gained a pound. Another drank a lot of Tab.

Of the *program* people, some simply used the programs as a tool for losing weight, but now they maintain on their own. Others continue to attend group meetings faithfully and/or go back to the program when they start to gain weight. (See Chapter X, "Don't Go It Alone," for more on group support.) Here's what some of the program people had to say:

- "I was nearly 40 pounds overweight when I joined Weight Watchers. When my sister-in-law found I had signed up for the program, she said, 'I've never known anyone who was in the Weight Watchers system who didn't gain all the weight back.' Those were fighting words for me!" (She lost 57 pounds with Weight Watchers and has kept it off for 19 years.)

• "For the most part, I have kept my weight either below or around 200 pounds for the past 5 years." (This 6' man once weighed 382.) "I truly credit my weekly attendance at Health Management Resources maintenance classes."

• "I get tremendous support from TOPS—my chapter and state-wide. You talk about what's bothering you. There's a family feeling." This woman lost 62 pounds, which she's kept off for 4 years.

Some program people lost their weight in stages, with a variety of methods:

• "10 pounds through Shaklee, 10 through Omnitrition, the other 15 through better eating and exercise." (It took this woman 6½ years to lose 35 pounds, but she did it.)

• "I started with Nutri/System, and it was a very good program for me to start with. . . . I signed up to lose 30 pounds, and I did [3 years ago]. I joined Diet Center 7 months ago to lose the last 15 pounds."

What Do the Studies Show?

BEFORE DISCUSSING how to find a weight-loss plan that's right for you, let's look at some research findings on success stories. Studies suggest that people who maintain weight loss are more likely to devise their own weight-loss programs than to seek an outside solution to their problem.

Not long ago, a study conducted at Kaiser Permanente Medical Center offices in Fremont, California, compared a group of women who had maintained weight loss with women who had gained back lost weight. The maintainers shed pounds by devising personal "plans to fit their lives." The plans usually included regular exercise and a new eating style that consisted of consuming less fat, less sugar, more fruits and vegetables and much less food than previously. (By far, this approach was mentioned most often by *Thin for Life* masters as well.) Like Ernie L., with his occasional spareribs, the maintainers did not completely restrict their favorite foods and made efforts to avoid feeling deprived.

In contrast, regainers were far less likely to have exercised to lose weight and, instead, were more likely to have lost by taking appetite suppressants and shots, fasting, going to weight-control groups or to hypnosis or by going on diets in books or magazines. While dieting, they denied themselves foods they enjoyed, and they felt deprived. Compared with the regainers, the successful women seemed to have more of an ability to "look within" and to depend less on outside help. They also used dietary strategies they could live with permanently.

Dr. Susan Ross found, too, that most of the people in her study had developed their own plans based on previous knowledge and experience. "Each person chose the foods and habits he/she was willing to forgo and created a diet plan that incorporated all that was needed to avoid feelings of deprivation." The key to success seemed to be that each individual devised or voluntarily chose his or her own approach to weight loss and maintained control over it. As Ernie L. puts it, "You have to look at your eating style and see what you crave and within that style, what will work for you. What are you willing to do?"

Does all of this mean that you can't find success with formal weight-loss programs? Certainly not, since close to half of the masters found success with them. I had the opportunity to speak with Ed Grattan, M.A., who interviewed each of the 82 weight maintainers in the University of Iowa College of Medicine study (page 25) for 1½ hours. "What was critical was when people took ownership, and a weight-loss program became *their* program," he said. "For instance, even though Mary may have gone to Diet Center, it became her program because she individualized it, making subtle changes in portions or foods." By changing the program, people became responsible for anything that might happen in the future.

Take *Thin for Life* master Violet Y., who, at the age of 64, went to Weight Watchers. That was 20 years ago, when the food plan was much stricter. "I attended meetings quite regularly and usually lost at least a pound or two. I did not fully comply with Weight Watchers suggestions. Also I am a 'chocoholic,' so every day I ate three chocolate chips!" She lost 57 pounds, which she's kept off to this day. But she did it her way.

Whatever method you choose, you have to find a way to make it your own—so it's your plan and you're in control. Ernie L. believes that one of the reasons he was ready to lose weight once and for all was that he resolved some spiritual issues that led him to take control of his life. After deciding to leave behind his religious ties, he found, "I then became responsible for me. No church or parents were guiding my life."

This was Ernie's way. But it's important to realize that the very act of devising your own weight-loss plan is a way of taking responsibility for your life and your weight problem. It's also a means of increasing your sense of self-efficacy, that sense of how competent and effective you really can be at controlling your weight.

Learn From the Past

NOT ANOTHER DIET! When you think about trying to lose weight *again,* you're faced with your past history—that long line of diets and other methods you tried unsuccessfully to control your weight. These efforts can serve as cruel reminders of failure. Or, as psychologists Brenda L. Wolfe, Ph.D., and G. Alan Marlatt, Ph.D., propose in *The Weight Control Digest,* you can use your past attempts at weight loss as "a rich library of what worked and what did not." (They note, too, that past weight-loss attempts show your potential for change.) *No matter what you weigh, how many times you've lost and regained weight—you are more knowledgeable now than you were before each weight-loss effort of the past.* Ernie L. says, "You get to be an expert only because you had so many failures."

As Weight Watchers psychologist Ronna Kabatznick puts it, "When you're learning to ride a bike, it's highly unlikely that you'll do it right the first time. And it's human to fall and scrape your knees. It's the same way with trying to lose weight—you'll have setbacks, but you learn something with each attempt." Look to your past experiences to identify what did and didn't work for you. Says master Sam E., who's lost 35 pounds and kept them off for 10 years, "If you hate fish, don't eat it just to lose weight."

Since you already have a sense of what will and won't work for you, start out by making two lists. Here's a sample:

What worked

occasionally having a treat

eating 3 meals a day

saving up calories for parties

limiting red meat

packing my lunch the night
  before

What didn't work

strict dieting

skipping lunch

drinking tons of water

eating grapefruit 5 times a day

For more help in figuring out what worked and didn't work, ask yourself the following questions while reflecting on your last two or three attempts at weight loss:

• Think about the food plan or diet you used—was the calorie level too high or too low? What foods could you have? What foods couldn't you have? Was this just right or too restrictive for you? Was there much food preparation or shopping involved? What did you do to make the food plan work for you? (For example, did you make a special effort to keep plenty of fruits and vegetables on hand?) Would any of this be right for you now?

• How did you feel—both physically and mentally—on past weight-loss plans? Think about what made you feel good and bad.

• What sort of exercise plan did you follow? Was it realistic, one you could fit into your current routine? How could you modify it?

• What were the most difficult and easiest aspects of this plan?

• How did you modify your daily routine? Were there new activities you adopted that were helpful? (For instance, did you stop going grocery shopping right before dinner, when temptation levels are high?)

Call your answers to these questions into play as you finally decide upon a weight-loss program. For example, if you really hate dieting and can't bear the thought of going on another diet, you might benefit from one of the nondieting approaches to weight loss, such as the 6-Week Nondieting Weight-Control Plan (page 109). If, like Ernie L., you love carbohydrates, don't choose a food plan that eliminates them. If you feel you can't lose weight on a plan that allows you to eat sweets, then choose one that temporarily cuts them out. (Remember, though, that most successful maintainers do not deny themselves favorite foods; they eventually learn how to control them.) If you hated swimming the last time you lost weight—it took too much time to drive to the pool—then you might want to consider an at-home exercise program or something you can do outside your front door, like walking. (For more on exercise, see Chapter VII, "Move It to Lose It.")

Consider the possibility of returning to a plan that worked for you in the past. If it helped you before, it may help you again. Moreover, you may find that a weight-loss program you attended in the past is better than before, since good programs change with the times.

In reflecting on her past weight-loss attempts, Donna C. says, "My problem was that I focused on 'the diet' and what you had to give up. I was either 'going on' or 'going off.' It was feast or famine. I needed the lifestyle-change aspect." And that's how she finally lost her 108 pounds: by attending a several-month class on behavior modification and lifestyle change taught by a registered dietitian.

Ann F. also learned a great deal from her past experiences. (She had plenty to draw from: she estimates that she tried to lose weight 20 to 30 times before she finally lost her 220 pounds.) She had been on many diets that were highly restrictive. She told me, "The more extreme the diet, the more I failed. These diets made me feel physically sick and depressed, probably because I did a lot of them." Ann also learned that "eat-only-one-food, strict-rules diets" set her up for failure. "I wanted whatever I couldn't have. Now I feel there's no such thing as good and bad food." Looking back on her experiences, she found Overeaters Anonymous to be too focused on food and binge eating for her liking. With Weight Watchers, she acknowledges that although she did not lose weight and keep it off with their program, "Their reasonable diet may have helped to establish my current habits." Because of her massive weight problem (she once weighed 380), Ann finally had gastric surgery (see page 79). But she still has to do what most of the other masters do to keep the weight off: eat less and engage in more physical activity. Her secret of success is, "I eat what I like, eat moderately and exercise. I try to eat a low-fat, balanced diet."

Think about your past experiences and draw from them as you make the decision about your final weight loss plan.

Finding the Right Match

T HE PROBLEM WITH SOME WEIGHT-LOSS PROGRAMS and regimens is that they try to make you think there is one right way to lose weight. As we've established, however, the approaches used by the masters were highly variable.

I can't even tell you that the experts are always right in their recommendations about what approaches will work for what people. For instance, some experts tend to favor more aggressive approaches, such as very-low-calorie medically supervised diets (see page 75) or residential weight-loss programs, for people who have large amounts of weight to lose. Indeed, for someone with more than 100 pounds to take off, it can be far more motivating to follow a plan that allows for more rapid weight loss than one that allows just half-a-pound-a-week weight loss.

Nevertheless, some "big losers" among the masters did just fine on less extreme plans. Bob W. credits his 250-pound loss to Weight Watchers. (He's kept it off for 21 years.) "They taught me what to eat and how to cook low-calorie meals. Through the Weight Watchers program, I received much moral support." Then there's Joseph M., who, 19 years ago, lost 115 pounds by following his own self-styled diet based on Weight Watchers that included lots of fish (twice a day), vegetables and fruit. "I never went to Weight Watchers [although his mother did, and sent him diet information]. I'm not into 'rah, rah' stuff."

So how do you find the right match? Says Joseph M., "You have to search it out." That is, you have to do some investigation, some research to sort out what you like and don't like about various weight-loss approaches. When Alisa S. was ready to lose weight once and for all, she did her homework by touring her local library diet section. "I found one book that talked about the emotional side of being fat, the purposes of eating and not eating and a diet-for-life plan. That gave me the grounds for a 25-pound loss for [the past] 7 years."

Following are some questions you can ask yourself to help figure out what's right for you as you investigate various approaches:

• **Are you a "program" person or a "self-styler"?** A group person or a loner? Do you find it helpful to be with others who have the same problem or do you prefer to deal with things on your own? If you lean toward groups, does the one you're considering have enough members of each sex to suit you?

♦ **How much money do you want to spend?** The most expensive programs tend to be residential programs, medically supervised very-low-calorie plans and those that supply you with food. "The good news for dieters is that there is no association between cost and effectiveness," note Tufts University Medical School's Johanna Dwyer, D.Sc., R.D., and Diana Lu, M.S., R.D., in a review of popular diets. (When comparing costs, be sure to get a written estimate of the entire program, including maintenance.)

♦ **Does the program or plan in question support your personal weight goal** (see page 52)? If an unrealistically low goal is imposed upon you in any way, it's a tip-off that the approach is less than ideal.

♦ **To what extent is exercise emphasized?** Are the suggestions realistic for your lifestyle? Is there medical supervision of exercise?

♦ **Do you prefer working with professionals,** such as psychologists, dietitians, nurses and physicians? Or do you find groups led by laypeople to be more helpful?

♦ **Do you do well on diets or have you had it with dieting?** Although a number of masters said that they did best when they threw away all diets, planned diets did work for many masters. Says Arizona obesity expert Dr. Susan Olson, "A diet for a short period of time can be a motivation. If it doesn't work, chuck it." Diets do not necessarily set you up for failure—it's how you perceive them and use them. It's important that diets be viewed as tools—not long-term solutions to weight problems. (See page 317 for "The Jump-Start Diet," a fairly aggressive diet on which you lose some weight quickly so you are motivated to proceed.)

♦ **Can you tailor or modify the diet to suit your own needs,** if not in the beginning, later? Does the program discourage this?

♦ **How much freedom of choice do you need?** If you can't bear the thought of liquid meals or prepackaged foods and know you've gone off them quickly in the past, try something different this time. On the other hand, some people prefer a more drastic approach to get them started.

♦ **If you're considering a program, how frequent are the sessions?** Is this compatible with your lifestyle?

◆ **What is the maintenance component of the plan?** (Experts advise you to spend at least one month in a maintenance program for each month that you spend losing weight.) Will you be taught skills for life? Do you go back for group meetings or appointments? Is this included in the original cost?

◆ **Does the plan have the right emphasis on nutrition and food preparation for you?** If you rarely cook for yourself, then a program with a heavy emphasis on food preparation may not be for you.

◆ **If you are an emotional and/or binge eater, does the plan offer a way to help you?** Will the plan enable you to develop more positive-thinking skills?

There are no right answers. You have to decide if any one particular approach suits you and your needs. (For reliable weight-loss programs and books on the subject, consult the list on page 81.)

Give Yourself Time

W HATEVER MEANS YOU CHOOSE to get the weight off, it's important to be patient. You didn't gain the weight overnight, and you can't expect to lose it overnight (or in a week or a month) either. In fact, the vast majority of masters took 6 or more months to reach their goal weights. Many took 2 or more years.

If you decide you're a program person, the longer you stick with it, the more weight you're likely to lose. A review of 105 studies on behavioral weight-control programs revealed that duration of treatment was the single most important factor positively associated with weight loss. (Often offered by local hospitals, behavioral programs typically last for 12 to 25 weekly sessions and are for small groups of participants. Such programs may be led by dietitians, psychologists, nurses, exercise specialists or some combination of those, and they usually include behavior-modification techniques [see page 102], positive-thinking techniques [see Chapter VI] and sensible low-calorie diet advice.) The idea is that a longer program gives you more time to practice the skills necessary for maintenance before you venture out on your own.

To test this theory, weight-maintenance researcher Michael G. Perri, Ph.D., of the University of Florida, and colleagues studied people who took part in either a 20- or 40-week behavioral weight-control program. Study participants in both groups were taught the same skills but at a different rate. By week 20, both groups had lost the same amount of weight. But by week 40, the members of the extended group continued to lose weight, while the 20-week group did not. Those who had participated in the lengthier program also kept off significantly more weight 32 weeks after the program had ended than did those who were in the shorter program. Both groups did, however, regain weight after their weight-loss program ended: on average, people in the 40-week group regained 33 percent of their weight, while the 20-week individuals gained back fully half of their lost weight.

In a recent issue of the journal *Addictive Behaviors*, Brenda Wolfe, Ph.D., a psychologist and director of research for Jenny Craig International, hypothesizes that the reason the participants in Dr. Perri's study regained the weight is that they never lost enough to perceive themselves as successful. Although the people (mainly women) in the 40-week program lost an average of about 30 pounds, their average starting weight was well over 200 pounds, and they may have still seen themselves as overweight.

In contrast, Dr. Wolfe found far more success in a group of 267 women who stayed in weight-loss programs long enough to reach their goal weights or weights that they found acceptable. (The women were recruited from Jenny Craig weight-loss centers across the country.) Dr. Wolfe found that 8 out of 10 women remained within 10 percent of their goal weights 1 year after they had left the program. Her findings suggest that people who stay in programs long enough to reach or come close to their goal weights are more likely to maintain weight loss.

Is It Legit?

THE FOLLOWING ARE TIP-OFFS that a weight-loss plan may be less than reputable:

• **Suggestions that weight loss will be quick and easy.** For most people, it's not. Unless you're in a medically supervised program, steer clear of programs that promise more than 2 pounds loss per week after the first week or two.

• **Diets that overemphasize one food or food group.** They may be unbalanced, and you won't be likely to stick with them.

• **Claims that you can eat all you want and still lose weight.** That's impossible.

• **"Guaranteed, forever" results.** There are no guarantees, even with the best of programs.

• **Claims that dealing with sensitivities or allergies will "cure" your weight problem.** Overweight is not caused by sensitivities or allergies.

• **Offers of foods or supplements that burn off fat.** There are no known combinations of foods or special supplements that you can take to burn off fat.

• **Unscientific remedies, such as body wraps, injections, herbs and cellulite treatments.**

• **Promises of secret or breakthrough findings.** If there were a breakthrough, you'd see it on the front page of your local newspaper.

The Question of Safety

IF YOU CHOOSE to follow a formal diet, how can you be certain of its safety—be it a "program" diet or a "self-styled" diet? Let's start with the most aggressive diets, *very-low-calorie diets* (**VLCDs**), which are meant for people who are more than 40 percent overweight according to height and weight tables. VLCDs are particularly helpful when someone needs to lose weight quickly because of urgent health problems. Average losses are 3 pounds per week for women and 4 pounds for men for up to 12 to 16 weeks, the recommended duration of VLCDs. Because they can have serious side effects, *VLCDs should* *be followed only under careful medical supervision; they are not meant for self-styled dieters.*

VLCDs provide fewer than 800 calories per day, with most of the calories derived from protein. There are two types of VLCDs: those that use animal protein foods—such as red meat, fish and chicken—and those that use high-protein liquid formulas. Special supplements are needed as well. (VLCDs are a modification of total fasting; protein is added to prevent your body from breaking down its own protein, which can be dangerous. Total fasting is not recommended under any circumstances because of the excessive losses of body protein, water and nutrients.)

Beware, too, that on VLCDs metabolic rate can drop, possibly making weight loss more difficult with time. Moreover, if the diet makes you tired and less active, your calorie needs can drop further. Exercise may help to offset the decrease in calorie needs on any weight-loss diet, but strenuous exercise is not recommended on VLCDs.

In their review of diets, Dr. Dwyer and Ms. Lu are quick to point out, "VLCDs are not panaceas; they are simply a rapid way to lose weight." They should be used as only one part of a comprehensive program that includes behavior modification, cognitive restructuring, exercise, education about nutrition and the transition back to "real foods" and a strong maintenance program. The ideal staff for such a program includes a physician, registered dietitian, psychologist, nurse and exercise physiologist—all specially trained in the treatment of overweight people.

Interestingly, new findings suggest that there may be no weight-loss advantage in consuming fewer than 800 calories per day. Moreover, although more research is needed, the ongoing studies of Syracuse University's Dr. Wadden and colleague Robert Kuehnel, Ph.D., suggest that it may be beneficial to add a daily meal of conventional food to liquid diets. They suspect that this meal of "real" food may reduce anxiety and problem eating, as the dieter winds down on the program.

Low-calorie diets—in the 800-to-1,200-calorie-per-day range—should also be undertaken only with a physician's approval and ongoing supervision, particularly if you have a lot of weight to lose and/or medical problems. The lower the calorie level, the less likely the diet is to be nutritionally adequate. Multivitamin-mineral supplements are usually recommended, as are iron and calcium supplements for many women. (Note, however, that there is no reason to exceed Recommended Dietary Allowance [RDA] levels of any vitamin or mineral.)

Diets providing 1,200 or more daily calories are likely to be nutritionally adequate if they're carefully planned according to the Food Guide Pyramid (see page 109). To play it safe, however, it doesn't hurt to take a multivitamin-mineral supplement. In general, such diets should provide the following *minimum* amounts of these nutrients each day:

 ◆ 50 grams of protein (63 for men)
 ◆ 100 grams of carbohydrate, predominantly complex carbohydrate from grain products, fruits and vegetables
 ◆ 6 to 8 eight-ounce cups of water or noncaffeinated liquids (A number of masters told me that drinking lots of water helps them.)

Moreover, no more than 30 percent of your calories should come from fat.

If you are someone who likes a formal diet plan—as did a number of the masters—you may want to consider the Jump-Start Diet on page 317. It will allow you to lose weight fairly quickly in the beginning, so that you become motivated to keep losing.

The Mathematics of Weight Loss

S IMPLISTIC AS IT SOUNDS, if you want to lose weight, you have to eat fewer calories than you burn off each day. You can do it by cutting back on calories or by increasing your activity level so you expend more calories. But the best method is some combination of the two.

The average American woman eats about 1,800 calories a day; for men the figure is 2,800 calories. (Men tend to have higher calorie needs because their bodies have a greater percentage of muscle tissue and less fat than those of women; muscle tissue burns more calories than fat.) Assuming that a woman is maintaining her weight on 1,800 calories a day, how much will she lose on a 1,000-calorie-a-day diet? Since she's burning off an extra 800 calories each day—above and beyond the calories she's consuming—her calorie deficit for 1 week would be 7 days x 800 = 5,600 calories. Divide 5,600 by 3,500 (the approximate number of calories in a pound of body fat), and she should lose about 1½ pounds a week on her 1,000-calorie diet. Of course, weight loss is often greater in the beginning, presumably because of body-water losses.

Be aware, however, that weight loss is highly variable from one person to the next—depending on one's overall size, activity level and metabolic rate. Thus, some people on the same diet lose more weight than others do. In one study, published in the *American Journal of Clinical Nutrition,* a group of 108 obese women who were placed on an 800-calorie-a-day diet for 21 days lost anywhere from 2 pounds to 28 pounds. Some women did not lose any weight at all until day 13 of the diet.

Where do the calories you expend each day go? Fully 60 to 75 percent of them are used for your resting metabolic rate (RMR). RMR is the energy required to run the body at rest—to do the bare minimum: breathe, keep your heart pumping and regulate body temperature. Another 10 percent of your calories are used to digest and process food that you eat. The remaining component of calorie expenditure— physical activity—is the one over which you have the most influence. Even if you're not physically active, 15 to 30 percent of calories are used on everyday activities.

In Chapter I, we talked about how a low metabolic rate relates to the development of a weight problem and how variable the rate can be among people of similar size. The University of Pennsylvania's Obesity Research Group conducted a study measuring RMR in a group of overweight women of the same weight, age and height. Individual RMRs for these 5 women were: 1,263, 1,523, 1,778, 1,979 and 2,152 calories per day. "If these 5 women consumed a 1,200-calorie diet for 3 months, their weight losses would be 11, 20, 28, 35 and 40 pounds respectively," says Gary Foster, M.S., who helped with the study.

The differences in RMR explain in large part why some people lose weight so much more easily than others. Just as certain individuals have thick, shiny hair while others have thin, limp locks, some people have slower metabolisms than others. If you're a slow loser, Weight Watchers psychologist Dr. Kabatznick points out, "You have to learn to see small amounts of weight loss on a steady basis as success—at least you didn't gain." Of course, as mentioned earlier, even if you have a low RMR (which you have little influence over), you still have control over the number of calories you expend in exercise.

We've also talked about how metabolic rate drops with dieting—it's the body's way of adapting to a state of semi-starvation. As an act of self-preservation, the body, in effect, says, "You're not feeding me enough calories, so I'll slow down the rate at which I burn them." RMR also decreases after you lose weight because you weigh less. (It should make sense, for instance, that if you maintained your old 200-pound weight on 2,400 calories a day, you won't be able to eat that much if you want to maintain your weight at 150 pounds.) The good news is that dieting per se does not appear to lower RMR permanently, as some people believe. The decrease is no more than that expected because you weigh less. (The same thing, however, may not be true for those who are *always* on a diet, who may have lowered their metabolic rate through chronic dieting.) Unfortunately, RMR does drop as people age, mainly because the body contains proportionately more fat tissue, which is metabolically less active than muscle tissue. A major reason that calorie needs tend to drop in older people is that they are often less physically active. The good news is that exercise may offset at least some of this change.

Surgery and Drugs

SOMEONE WHO IS 100 percent or more overweight, has medical problems and has failed on more conventional weight-loss plans may be a candidate for surgery for weight loss. Two of the masters I interviewed lost weight with surgery. Ann F. once weighed 380 pounds, and Lisa B. was once as heavy as 385. Both have kept off more than 200 pounds. Although their weight loss primarily resulted from the surgery, to maintain their new weights, both Ann and Lisa exercise regularly and are careful about what they eat.

The two most commonly used forms of surgery in essence "shrink" the stomach so you can't eat as much. (One is called gastric bypass, and the other is vertical banded gastroplasty.) Surgery typically helps people lose at least half of their excess weight within 1 year. But because it is possible to stretch the "shrunken" stomach by repeated overeating, the weight can be regained. According to Richard Atkinson, M.D., Chief of Clinical Nutrition at Hampton Veterans Administration Medical Center in Virginia, the surgery should be done only by an experienced surgeon who does several such operations per month. You also need to know what kind of follow-up care you'll receive. "If the surgeon tells you, 'I'll do it, then you'll be seen by your local doctor,' that's not good enough." You will need regular follow-up visits with a physician who is knowledgeable about the procedure—be it the surgeon himself or an internist who has a formal collaboration with the surgeon. It is critical that your return visits include education about nutrition, exercise, lifestyle change and behavior modification.

Dr. Atkinson adds that you should talk with people who have had the surgery. "It's a serious step. It should be done only if you can't lose weight any other way or if you have critical medical problems like diabetes or high blood pressure. It's serious surgery, and there are some unpleasant side effects. You'll never be able to eat huge meals again."

As far as appetite-suppressant drugs are concerned, people who lose weight while on them tend to regain once the drugs are stopped. Although many of the masters had tried such drugs in the past, none found long-term success with them.

Reasonable Weight-Control Guides

PROGRAMS

Fewer than 600-800 calories per day:
Health Management Resources (HMR)
Medifast
Optifast

800-1,200 calories per day:
Diet Center
Diet Workshop
Jenny Craig Weight Loss Centres
Nutri/System
Weight Watchers

BOOKS

Breaking the Diet Habit by Janet Polivy & C. Peter Herman. 1983. New York: Basic Books, Inc.

Buddy Diet by Helen Ashton Tedder and Marlene Johnson. 1992. New York: Warner Books.

Callaway Diet by C. Wayne Callaway. 1991. New York: Bantam Books.

Diets Don't Work by Bob Schwartz. 1982. Houston: Breakthru Publishing.

Fat Attack Plan by Annette B. Natow and Jo-Ann Heslin. 1991. New York: Pocket Books.

Fit or Fat Target Diet by Covert Bailey. 1989. Boston: Houghton Mifflin.

Keeping It Off by Robert H. Colvin and Susan C. Olson. 1989. Arkansas City, Kansas: Gilliland.

LEARN Program for Weight Control by Kelly D. Brownell. 1994. Dallas: American Health Publishing Co. 1-800-736-7323.

Living Without Dieting by John P. Foreyt and G. Ken Goodrick. 1992. Houston: Harrison Publishing.

Maximize Your Body Potential by Joyce D. Nash. 1986. Palo Alto: Bull Publishing Co.

Now That You've Lost It by Joyce D. Nash. 1992. Palo Alto: Bull Publishing Co.

The Setpoint Diet by Gilbert A. Leveille. 1985. New York: Ballantine Books, 1985.

T-Factor Diet by Martin Katahn. 1990. New York: Bantam Books.

Truth About Addiction and Recovery by Stanton Peele and Archie Brodsky. 1991. New York: Fireside Books.

Weight Control Digest newsletter. American Health Publishing Co., 1555 W. Mockingbird Lane, Suite 203, Dallas, TX 75235.

Weight Maintenance Survival Guide by Kelly D. Brownell and Judith Rodin. 1990. Dallas: American Health Publishing Co.

Note: This is by no means an exhaustive list. There are other legitimate weight-loss programs and books. An excellent reference that evaluates many different approaches is Diets That Work *by Deralee Scanlon. 1992. Los Angeles: Lowell House.*

IV

Accept the Food Facts:

Featuring a 6-Week Nondieting Weight-Control Plan

MOST MASTERS PEACEFULLY ACCEPT their new way of eating: they know they can't eat whatever they want and they know they can't go back to their old food habits. They have learned how to make low-fat eating enjoyable, and they have accepted certain food facts.

Susan C.'s Story

AS I INTERVIEWED SUSAN C., I had a hard time distinguishing the difference between how she ate while she was losing her 100-plus pounds and how she eats now. There are many similarities. When Susan lost weight, she cut way back on meat. She still eats little meat. While losing, she "religiously" ate three regular meals a day. Same behavior now. With every 10-pound drop, Susan would treat herself to a favorite food. Now, at maintenance, she includes plenty of treats. "Yes," she says, "I eat pies, cookies, cakes, drink wine and Scotch—but in moderation." Today, she weighs 132. Fifteen years ago, she carried about 250 pounds on her 5'7" frame.

In retrospect, Susan C. says that her 31-year difficulty with her weight was the result of eating at every time *except* mealtime. "At the age of 9, I was given a cookbook and told to cook for the family when my mother went to work. I could never understand why I had a weight problem because I never ate much at the table. But as I cooked, I would eat. As I cleaned up, I would eat some more. If I made cookies, half of the dough would be gone before it hit the sheets. But I never ate the cookies."

Susan also attributes her former weight problem to her Scandinavian and Portuguese food heritage. "Meat was usually eaten three times a day. It was meat, potatoes and gravy." That tradition, along with her penchant for picking as she cooked, landed Susan in size-18 dresses by the time she was a freshman in high school. "Can you imagine being 16 and wearing a size 44-D bra?" she asked.

From her earliest memories, Susan was heavy. "I have a picture of me as a baby from when I won a contest. I was the happiest, most chubby baby." She recalls many hardships as a child. "My brothers and sisters were slender, and I could never eat the foods they did because I was too fat. I always had to bring my lunch to school because I couldn't eat what the other kids did. My mother would pick me up after school, and I'd go home and eat cottage cheese." Children called her names, and she wore "sack" dresses. "Once my mother made me a crinoline dress, but I looked like a flying hippopotamus in it."

By the time she was in college, Susan weighed 250 pounds. She met a man who wasn't concerned about her weight and married him in her sophomore year. "I would diet, and it never worked out. But it didn't bother him." Like most masters, Susan tried to shed pounds many times and in many ways before she found success. "I tried all the current fad diets available at the time: egg diets, grapefruit diets, eat-everything diets, liquid diets, cottage-cheese diets and so on." But she never lost more than 5 pounds with any of these schemes.

"I was thoroughly convinced that I'd be fat for the rest of my life. I was sure it was the result of an outside problem—my metabolism, my thyroid, a medical problem that would never be resolved. I believe I know all of the excuses for being heavy and most of the avoidance methods for facing the truth."

What finally turned the tide for Susan? She says, "There didn't seem to be any one particular thing or event. I really believe that psychologically I was ready. Something finally clicked in my head." (There's that "click" again.) Her weight loss began when she happened to drop several pounds right before she and her husband moved from Oregon to Southern California, where Susan had access to a swimming pool. She started to swim, which she loves, and noticed some more weight coming off. A spiral began. "I found that it was really possible to lose weight, and I decided to keep up the momentum through exercise and a change in my eating habits."

Exercise was critical to Susan's weight-loss efforts. "I bought a 10-speed bicycle and rode it for 10 miles early every morning. Then I'd swim 50 laps a day—rain or shine—and I did floor exercises two to three times a day." She kept all that up for about a year, the length of time it took to lose most of the weight. What about now? Susan says, "I exercise, but not fanatically." Actually, Susan is one of a minority of masters who has no formal exercise program. But she makes an effort to be physically active: "I walk a little more, climb more stairs, stretch a little more, and sometimes I do floor exercises. In the winter, I shovel snow a lot and wash my car. I try not to sit around. In the summer, I get up early and do work in the garden and yard. I'm conscious of not sitting on my rear end all day."

How did she eat when she was losing weight? Much the way she does now. "I stopped eating a lot of meat and concentrated on vegetables, fruits, fish, chicken and cottage cheese. I never would have dreamed that cutting out meat would make a difference. I also love dairy products: cream, cheese and butter. But gradually, I cut back and learned I could live with less. I also ate at very specific times, three meals a day. My husband would take me for a pizza or ice cream soda once a month. I eagerly anticipated that treat. After a while, I no longer needed that incentive, and as my eating habits changed, so did my longing for certain foods.

"This worked for me but may not for someone else. You have to ask yourself what will suit your lifestyle. Then keeping the weight off will come easier." Susan found that strict diets of the past, "where I ate half a cup of cottage cheese, half a grapefruit, 3 ounces of meat and half a cup of beans, and having to be the only one eating like that made me feel like I was punished. You don't need to be regimented—just have some discipline and stop cheating on yourself."

In general, Susan has cut down on fats and tries to stay away from fried foods of any sort. She eats mostly vegetables, grains and some cheese, like part-skim mozzarella or farmer cheese. She eats meat only about once a week. Breakfast typically consists of cereal, fruit and bread. Lunch might be cottage cheese and fruit, a salad and fresh vegetables. Dinner is usually whatever she cooks for her husband—Italian, Indian, Thai—but Susan doesn't eat as much as he does. She also finds drinking water to be helpful in controlling her weight: she consumes 8 to 10 glasses a day.

Susan's childhood penchant for cooking is still with her. She makes her own bread, cakes, cookies, jams and jellies, pasta and sauces. "My husband is Italian, so we eat a lot of pasta—but not with cream. I might make homemade sausage, but I'll just eat a few pieces. If we have Parmesan cheese, which is full of calories, it's not in the recipe, just sprinkled on top." Lately, Susan has been enjoying Indian cookery. "It calls for quite a bit of oil, so I let the finished dish sit and remove the fat from the top." But Susan loves chicken skin, so she broils the chicken and allows herself the skin. And she eats real butter, but only in small amounts.

As she cooks, Susan has learned not to taste any more than is essential to the success of a recipe in an effort to overcome her old habit of eating a whole meal before she ever got to the table. "When I'm clearing the table, if I feel tempted to eat something left behind, I dump it in the garbage disposal quickly."

I was surprised at the number of tempting foods Susan is able to keep around. "At the moment, there's a jar of peanuts sitting on my counter." But Susan has learned how to handle her highest-temptation foods. "I have a bag of cashews in my cupboard, but I don't start because I know I won't be able to stop." She admits to an occasional urge to go on a food binge. "So I go downtown and buy an expensive candy bar. It takes care of a craving. I give in to it, and it satisfies me. Then I go on with my business. Once I allow myself to have it, I don't have to worry anymore."

If things get out of hand, it's just for a short time. Susan recently made a sumptuous strawberry-rhubarb pie and found herself eating three slices in one day. So she said to herself, "Hmmm, that's full of calories. You can't have pie three times a day."

Susan finds it critical to weigh herself daily. If the scale creeps up a few pounds (she never lets herself gain more than 5), she cuts back for a few days. "I might have grapefruit and dry toast for breakfast, a salad with apple and cheese for lunch, then a normal supper, but less of it. Within a few days, I'm back down again. I ask myself, 'Was it worth it?' No, it wasn't."

In short, Susan has been able to maintain a 100-pound-plus weight loss for many years, yet she still has a nice food life. It's not one of sacrifice and denial, but instead one involving moderation, tradeoffs and pleasure in knowing what she really wants to eat and what she can forgo.

The Many Ways of Maintenance

WHEN I ASKED EACH MASTER "What are the three most important things you do to keep your weight down?" I got more than 90 different answers. Here are some of their responses:

- "Make weekly menus and shop to fit the menus."
- "Monitor fat intake."
- "Eat differently—more fruit, less sugar/fat."
- "Eat nutritious meals—reasonable amounts."
- "Eat the bad things only on Saturday."
- "Avoid old 'problem' foods: *excess* pasta, bread, butter, sour cream. I don't eliminate, just watch quantity."
- "Portion control of foods."
- "Eat oatmeal every morning—no sausage, bacon or eggs."

It soon became obvious that there are just as many ways to maintain weight as there are to lose it in the first place. But, again, I was struck by certain "food facts" that emerged from the stories of the masters.

FOOD FACT #1
The masters stop seeing the way they eat as dieting.

I have an overweight friend who does all the "right" stuff when she's trying to lose weight. Vegetables in cream sauce make way for plain, steamed versions. She eats more chicken and fish in place of fattier meats. Diet salad dressing takes the place of chunky blue cheese. The freezer is filled with frozen yogurt. Then, after she sheds 30 pounds or so, she gets sick of the new way of eating. All of the changes are reversed, and on go the pounds—again. My friend lives in one of two states: she's either on a diet or off one.

Susan C., however, never used the word "diet" to describe how she lost weight that final time nor to describe the way she eats now, even when she cuts back for a few days to lose a few unwanted pounds. The way she eats has simply become a way of life for her. When Arizona researchers Drs. Robert Colvin and Susan Olson conducted their first interviews, they found themselves saying, "You're telling us what you eat *now.* How about when you were losing?" The typical puzzled reply of the masters: "*Of course* it's the same food—how could you ever go back to what you ate before?"

In a recent article on preventing weight regain, psychologists Brenda L. Wolfe, Ph.D., and G. Alan Marlatt, Ph.D., state, "The first essential step in *preventing relapse* is eliminating the artificial boundary between *weight loss* and *weight maintenance.*" The masters recognize this: they see that the strategies to lose weight and those to maintain weight are essentially one and the same.

Diets can be useful tools to get you started on weight loss. But, as Weight Watchers psychologist Dr. Ronna Kabatznick points out, "The difference between weight loss and maintenance is only a couple of hundred calories for many people. It's an extra sandwich or an extra dessert. You have to close the gap between the effort it takes to lose weight and to keep it off."

Here's what the masters have to say about breaking away from the diet mentality:

• Sam E., who lost 35 pounds 10 years ago, reiterates, "People need to realize that what they are doing now to get the weight off has to be what they are willing to do once the weight comes off." Like a number of masters, Sam lost weight when she stopped dieting and adopted a lifestyle of healthy eating.

• Nancy K., who's kept off 60 pounds for 5 years: "I lost weight when I quit dieting and just watched what I ate."

• Linda W. lost her 39 pounds 6 years ago when she "decided to just try to cut back rather than going on an all-out starvation diet."

• Cathy C.: "When I stopped thinking about food and dieting, I started losing weight." She lost 38 pounds and has kept it off for 11 years.

• Rose F. has lost 35 pounds and is still losing: "The secret is I never really denied myself anything that I really wanted. I just cut back a little each day and stayed with it. My original plan was to quit gaining and start losing without torturing myself."

• Bob W., who has lost 250 pounds and has maintained that loss for 21 years, says, "I keep the weight off by continuing to do what I did to lose it."

I was impressed by the similarities in the way other masters ate "then" (when they were actively losing weight) and how they eat now.

• Marie D. **Then:** "Ate low-fat healthy foods (fruits, vegetables, whole grains) and ate only when hungry." **Now:** "Concentrate on eating unprocessed foods, whole grains, little meat, low-fat foods and eating only when hungry."

• Linda G. **Then:** "Ate smaller portions, watched fat and sugar intake." **Now:** "Modest portions, less fat, less sugar."

• Don C. **Then:** "Ate low-fat, low-sugar, high-fiber." **Now:** "Try to maintain low-fat, high-fiber diet and minimize between-meal snacking."

• Mindy B. **Then:** I decided to cut out all fat from my diet. I ate no meat, but I did eat chicken and fish." **Now:** I don't eat meat, and my fat intake is minimal. I eat fruit, raw vegetables, lots of yogurt, rice, potatoes and chicken and fish."

Accepting that you have to make permanent changes in the way you eat doesn't mean a lifetime of hardship but does mean some sacrifice and delay of gratification. Donna C. is one who admits it's a struggle to keep off her 108 pounds. She adds, "But it's worth it! My life has changed dramatically for the better, and I love it!"

Pat B. also feels great about her choice to adopt a new way of eating. "I'm lazy. I don't ever want to have to do it [lose weight] again. I don't ever want to be that unhappy again." She's kept off 84 pounds for 10 years.

FOOD FACT #2
The masters survive the transition from weight loss to maintenance.

Even with a change in attitude, the transition from losing weight to maintenance is not always easy. There's no question that most people do eat less while losing and get to eat more afterward. The difficulty is making the decision about what foods to add at maintenance, particularly for people who have lost pounds quickly through a more structured weight-loss plan and/or a strict diet. Kevin C. lost his 45 pounds in 5 months and admits, "Maintenance was a nightmare. You're probably better off if you lose weight slowly so you have more time to make behavioral changes." If you're a program person, you should stay with the program through the maintenance phase.

For many masters, learning what to eat at maintenance seemed to be a trial-and-error process. Of the difference between her current eating routine and the one when she was slimming down, Susan C. says, "When I was losing weight, I wouldn't eat pasta because I thought it was more fattening. I would eat my meat plainer and [skipped] most desserts. I was more focused then than now, but I don't recall a transition period. My maintenance eating just seems to have evolved from changing my eating habits." (The remaining Food Facts will help you establish maintenance food habits, as will the "Nondieting Weight-Control Plan" on page 109.)

Of course, it's easier to "settle in" to maintenance food habits if you discover the value of exercise as you're losing weight or shortly thereafter. Brian L. felt a need to cut out sweets as he was losing his 20 pounds (he's 5'5") 15 years ago. But when he started running shortly after he lost the weight, he found that he could include his treats.

Another difficulty in making the transition is finding your "comfortable weight" (see page 52). Many masters initially dropped to a weight that was too low for comfort. For example, Brenda Z. says, "My goal of 135 was hard to maintain. I can maintain and not 'fight my body' at 140 to 145."

Susan C. still views herself as heavy and wishes she had been prepared for feeling this way as she was losing weight. Similarly, Jeffrey B. continues to see himself as "a fat person, even though I've had the weight off longer than I've had it on. I still have to work to believe it when my friends say I look better at 180 than at 150." (He's 6'1" tall and weighed 235 pounds 22 years ago.)

FOOD FACT # 3
The masters see the beauty of low-fat eating.

In addition to the two major ways to lose weight, eating less or exercising more, the experts say there may be a third way: eating fewer fatty foods. In fact, the masters seldom talk about calorie intake; fat has become the focal point. When asked the three most important factors in keeping their weight down, the number one food-related response from the masters was "watch my fat intake."

Patsy B. (73 pounds, 3 years): "I basically cut all fats from my diet. It's wonderful, and I really do eat a lot. I buy fat-free [products] and sometimes these things cost a little more, but they are worth it."

Shirley C. (26 pounds, 12½ years): "Even when eating out, which I do at least twice a week, I tell waitpersons I'm allergic to butter. I eat fish out—but seldom, if ever, meat. I'm careful but happy in my eating habits."

Marie D. (32 pounds, 3 years): "I focus on eating a low-fat diet and eating only when I'm hungry. I eat as much as I want of healthy foods."

Donna C. (108 pounds, 3½ years): "I cut way down on fat intake; the rest of the calories take care of themselves!"

Ann B. (35 pounds, 3½ years): "Restricting the level of fat in my diet made a huge difference in losing my final 10 pounds. I found I could eat almost anything and as much as I wanted, as long as my total fat intake was less than 20 percent."

Edith S. (56 pounds, 3 years): "I never starved myself as I had done many times before. I ate all the complex carbohydrates I wanted. I cut all the fats out of my diet that I could and only ate small amounts of chicken, turkey or fish. I used nonfat milk, yogurt and cottage cheese. I also quit frying. I never had hunger pangs or felt weak like before. I still follow the same program."

Several studies indicate that when people are allowed to eat as much as they want of low-fat foods, they consume fewer calories than if they are allowed to eat unlimited amounts of high-fat foods. In a study at Cornell University, researchers compared the weights of a group of women who followed an 11-week diet providing 20 to 25 percent calories from fat with their weights when they followed a diet with 35 to 40 percent of calories from fat for the same length of time. (The women rated the two diets as equally palatable.) Even though they were allowed to eat as much food as they wanted on both diets—and were actually encouraged to snack—on average, the women ate about 300 calories less per day and lost twice as much weight on the low-fat program—about 5½ pounds in 11 weeks.

This research suggests that if you pay attention to your fat intake, you can lose weight without paying much attention to calories. Why would this be? In the first place, fat is the most fattening nutrient: each gram of fat (a gram is about ⅓₀ of an ounce) provides about 9 calories, while a gram of protein or carbohydrate each provides about 4 calories. Thus, any time fat is added to a food—a tablespoon of oil to a salad or a dollop of real mayonnaise to water-packed tuna—it markedly raises calories. (Fat is, in essence, any food that's greasy to the touch: butter, oil, margarine, mayonnaise, regular salad dressing and cream cheese. Whole-milk dairy products and cheeses tend to be high in fat, as do many lunch meats and marbled fresh meats.) Thus, if you cut back on fat, you automatically cut back on calories. (For details on cutting back on fat, see "The Basics of Low-Fat Eating" on page 106.)

In the second place, the body seems to have a highly efficient way of storing food fat as body fat. Dietitians used to say that all calories are created equal. That is, they believed you would be just as likely to gain weight if you regularly overate by 500 fat calories as you would if you consumed 500 too many carbohydrate calories. But it now appears that you're more likely to gain weight by overeating fat calories because your body has an easier time converting them to body fat.

This notion is supported by a study published in the *American Journal of Clinical Nutrition* showing that women who switched from the typical American level of a 37-percent-fat diet to a 20-percent-fat diet for 20 weeks lost a significant amount of weight (they also lost 11 percent of their body-fat weight)—even though the researchers kept *adding* calories. The number of calories required for weight maintenance actually increased the longer the low-fat diet was followed.

When her doctor ordered her to lose weight after her legs "gave out," Holly L. headed for the library. "The fact that I could have generous amounts of carbohydrates, fruits and veggies in exchange for fat put me on the road to a 54-pound loss of weight." She adds, "Now, at age 72, I walk at a fast clip 6 days a week, bend and stretch with not a worry in the world about ever gaining it back." She described how she follows her low-fat food plan at buffets and as she travels: "I always find something on the menu that is suitable. This has been my way of eating for the last 3 years, and I'm happy with life. It's a whole new world being normal in size and not having to worry about gaining weight again." Today, Holly weighs 160, down 97 pounds from her high of 257.

Of course, another critical bonus of cutting back on fat is that it will lower your risk of cardiovascular disease and, possibly, certain types of cancer. Be especially careful to avoid saturated fat (whose major source is whole-milk dairy products), meats (especially fattier cuts) and coconut and palm oils.

None of this means that if you cut back on fat, you can eat unlimited high-carbohydrate foods like low-fat crackers, pretzels, pasta, bread and rice and still lose weight. It just means that if you lower fat intake and eat proportionately more carbohydrates, it should be easier to lose weight and easier to maintain that loss. A too-rigorous regimen can create problems. Obesity researchers Drs. Kelly Brownell and Thomas Wadden point out that if fat intake is too low—for example, less than 20 percent of your total calories—people often have trouble sticking with the regimen.

FOOD FACT #4
The masters develop—and enjoy—new tastes in food.

The masters have discovered the satiety value of fruits, vegetables and grains like breads, cereals, pasta and rice, which have bulk and are filling without providing many calories.

Edith S., who's kept off 56 pounds for 3 years, says, "I eat 5 starches a day, 4 vegetables, 3 fruits, 2 servings of nonfat dairy products, 1 serving of protein-rich foods. This is my daily goal, and I usually keep close to it. I stress high-fiber foods, as they seem to keep me from feeling hungry."

Consider one study by researchers at the University of Alabama, Birmingham, in which 20 people were served a 5-day diet with a large amount of fresh fruits, vegetables, whole grains and dried beans with very little fat. For another 5 days, they were served a diet high in fats and sugary foods with minimal fruits, vegetables and grains. On both diets, the participants were allowed to eat as much as they wanted. The researchers kept track not only of how many calories were eaten on each diet, but also of satiety or "fullness" ratings. The participants reached a point of satiety on the first diet at an average daily calorie intake that was *one-half* that of the diet high in fat and sugar—1,570 calories versus 3,000 calories! On the high-fat diet, the participants had a tendency to eat beyond "pleasant fullness." And it wasn't that the high-fat diet tasted better—the two diets were rated as equally tasty. The authors of the study noted that it took people significantly longer to eat meals on the lower-fat diet, which may help to explain their sensation of fullness at a lower calorie level.

This short-term study suggests that diets rich in fruits, vegetables and grains, which are at the same time low in fat, help you to eat fewer calories and are more satisfying for the calories. That makes sense, considering the following example: a 1-ounce bag of potato chips provides about 160 calories along with 11 grams of fat, while a 6-ounce baked potato, which has the same number of calories, has next to no fat and is far more filling.

Sadly, there is a pervasive attitude that anything good-tasting is automatically bad for you and, conversely, that all the good-for-you foods taste bad. Yet many of the masters seem to celebrate their new way of eating and have found ways to enliven foods and enjoy new taste sensations. Instead of dwelling on what they can't have, they focus on what they *can* have.

Carole C. (40 pounds, 20 years): "I learned to cook super low-fat. If it didn't taste good, my husband wouldn't eat it. I use lots of herbs and spices. I never feel deprived. Now, I just don't like the feeling of greasy, fatty foods. I'll eat a whole baked potato with low-fat cheese and chopped green onion: it's heavenly. We don't keep high-calorie foods in the house. We have other enjoyable things, like fresh strawberries."

Tom J. (75 pounds, 27 years): I never sit down to a plate of protein. I eat lots of vegetables, fruits and legumes instead of meat. I know how to cook and can make a vegetarian meal that's better than most people's idea of a regular meal. I use lots of garlic, spices and herbs."

Holly L. (54 pounds, 3 years): "I get several health-conscious magazines now. They have recipes and tips that I use. Mostly I've changed my habits and find those to be second nature now. After 5 or 6 months, I was no longer interested in eating the way I had."

Ernie L. (45 pounds, 12½ years): "I started stir-frying and putting it on pasta. For me, it was heaven. I love to cook, and I'm very creative."

Leo P. (46 pounds, 3½ years): "What I have done is kept myself from feeling as if something was being taken away from me. I have developed a new taste for food. When I'm cooking, I will use a combination of common herbs and spices to enhance the food's flavor."

Shirley C. (26 pounds, 12½ years): "I love to cook and convert all my recipes to low-fat, nutritious selections. Low-fat, high-carbohydrate cooking is so easy. All you have to do is take a few extra minutes to read labels!"

Marie D. (32 pounds, 3 years): "I obtain great satisfaction from cooking and baking quality, healthy dishes."

And the pay-off is worth it, as Gail O. explains of her eating habits and her 79-pound weight loss of 3 years: "I eat lots of carbohydrates, vegetables and fruits, chicken and fish, very little red meat. My food rewards are pretzels, raisins and a glass of red wine about four times a week. I went from a size 18/20 to a size 2/4 petite. Healthwise, I have normal blood sugar, blood pressure and cholesterol levels; all were high when I started." Ron K., who's been down 61 pounds for 5 years, says, "By 'eating smart,' one can live a normal life and not be an overweight recluse."

I was curious to see if the 20 masters who had lost 100 or more pounds had to work harder or eat more stringently during maintenance than did the people who had lost less weight. (All but 3 of the 20 had been overweight since childhood.) When asked to rate the degree to which they agreed with the statement "It is a constant struggle to keep my weight down," on a scale of 1 (agree) to 5 (disagree), the average response was "2.3," compared with the average response of about "2.7" for masters who took off fewer than 100 pounds. Although there was wide variation in responses, maintenance does appear to be somewhat tougher for certain people who were once extremely heavy.

But none of these people seem to regret what they had to give up. Doug S., who's lost more than 100 pounds twice in his life (he's kept off 108 pounds for the last 4 years), admits, "It's hard, it's really hard. But I know how much better I feel about myself. It's definitely worth it."

Master Kim W., who's kept off 27 pounds for 7 years and now works as a personal-fitness trainer, has a motto: "How bad do you want it?" She says, "I use this with clients when they complain about giving up certain foods. If you want to lose weight badly enough, you'll do what it takes."

Contrary to the popular belief that "naturally thin" people get to eat whatever they want, one study suggests that they eat much the way the masters do. In the study on successful maintainers conducted at the Kaiser Permanente Medical Center (page 66), the researchers also examined eating habits of women who had never been overweight and found that these women consciously worked to stay trim and in shape. If they gained some weight—say, after a vacation—they made an effort to eat less until their weight returned to normal.

FOOD FACT #5
The masters indulge themselves but spend their calories wisely.

One of the ways the masters manage to eat healthfully over the long term is by not denying themselves favorite foods. Carole C. told me, "If I want it, I have it. On Mother's Day, I was given a huge chocolate 'turtle,' and it was wonderful." Marie D. says that one of her top three strategies for keeping her weight down is "allowing myself treats and desserts occasionally but enjoying smaller quantities." She finds that eating a little more food and a few treats on weekends helps her to maintain a healthful diet all week. Linda W. adds, "I found that when I get hungry for a high-fat food, I eat it. A slip-up every now and then is better for me than the craving." As Susan C. explains, "You eventually learn that you can occasionally eat those things [high-fat foods] and still lose weight." (To learn how you can develop this no-guilt attitude, see "Don't Let Lapses Become Relapses," on page 142.)

Some masters, however, choose not to eat regular treats. Instead, they decide to view more healthful foods, such as fresh fruits, as rewards. Or they develop their own low-fat recipes for "splurge" foods. (See "How One Master Eats Very Lean and Loves It" on page 122.)

All the masters take steps to control their highest-temptation foods. Susan C. avoids buying aged cheeses because she can't stop herself from eating them. Ernie L. says his first line of defense is in the grocery store. "I shop very sensibly. If all that's in the fridge is apples and grapes, then that's what I'll eat. But if I know there's a half-gallon of butter-pecan ice cream [his favorite] in the house, I'll work on it 'til it's gone." Holly L. says, "There are certain things I do not have in the house, like chips and high-fat cheese. Sweets have never been a real problem for me. But when I do buy them, I get the no-fat ones."

The masters also make conscious choices about how to spend their calories. Jeffrey B. made it clear that he doesn't waste his calories on foods he doesn't really care for. "I decided that if I am going to eat something, it has to taste good. If I'm going to spend calories, it's not going to be on a bologna sandwich."

Part of the choice-making process is trade-offs. That is, if you have a higher-calorie or fatty item, you may have to forgo something else. "I'll sit down and eat half a pizza, but I won't eat dessert," says Susan C. "One day I may have butter but no jam on my bread. The next day, it's jam with no butter." Sometimes she has pie or cake for breakfast, then she eats more lightly at lunch. Kelly D., who has maintained a 55-pound weight loss for 4½ years, told me, "If I want to have a cocktail or two before dinner, I will eliminate dessert. If I want a dessert, which is a treat, I eliminate the cocktails." Cam L. "splurges" on fried oysters but has them with a plain baked potato and salad with no dressing.

Steve S., one of the more disciplined masters I interviewed, once weighed 435 pounds and now tries to eat at least 35 servings of fruits and vegetables each week and tries to consume no more than 25 percent of his calories from fat. He's been able to maintain a 210-pound weight loss for 13 years. But, he adds, "I get to eat the things I really like, like ice cream and pizza. I rarely order fried food or steak. And I don't keep high-fat foods around my home or office."

Do the masters lose their love of eating? "It's an understanding that I will always love food—its preparation, fine restaurants, eating with friends, junk food—all of it," says Karen S. "Having kept my weight within 5 pounds for the last 15 years, I also know that if I eat a large quantity of a food that's not the best (like tortilla chips), I will not shoot back up to my original weight." Says Nancy R., who's kept off 55 pounds for 3 years, "My main problem, as with many overweight people, is that I love to eat—even with the diet plan, education and rethinking on what and how to cook, I still just love to eat, and I'm not sure that will ever change!"

Nor should it. For most people—heavy, thin, average and formerly heavy—food is one of life's pleasures. Master Rosetta F. says, "I never did plan to quit the thing that I enjoyed the most. That is, when I am eating a large meal with friends or family, I just enjoy the food and company and tell myself that I owe it to myself to do this because I have been so good for so long."

Connye Z., who's kept off 34 pounds for 5½ years, has accepted the limitations and admits that sweets are a weakness for both her and her husband, so she doesn't buy them often. "If it's there, we know we will eat it right away! However, there is nothing I cannot eat. I never told myself I can never have another chocolate doughnut. No food is forbidden to me, so I'm not deprived."

How can you start to learn to spend your calories wisely? Try answering the following four questions for yourself:

1. What are my food strengths—things that can really work to my advantage in keeping weight off? If you love fruits and vegetables, for instance, how can you capitalize on that? Perhaps you can stock up at the supermarket and make a concerted effort to eat at least two with every meal.

2. What foods are really important to me? Make a list of the ones you really love—whether French fries, hot fudge sundaes, rib-eye steaks or chocolate chip cookies. Ask yourself under what circumstances you can eat a controlled amount of these foods. Some people find that it's best to buy a one-portion package and savor every bite. Others find it easiest to have such items in restaurants, where portions are controlled.

3. What foods do I really need to keep out of the house? If at all possible, get rid of foods that you have difficulty controlling.

4. What foods can I forgo and not miss too much? Maybe you really don't mind bread without butter or margarine—as long as it's fresh and warm.

FOOD FACT # 6
The masters learn to listen to their bodies.

Several masters told me one of their major ways of controlling weight is to try to eat only when they are hungry. Kathleen H. says, "Don't eat just to eat! If you are not hungry, don't eat. If it takes more than 5 minutes to decide what to eat . . . I'm not hungry! If you need to eat but are not hungry, eat an apple and a glass of water."

Susan C. said, "I don't like the way overeating makes me feel." One of Nancy K.'s important strategies for keeping off her 60 pounds is, "I don't eat 'til I'm stuffed—even at holidays."

On the other hand, the masters find that it's important not to let themselves get too hungry. "I refuse to starve myself," states Cathy C. And Mary S. advises, "Don't ever let yourself get hungry; it leads to disaster." The problem with allowing yourself to become ravenous is that it lowers your resistance, and you're less likely to make wise choices. If, for instance, you let yourself get to the point of faintness after a long day at work, you're more likely to stop for a fast-food burger, fries and a shake than to go home and make yourself fish, baked potato and vegetables.

Many people have been on and off diets so much that they don't even know when they're really hungry and when they're full. As Janet Polivy, Ph.D., and C. Peter Herman, Ph.D., point out in *Breaking the Diet Habit,* many of us were brought up as members of "the clean-plate club," taught to finish everything set before us. To get in touch with physiological hunger, try some of the following behavior-modification techniques:

◆ Put your fork or spoon down between bites and drink water or a no-calorie beverage frequently during a meal so you have time to consider whether you're really hungry for more.

◆ Stop eating for 1 or 2 timed minutes at several points throughout your meal, and use these breaks to ask yourself if you are still hungry.

◆ Put only half to three-quarters of the food you usually eat on your plate. Have second helpings only if you are truly hungry.

◆ Take a break from eating for about 20 minutes and return to the table only if you find you remain hungry.

Drs. Polivy and Herman find that such techniques are helpful for people who, out of mere habit, eat more than they really need. However, the techniques may not be sufficient for binge eaters, particularly those who eat to fulfill emotional needs. (For guidelines on handling emotional eating and binge eating, see Chapter VIII.)

FOOD FACT #7
The masters develop consistency in their way of eating.

When I asked the masters to describe their daily eating habits, nearly half made a point of saying that they eat three meals a day. Quite a few eat several snacks in addition to their regular meals, and some eat just two meals a day. Many of the masters could tell me exactly what they regularly eat for breakfast, lunch and dinner. Ron K. maintains that consistency is one of the keys to his 61-pound weight loss of 5 years. "By eating primarily the same foods on a daily basis, I can keep track of my caloric input."

It appears that distributing your calories throughout the day is important to weight control. In a recent study in which 52 moderately obese women either ate three meals a day (including breakfast) or two meals a day (with no breakfast), it was found that the breakfast-eaters tended to eat more nutritionally balanced meals that were lower in fat. Those who ate breakfast also ate fewer impulsive snacks. Surprisingly, women who used to skip breakfast but were then asked to eat it lost slightly more weight than did those who already were accustomed to eating breakfast.

Not every master eats three square meals a day, though. Ernie L., the master profiled in Chapter III, maintains his weight easily on two substantial meals a day, but like many other masters, he can tell you exactly what those meals consist of.

What's the best advice? If you are a meal-skipper, you might want to try a week or two's experiment of eating a small meal at the times you usually don't eat; it may help you to eat less at other times. It does seem to be important to sit down and eat at least two planned, well-balanced meals, with some low-fat protein, vegetables, fruit and a grain or two each day. None of the masters I interviewed were "grazers" who nibbled all day long.

One way to get yourself into a regular meal routine, as well as to get a handle on between-meal snacking, is to keep a diary of what you eat, listing every single food and beverage, as well as the portion size and when it's eaten. A number of studies indicate that people who keep food diaries lose more weight and keep it off longer than those who do not. *Quite a few masters mentioned that keeping a food diary is one of the most important things they do to keep their weight down;* more than a third mentioned that they keep a diary or count calories if their weight rises. "Once a day, I write down the food items and their calories," admits Lois M. "It forces me not to kid myself about food. Some days I do better than I thought, and on others it's the opposite."

A number of masters also make an effort to control the portions of the food they eat. "I measure my portions," states Mary S. "They tend to grow in size." It makes sense to keep track of what and how much you eat, at least for a while, because several studies reveal that overweight people have a tendency to underestimate the amount they eat. Recently, researchers reported in the *New England Journal of Medicine* that a group of 10 overweight people who estimated their average daily intake to be just over 1,000 calories were actually consuming 2,081 daily calories. According to the researchers, the participants were not trying to be deceptive; rather, they seemed to be in a state of denial about how much they really ate.

In addition to writing down food items, you may want to keep track of calories or grams of fat (see page 123, "Fat Content of a Sampling of Foods") for a while—at least until you feel you are more in touch with your real hunger.

If a food diary doesn't seem to help, then stop keeping one. Marie D. has found that counting calories or measuring portions doesn't work for her. What is effective is eating a low-fat diet and eating only when she's hungry. But she knows exactly what she eats during her three structured daily meals.

More on Behavior Modification

THE TRADITIONAL USE OF FOOD DIARIES has been to identify patterns and problems in eating habits: to see if you're eating too fast, eating while you do other activities (like watching TV, which is apt to distract you from paying attention to your food), eating at certain times of the day (because it's coffee-break time, not because you're hungry) or eating because you have a lot of scrumptious foods sitting around your home.

Ten years ago, in keeping with the state-of-the-art techniques for working with overweight people, I instructed my patients to follow certain behavior-modification techniques in order to correct problem eating habits:

• Slow down your rate of eating, put your fork down between bites of food; chew and swallow what's in your mouth before going for the next bite.

• Make eating a singular activity—that is, don't do anything else: don't watch TV, read a newspaper or do office work.

• Keep highly tempting foods out of the house. If you must keep them around, store them out of sight and make them hard to get to.

• Eat all of your meals at the same place and while sitting down, at a table.

+ Serve your food on a smaller plate, so it looks like you have more to eat.

+ Always leave a little food behind at the end of a meal, so you break the habit of cleaning your plate.

+ Avoid shopping when you're hungry because your resistance will be low. Shop from a list and stick to it, so you don't buy a lot of extras.

+ Plan ahead: think about what you'll eat for meals, as well as before going to social events and restaurants.

One day, however, the following thought hit me: "*I* like to read the newspaper while I eat breakfast and lunch; I *enjoy* my food *more* when I read while I eat, and it doesn't keep *me* from paying attention to my food." Not long after, a patient who had been in the habit of eating in front of the television said to me, "I ate *more* when you told me to shut off the TV!" Some patients felt these techniques were just plain silly and uncomfortable.

Not many of the masters mentioned behavioral techniques as important. Drs. Colvin and Olson, in fact, found that the successful maintainers in their study ignored behavior-modification techniques "almost totally." Just as with every other technique for weight control, you may have to experiment to see if these tips help you.

Here are some that the masters found to be helpful:

+ Nancy K.: "I don't tempt myself with any favorites (potato chips) in the house." At dinnertime, she fixes herself a lunch-size plate of whatever else she makes for the family. Sometimes, she has seconds.

+ Rosemary O.: "I have selected my kitchen and dining room as designated places to eat. I avoid eating in the den, etc." When she knows she's going out, she plans ahead by "banking calories"—that is, by saving them up so she never feels she's on a diet.

+ Ernie L.: "Food waste really bothers me. I know I won't leave food behind on my plate. So I buy foods in controlled portion sizes, like a 6-ounce steak."

+ Karen S.: "I attempt to mimic my thin husband's eating habits, particularly his slow speed of eating."

+ Julie J.: "I don't eat food when I can't sit and enjoy it."

• Mindy B. finds it helpful to avoid cleaning her plate of food and to "wait 15 minutes to see how full you really are after your meal."

• Joanna M.: "I keep cookies, candy and other goodies in the freezer so I know they'll be there a while, and I don't feel compelled to enjoy them before they get stale." After a meal, she removes "triggers," such as dishes and packaged foods that might compel her to eat more. To get the food taste out of her mouth, Joanna ends each meal or snack with a hot drink, carbonated beverage or small mint.

The masters who find these behavior-modification techniques to be beneficial did not just use them while they were losing weight, they continue them during maintenance.

How the Former Galloping Gourmet Converted to Minimax

As you may know from his Public Television and Discovery Channel series, Graham Kerr, the gallant wine-drinking, cream-and-butter-sloshing Galloping Gourmet of the early '70s, is back with a whole new way of cooking and eating. If the man who was "once paid $10,000 a day to recommend the addition of fat, salt and sugar to recipes" could adopt the low-fat way of life, anyone can. Moreover, Kerr's dietary changes also illustrate how switching to low-fat habits can bring about weight loss.

At his all-time high, Kerr weighed 225, which he brought down and held at about 215 through most of his years as the Galloping Gourmet. Since he switched to low-fat eating about 20 years ago, his weight hovers around 200. (He's 6'3" tall.) He recalls that in 1971, his blood cholesterol was a none-too-healthy 260; now it's 165, well below the recommended cutoff of 200.

The turning point in eating habits occurred for Kerr when he was on a two-year boat cruise, recuperating with his wife from a car accident. He recalls the date: "It was May 18, 1971. We had just eaten a rich meal from a famous restaurant. There were probably 170 grams of fat in that one meal. Everyone on board felt sick. I said to myself, 'I've gone to bed many times before feeling greasy, awakening with my mouth feeling coated with fat.' And the room would be spinning, in part because of the wine and Cognac." Kerr wondered if he'd been "subclinically sick" for many years and decided to remove fat and hard spirits from the boat's menu. "Within weeks, everyone felt better. I understood that my body didn't like what it had been doing."

Kerr admits that he soon became a "health-food extremist." He recalls his wife complaining, "There's nothing left to eat." He goes on, "She tossed the bologna across the floor and started throwing everything away. At that point, I realized I had gone too far. I had no joy left at my dinner table. I realized that the table is where we come for love and regeneration, but I had turned it into a place of 'No, you don't eat that.'"

Today, as he chooses his daily foods and designs his recipes, Kerr's guiding question is, "What is the least I can put in my body that will give me the most vitality, and P.S., can it taste good, too?" His "Minimax" approach means cooking with minimum risk from fat, sodium and cholesterol but with "maximum creativity by using aromas, colors and textures." He and his wife, Treena, who has had to modify her diet because of a heart attack and stroke, see their way of eating as "a joint venture. We don't focus on what we can't have but on enhancing what we do have. We *can* eat much more than we *can't* have."

What *does* Kerr have? He starts his day with homemade "caremush," consisting of oats, a few raisins, some nuts and seeds and nonfat milk. Lunch is usually vegetable soup with grains and beans in it, plus a "great" piece of bread with some herb-seasoned yogurt cheese. A typical dinner would consist of a 2-ounce portion of chicken or fish, pasta or a baked potato—sloppy-joe style with a low-fat sauce—along with two or three vegetables. For dessert, Kerr may have plain yogurt flavored with vanilla and honey, served over fruit.

I asked Graham if he ever treats himself, indulging in occasional high-fat foods. He responded, "My memory menu could easily go to goose liver in a Madeira sauce or a rich, wonderful ice cream. There is a part of me that says, 'God, I'd love to eat that.' But I know I'd feel less than well. I'm the sort of person who could easily gain 20 pounds if I relent." Instead, his indulgences are foods like English muffins with marmalade, perfectly cooked sweet potatoes, brown rice with kidney beans, or spinach with cilantro, red pepper and lemon. He says, "You *can* find comfort in food that is good for you."

Kerr's advice for making the switch to low-fat eating is simple. "Whatever you know has fat in it, halve it. For instance, if you order French fries, only eat half of them. Then triple the amount of fruits, vegetables and grains that you'd have with that food. Always replace food that has fat with food you adore that doesn't."

The Basics of Low-Fat Eating—Going by the Numbers

WHERE DO YOU START? How do you know what "eating low-fat" actually means when it comes to making food choices? Some people count grams of fat in everything they eat until they get a feel for various foods and how much fat they can consume on a daily basis. The table on page 123 gives you a sense of the number of grams of fat in basic foods. (See also page 128 for recommendations on comprehensive fat counters.)

The following steps will help you determine how many grams of fat you can consume each day:

1. Decide on your calorie level. To go on a low-calorie diet on your own for any length of time, women should drop no lower than 1,200 calories a day; men no lower than 1,500 calories. But you may want to see what happens just by cutting back on fat and thus shoot for a calorie level somewhat higher. Once you reach your maintenance weight, you should be able to consume more calories. (Hard and fast numbers are not available since calorie needs are highly individual and depend on your activity level.)

2. Set your goal for percentage of calories from fat. Major health organizations recommend that no more than 30 percent of calories come from fat, but a number of masters eat considerably less than that, about 20 percent. Yet it may be tough to make such a drastic jump from your current diet. Perhaps it makes sense to start at 25 or 30 percent and go lower if you think you can later.

3. Figure out how many grams of fat you can eat each day for your chosen calorie and fat levels. Use the chart below to guide you.

If your calorie level is:	Your total daily fat gram allowance is: % of calories from fat		
	30%	25%	20%
1,200	40	33	27
1,300	43	36	29
1,400	47	39	31
1,500	50	42	33
1,600	53	44	36
1,700	57	47	38
1,800	60	50	40
1,900	63	53	42
2,000	67	56	44
2,100	70	58	47
2,200	73	61	49
2,300	77	64	51
2,400	80	67	53
2,500	83	69	56
2,600	87	72	58

To determine the amount of fat you can eat at any particular calorie level, multiply the calorie level times the percentage of fat you want— say 2,000 x .25 = 500, which is the total number of calories contributed by fat. Take that number and divide by 9 (since there are 9 calories in each gram of fat), and you'll have your daily quota for fat, which, in this example, is 56 grams.

By paying attention to the grams of fat in various foods, with time you'll get a sense of how to budget your fat grams. Let's say you've selected a 1,400-calorie level with 25 percent of those calories from fat. The chart indicates that your daily fat quota is 39 grams. If you see that a serving of a particular food provides 10 grams of fat, you'll know that's fairly steep since it provides about one-fourth of your allowance for the day. Should you choose to eat that higher-fat item, you'll know to watch more carefully the other items you eat that day.

Remember that what's important is your *average* intake of fat over time—there's no harm in an occasional meal or even an occasional day of high-fat eating.

The new nutrition labels make it easier to keep track of fat, as grams of fat per serving are listed on all processed foods regulated by the Food and Drug Administration. A point of confusion, however, on the new labels is their listing of "% Daily Value," which is based on a 2,000-calorie diet with 30 percent of the calories coming from fat. Unless that's exactly the calorie and fat level you've selected, it's best to ignore "% Daily Value" for fat. Instead, pay attention to *total grams of fat per serving* and see how that food fits into your daily fat budget.

Your best bet, if you want to cut way back on fat—and eat a nutritious, well-balanced diet at the same time—is to consult with a registered dietitian. You can ask your physician for a referral, call the outpatient dietary department of your local hospital to set up an appointment with one of its dietitians, or call the Consumer Nutrition Hotline: 1-800-366-1655.

Making Food Shifts:
A 6-Week Nondieting Weight-Control Plan

Y OU DON'T *have* to count grams of fat in everything you eat. Studies suggest you can markedly lower fat intake by making some relatively painless shifts within each of the food groups in the Food Guide Pyramid (see below), a new way of understanding the basics of healthful eating. Foods at the base of the Pyramid are supposed to be the foundation of a good diet, while items at the tip are meant to be eaten in lesser amounts.

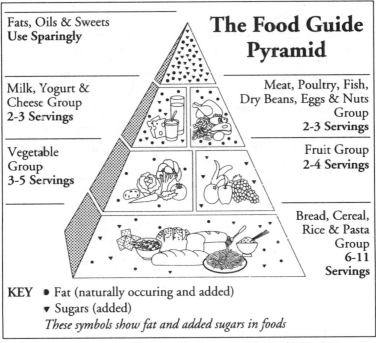

The Food Guide Pyramid

Fats, Oils & Sweets
Use Sparingly

Milk, Yogurt &
Cheese Group
2-3 Servings

Meat, Poultry, Fish,
Dry Beans, Eggs & Nuts
Group
2-3 Servings

Vegetable
Group
3-5 Servings

Fruit Group
2-4 Servings

Bread, Cereal,
Rice & Pasta
Group
**6-11
Servings**

KEY ● Fat (naturally occuring and added)
▼ Sugars (added)
These symbols show fat and added sugars in foods

Source: U.S. Department of Agriculture/U.S. Department of Health and Human Services

The most important fat-saving shifts are to use less fat and oil in cooking and on foods, change from whole- to skim-milk dairy products and consume less meat (most importantly hamburger, which is one of the fattiest meats, and high-fat processed meats, such as salami and sausage). At the same time, more of your calories should come from low-fat grain products, fruits and vegetables.

Many people, however, feel overwhelmed when they try to make multiple changes all at once. For this reason, the 6-Week Nondieting Plan has you take things one food group at a time, working on a single group for each one of 6 weeks. You can start with any food group, but since foods at the top of the pyramid contain the most fat, it makes sense to begin there. Each week, continue the changes from the previous week.

WEEK 1
Fats, oils and sweets

Fats include butter, margarine, vegetable oils, shortening, salad dressings, mayonnaise, cream, cream cheese and bacon. Use these items sparingly because they can markedly contribute to your fat and calorie budget. A study published in the May 1992 *Journal of the American Dietetic Association* of a large group of women who were trying to restrict their fat intake to no more than 20 percent of calories revealed that avoiding fats as a flavoring—for example, on potatoes and bread—was the single most important step in maintaining low-fat intake on a long-term basis. Cut back on fats as much as possible, and experiment with nonfat and reduced-fat products like nonfat mayonnaise, fat-free salad dressing and diet margarine. (Different brands vary not only in tastiness but also in fat levels.)

Sugar and low-fat sweets per se don't concern me too much as a dietitian, as long as the amounts are not excessive. Some masters treat themselves to no-fat or low-fat sweets, such as licorice, jelly beans and jelly (instead of butter). The problem is that many high-sugar foods, including ice cream, candy and cookies, also have a great deal of fat. Again, stick with low-fat or no-fat versions like frozen yogurt and reduced-fat baked goods. Beware, too, that many high-sugar foods are "empty-calorie" foods, providing calories but few or no vitamins and minerals. If you consume a lot of these on a low-calorie diet, you run the risk of nutritional inadequacies. You can save sugar calories by making the shift from regular to diet soda. One of my friends recently lost 10 pounds just by giving up regular soda. Alcoholic beverages are also typically considered part of this food group and can add significant calories to your daily intake. Some masters told me that they had much less trouble controlling their weight when they gave up alcohol. Master Ron K., who has kept off 61 pounds for 5 years, indicates that one of his most important weight-control strategies is to limit alcohol intake to 1 drink or beer at a sitting.

Goals for Week 1

◆ For 1 or 2 days, keep track of all the fats you eat, noting the exact amount. For the next several days, cut your fat intake in half. Then, if you feel you can, cut it in half once again.

◆ Take 3 foods that you would normally add fat to and try them without any fat. If that's unacceptable, try them with low-fat or nonfat substitutes. For instance, try a baked potato with just salt, pepper and chives. If it seems too dry, add a dollop of nonfat or low-fat yogurt or sour cream with chives.

◆ In cooking, try cutting the amount of fat that you usually use by at least one-third to one-half. (See "The Art of Low-Fat Cooking," page 118 and "22 Ways to Shave Fat From Your Recipes," page 121.)

◆ If you have a sweet tooth, try having no more than 3 small servings of desserts or sweet snacks this week, and/or switch to some of the low-fat sweets, such as sherbet, fig bars or jelly beans, listed in the chart on page 127.

WEEK 2
Meat, poultry, fish, dry beans, eggs and nuts group— the so-called protein foods

You can save a lot on your fat budget by eating more fish and skinless chicken in place of popular meats like hamburger and steak. Note that many types of fish and shellfish, such as sole, cod, orange roughy, clams, shrimp and scallops, have only 1 or 2 grams of fat per 3-ounce cooked serving, provided you prepare them without added fat. (Oilier fish like salmon and mackerel are higher in fat, but much of the fat comes from omega-3 fatty acids, which are considered beneficial.) Skinless roasted chicken breast has just 3 grams of fat in a serving. You can substitute fish and chicken for meat in many recipes.

Although it is not necessary to cut out red meats, a number of masters indicated that they limit them. Says Ron K., "I eat red meat once a week and have 3 to 4 ounces at the most." Another way to cut back on fat is to switch to lean cuts, such as beef eye-of-round, top round or tip round; pork tenderloin, boneless sirloin chop or boneless loin roast; veal chops or roast. You may also want to try some of the new low-fat cold cuts that have no more than a gram of fat per ounce. Since Americans tend to eat more protein than they need—and since protein foods often come packaged with a lot of fat—it's generally recommended that you keep portion sizes of meats small. Be sure to trim meats of visible fat, and use hamburger (even the lean type) as an occasional "treat" food rather than as a staple in your diet.

Note, too, that a number of masters enjoy the dried-bean family, which has next to no fat, and includes chickpeas, kidney beans, navy beans, pinto beans and lentils. As you can see from the chart on page 126, nuts and nut butters are quite high in fat and should be used sparingly. Eggs are not very high in fat, but because of their cholesterol content, the American Heart Association recommends no more than 4 whole eggs per week. (You can eat as many whites as you want; they're free of cholesterol.) Of course, you can undo the advantages of any low-fat protein food by using high-fat cooking methods, such as frying or sautéing in butter. Stick with broiling, roasting, grilling, baking, sautéing in little or no fat in a nonstick skillet, steaming and poaching.

Goals for Week 2

• Have 2 to 3 small servings of protein foods each day. For most adults, 2 servings is plenty. A serving is 2 to 3 ounces of cooked meat, poultry or fish (3 ounces is about the size of a deck of cards); ½ cup of cooked beans or 2 tablespoons of peanut butter. One egg or ¼ cup low-fat or nonfat cottage cheese, which is not as high in calcium as other cheeses and thus is not in the milk/dairy group, counts as an ounce of meat or ⅓ of a 3-ounce serving.

• If you have a food scale, weigh meats after cooking to assure that portion sizes are appropriate.

• Have fish or skinless breast of chicken or turkey a minimum of 3 times this week. Try substituting one of them in at least one recipe in which you would normally use red meat. Since prepackaged ground turkey breast can be quite high in fat, buy skinless turkey breast and have it ground. Use it in recipes in place of hamburger.

◆ Experiment with one of the lean cuts of meat mentioned above.

◆ Have at least 1 serving of beans as in vegetarian baked beans, mixed with pasta and vegetables, or in homemade low-fat soup, such as Jordan F.'s "Thick and Hearty Bean Soup" on page 268.

WEEK 3
The milk, yogurt and cheese group

Shifting from regular to reduced-fat dairy products can make a big difference: the more you can use nonfat (skim) or 1 percent-fat versions of milk, yogurt and cheeses, the better. (Cheeses should have no more than 5 grams of fat per ounce.) It pays to experiment, since some brands are much tastier than others. With time, you can get used to a new taste, as master Rosetta F. has: "I changed from whole milk to 2 percent and then to nonfat milk. I drank the 2 percent until I started to like it better and then changed to nonfat months later." Even though they may be low in fat, many yogurts are still quite high in calories because of the added sugar. Aspartame-sweetened yogurts are much lower in calories.

Goals for Week 3
◆ Have 2 to 3 servings from this group each day. (Teenagers, young adults to age 24 and women who are pregnant or breast-feeding should have 3 servings.) A serving is 1 cup of milk, 8 ounces of yogurt or 1½ to 2 ounces of cheese.

◆ If you haven't already switched to low-fat or skim milk, try Rosetta's technique of making the change gradually. (My family refused to drink skim milk until after my father had a major heart blockage, when I decided to switch without telling. My kids and husband never noticed the difference.) You may find that skim milk is fine for cereal, but not in your coffee. (Some people like evaporated skim milk in coffee.)

◆ Sample 2 or 3 kinds of low-fat cheese to see which you prefer.

◆ Try 2 new flavors of fat-free yogurt.

WEEK 4
The fruit group

The remaining food groups are those you can fill up on so you're less tempted to eat higher-fat items. Fruits are virtually fat-free, with the exception of avocados and olives, which are considered fats. You can save yourself calories from sugar by sticking with fresh versions and avoiding those canned or frozen in syrup. Many people find it more satisfying to eat a piece of fruit than to drink juices, which go down quickly and have little bulk. Says Rosetta F., "I switched to more natural foods by telling myself that 'fat goes to fat.' So I picked out fresh fruit instead of the cinnamon pull-aparts that I used to get. I discovered I liked nectarines, which I had never eaten before."

Goals for Week 4
• Have at least 2 to 4 fruit servings per day. A serving is 1 medium whole fruit, ¾ cup of juice or ½ cup of canned or fresh, cut-up fruit.

• Have at least 1 fruit serving with each meal: for instance, a banana on your cereal at breakfast, a juicy orange for lunch and a baked apple with cinnamon for a bedtime snack.

• Try a minimum of 2 less-familiar fruits this week, for example, an unusual type of melon, papaya or kiwi fruit.

• If you're in the dessert habit, have several different types of fresh, cut-up fruit instead at least 2 nights this week.

WEEK 5
The vegetable group

No fat to speak of here—again, unless you add it as butter, sour cream, mayonnaise or in frying. No shifting necessary—load up on vegetables.

Goals for Week 5
• Have at least 3 to 5 servings each day. A serving is considered ½ cup of cooked vegetable or 1 cup of raw vegetable. (On weight-loss diets, salad greens, such as lettuce and raw spinach, are usually considered "free foods" that can be eaten as often as you like.)

• Have at least 1 vegetable with lunch and 2 with supper. For example, at lunchtime have carrot sticks or cucumber coins (try them with nonfat salad dressing) to replace the crunch of chips. Supper might include a large spinach salad with mushrooms, red peppers and low-fat salad dressing, plus ½ cup of a cooked vegetable, such as broccoli.

• Try at least 2 less-familiar vegetables this week, such as okra, Brussels sprouts or winter squash.

• Experiment with various no-fat flavorings: dillweed on green beans, basil on zucchini or lemon juice and nutmeg on spinach.

WEEK 6
The bread, cereal, rice and pasta group
(Low-fat crackers are usually considered part of this group as well.)

For a long time, many people labored under the misconception that breads, cereals, rice and pasta are fattening. Luckily, this has been shown to be false, and these foods are now considered to be mainstays of a healthful diet. Not only are they low in fat, but these grain products tend to make you feel full. The key is to avoid *adding* fats to them or to use reduced-fat or no-fat products on them, such as diet margarine and nonfat mayonnaise. Shift away from higher-fat items like regular muffins, quick breads, oilier crackers and baked goods like doughnuts and cake. To boost your fiber intake, mainly use whole-grain versions of the foods in this group.

Goals for Week 6
• Have 6 to 11 servings from this group each day (6 servings are appropriate for most women; 9 servings for most men). A serving is 1 slice of bread; ½ cup of cooked cereal, rice or pasta; 1 ounce of dry cereal (check product labels for equivalents to 1-ounce sizes since they vary from ¼ cup to more than a cup); ½ English muffin, hot dog roll or hamburger roll or bagel; 3 graham cracker squares, 5 slices melba toast or 6 saltines; a 4-to-5-inch pancake. For portion sizes of other foods in this group, see the expanded list of complex carbohydrates in Week 2 of the Jump-Start Diet (page 324).

• Have 2 servings (men may want to have more) from this group with each meal. Breakfast might include an ounce of high-fiber cereal and a slice of whole-wheat toast with jelly, which has no fat. Lunch is easy—a sandwich with 2 slices of oatmeal bread. For supper, have a serving or two of pasta and a slice of warm Italian bread.

• Take at least 3 grain foods that you normally have with fat and try them without any; for example, plain warm whole-wheat bread or pancakes with syrup but without the butter or margarine. (If this proves unacceptable, try them with diet margarine or other reduced-fat products.)

• Have sandwiches with fancy mustard or fat-free mayonnaise instead of regular mayonnaise.

Here's how some of the masters have made food shifts:

• Tom J. (75 pounds, 27 years): "I eat very little meat, lots of vegetables, grains and beans and lots of fruit and pasta."

• Jean M. (60 pounds, 3 years): "Mine was a bad set of eating habits all my life: bacon, sausage, fried food, ice cream, candy." Now, she eats "every low-fat or fat-free food available," 3 to 4 fruits and a large salad with low-fat dressing every day, plenty of chicken and turkey, fat-free crackers and diet Coke.

• Carol B. (75 pounds, 6 years): "I eat 3 meals a day that are low in fat and high in complex carbohydrates." Specifically, she says the staples of her low-fat diet are "cereal, fruits, vegetables, pasta, seafood and chicken."

• Teresa M. (36 pounds, 4 years): "I eat lots of fruits and vegetables, no red meat—just fish, chicken and turkey. I stay away from high-fat foods. It's just not worth it to me to eat them."

• Leo P. (46 pounds, 3½ years): "I eat 3 to 4 fruits a day, grains, legumes, vegetables, very little if any fried food and limited meat."

• Vicki B. (61 pounds, 8½ years): "I eat a lot of whole grains and fruits and vegetables and cut down on fats."

Compare the following two days to see how making food shifts can greatly lower fat and calorie intake. (Approximate grams of fat are listed after items containing more than 1 gram of fat.)

Higher-fat day   Lower-fat day

BREAKFAST

Higher-fat day	Lower-fat day
1 oz. (1¼ cups) Cheerios (2)	1 oz. Cheerios (2)
¾ cup whole milk (6)	¾ cup skim milk
½ medium banana	½ medium banana
1 slice wheat toast with 1 teaspoon margarine (4)	1 slice wheat toast with 1 teaspoon margarine (2)

COFFEE BREAK

1 yeast doughnut (14)	English muffin with 2 teaspoons jelly

LUNCH

3 ounces bologna (24) on 2 slices rye bread with 2 tablespoons mayonnaise (22)	3 ounces very lean baked ham (3) on 2 slices rye bread with 1 tablespoon reduced-calorie mayonnaise (5)
1 ounce potato chips (11)	1 large carrot
2 chocolate chip cookies (6)	2 fig bars (2)

SUPPER

4 ounces roast leg of lamb, lean (9)	4 ounces broiled halibut (3) in 1 teaspoon margarine (4) with lemon juice
½ cup au gratin potatoes (9)	1 medium baked potato with 2 tablespoons reduced-fat sour cream (2)
large tossed salad with 2 tablespoons blue-cheese dressing (16)	large tossed salad with 2 tablespoons low-calorie blue-cheese dressing (2)
1 cup cooked spinach with 1 teaspoon margarine (4)	1 cup cooked spinach with lemon juice
1 cup vanilla ice cream (14)	½ cup vanilla ice milk (3) with ¼ cantaloupe

Higher-fat day		Lower-fat day
	SNACK	
3 cups microwave popcorn (6)		3 cups reduced-fat microwave popcorn (3)
8 ounces regular cola		8 ounces diet cola
Total fat = 152 grams		36 grams
Total calories = 2,603		1,594
% calories from fat = 53%		20%

The Art of Low-Fat Cooking

L ET'S FACE IT: fat does nice things for food. It adds moisture and what chefs call "mouth feel"—that smooth, velvety sensation. How do you make up for the loss of fat? First, you can still get a lot of the goodness of fat simply by cutting back—by using one-half to two-thirds the recommended amount of butter, margarine or oil in recipes. (Each tablespoon that you cut will save you about 100 calories and at least 11 grams of fat.) A number of masters leave fat out altogether and sauté in beef or chicken broth.

But many foods will surely miss the moisture and mouth feel that is no longer present when you remove some or all of the fat, so you have to add something back. You can substitute low-fat versions of the fats you take out, or add moist, low-fat ingredients like applesauce to baked goods. Low-fat or nonfat yogurt also works well to moisten certain dishes. In fact, many reduced-fat dairy products make good substitutes for whole milk, sour cream and cream.

Sometimes products with just a small amount of fat work better than those that are fat-free. Low-fat cheese products vary greatly in palatability, so experiment with them or try using a small amount of real cheese along with a low-fat kind.

Small amounts of flavorful fats, like butter, olive oil and sesame oil, can go a long way. A tablespoon may be all you need to enhance a recipe. Creative use of herbs and spices can also make up for the lack of fat. It helps, too, to use lemon and lime juice, as well as lots of vegetables in cooking. Aromatic vegetables like onions, garlic, peppers and celery can pick up the flavor of small amounts of fat and carry them through an entire recipe. Freshly squeezed lemon and lime juice, fresh herbs and spices and fresh garlic and onions deliver more flavor than dried and powdered forms. (Consult the list on page 128 for cookbooks and magazines devoted to the subject of low-fat cooking.)

Two Before and After Recipes From Masters

A NUMBER OF MASTERS are adept at low-fat cookery. Two of them submitted the original versions of the following recipes, along with their adaptations. Don M. was able to bring about more than an 85 percent reduction in fat in Mallory's Lean Delight, while Bonnie R. shaved off virtually all of the fat from Fruit-Filled Coffee Cake. (Grams of fat follow each ingredient containing significant fat. Directions for these recipes are on pages 290 and 313 respectively.)

Mallory's Lean Delight
with Don M.'s adaptations

Original recipe	Don's version
1 large onion, chopped	1 large onion, chopped
2 tablespoons butter (23)	(No butter)
1½ pounds ground beef (84)	1½ pounds ground turkey breast* (4)
15-to-16-ounce can tomato sauce	15-to-16-ounce can tomato sauce
1 can (6 ounces drained weight) pitted black olives, drained (18)	20 medium pitted black olives, drained (7)
16-ounce can cream-style corn	16-ounce can cream-style corn
1 tablespoon chili powder	1 tablespoon chili powder
(No salt)	½ teaspoon salt
8 ounces elbow macaroni (4)	8 ounces elbow macaroni (4)
6 ounces sharp Cheddar cheese (56)	(No cheese)
1 cup unseasoned bread crumbs (6)	1 cup unseasoned bread crumbs (6)
Serves 8	**Serves 8**

Use skinless turkey breast, and have it ground or grind it in a food processor.

Before:	After:
Fat = 195 grams	Fat = 25 grams
Calories = 4,229	Calories = 2,621
Per serving:	*Per serving:*
Fat = 24 grams	Fat = 3 grams
Calories = 529	Calories = 328

Fruit-Filled Coffee Cake

with Bonnie R.'s adaptations

Original recipe	Bonnie's version
1 cup oil (218)	1 cup unsweetened applesauce
1½ cups granulated sugar	1 cup granulated sugar
3 eggs (15)	1 egg, plus 4 egg whites (5)
3 cups all-purpose flour (4)	3 cups all-purpose flour (4)
1 tablespoon baking powder	1 tablespoon baking powder
2 teaspoons baking soda	2 teaspoons baking soda
1 cup sour cream (48)	1 cup nonfat sour cream
1 tablespoon vanilla	1 tablespoon vanilla
1 teaspoon almond extract	1 teaspoon almond extract
20-ounce can pie filling	20-ounce can light pie filling (any flavor)
2 teaspoons cinnamon mixed with 2 tablespoons granulated sugar	2 teaspoons cinnamon mixed with 2 tablespoons granulated sugar
Serves 12	**Serves 12**

Before:	After:
Fat = 286 grams	Fat = 10 grams
Calories = 5,990	Calories = 3,246
Per serving:	*Per serving:*
Fat = 24 grams	Fat = negligible
Calories = 500	Calories = 271

22 Ways to Shave Fat From Your Recipes

Substitute	For	Fat omitted (grams)
¼ cup butter, margarine or oil	½ cup butter, margarine or oil	46
¼ cup reduced-calorie tub margarine	¼ cup regular margarine or butter	22
1¼-second spray of vegetable spray	1 tablespoon butter or margarine	10
2 egg whites	1 large egg	5
3 tablespoons unsweetened cocoa	1 ounce baking chocolate	13
4 tablespoons chocolate syrup	4 tablespoons fudge topping	8
½ cup evaporated skim milk	½ cup heavy cream	44
1 cup plain low-fat yogurt	1 cup sour cream	45
1 cup "mock" sour cream*	1 cup sour cream	46
1 cup reduced-fat sour cream (2 g fat/2 tablespoons)	1 cup sour cream	32
white sauce made with 1 cup 1% milk, 2 tablespoons flour	white sauce made with 1 cup whole milk, 2 tablespoons flour, 2 tablespoons margarine	28
1 pound swordfish (raw)	1 pound pork shoulder (raw, lean only)	20
8 ounces Neufchâtel cheese	8 ounces cream cheese	32
4 ounces fat-free cream-cheese product	4 ounces cream cheese	40
⅔ cup plain low-fat yogurt	⅔ cup regular mayonnaise	113
⅔ cup reduced-calorie mayonnaise	⅔ cup regular mayonnaise	63
⅔ cup fat-free mayonnaise dressing	⅔ cup regular mayonnaise	116
4 ounces reduced-calorie cheese slices (2 g fat/ounce)	4 ounces Cheddar cheese	30
4 ounces reduced-fat Cheddar cheese (4 g fat/oz.)	4 ounces Cheddar cheese	22

Combine 1 cup 1% cottage cheese with several tablespoons skim milk in blender until smooth.

Substitute	For	Fat omitted (grams)
3 ounces reduced-calorie Swiss cheese slices, plus 1 ounce Swiss cheese	4 ounces Swiss cheese	18
8 ounces 1%-fat cottage cheese	8 ounces whole-milk ricotta cheese	27
1 cup applesauce	1 cup oil	218

How One Master Eats Very Lean and Loves It

UNLIKE SUSAN C., who frequently allows herself moderate amounts of higher-fat treat foods, some masters follow a more stringent eating plan. Don M. weighed 308 when he started the Optifast program, and it helped him lose his first 70 pounds. Then he switched to his own very-low-fat diet and lost another 41 pounds to bring him down to 197, his maintenance weight of 3 years. (He's 5'9" tall.)

When I described to Don how Susan eats, he said, "Oh, I couldn't do that. If you put a delicious high-fat food in front of me, I couldn't stop with a small amount." So how does Don eat? He describes a typical day with gusto. He starts with a breakfast of a large bowl of nonfat or very-low-fat cereal, such as shredded wheat or cornflakes, tops it with skim milk and sometimes adds fresh fruit. He may add a glass of juice, and for an occasional treat, he'll have a bagel with fruit preserves.

Lunch is often a huge potpourri of fresh, cut-up vegetables. "I'll have green pepper and zucchini strips, carrots, celery and a nice fresh tomato covering a dinner plate with a small bowl of nonfat salad dressing set in the middle as a dip. By the time I'm done, I'm stuffed." In the summertime, lunch might be a large fruit salad. "I've recently gotten into kiwi fruits and mangoes. I just love them mixed with pears and pineapple." I asked him if he gets hungry during the day, with so little protein to hold him from one meal to the next. (As a dietitian, I was tempted to say, "Don't you think you should add a little cottage cheese or tuna fish to that lunch?") He responded, "I don't get hungry. I never used to eat breakfast, so anything seems like a lot now."

Don saves his protein and his fat for his evening meal. (He figures he consumes 1,800 to 2,000 calories per day.) His dinner the night before we talked consisted of a boneless chicken breast marinated in nonfat salad dressing, skewered shish-kebab style and grilled. His accompaniments were fresh zucchini slices sautéed in a tiny bit of oil, plus pea pods and water chestnuts cooked with a touch of flavorful sesame oil. He also had a salad of fresh watercress topped with an orange-juice-based dressing. For dessert, Don had some figs. Twice a week, Don and his wife have homemade low-fat pizzas (see recipe on page 303). Interestingly, his wife has lost nearly 60 pounds—solely by following Don's low-fat plan.

His "splurge" might be a piece of angel food cake with fresh raspberry sauce. Don has also developed a number of low-fat sumptuous desserts like Too-Tasty-To-Be-No-Fat Chocolate Cake (page 312) and Black Bottom Cupcakes (page 310). He's experimented with countless low-fat products and knows which ones work best. Don, who teaches cooking classes, has his own cable-TV show, has published his own cookbook and writes a newspaper column—all on low-fat eating and cooking—has even been hired as a consultant at local hospitals to help dietitians counter the notion that low-fat food has to taste bad.

Don's motto is "lean and lovin' it." When you talk with him, it's clear he means it.

Fat Content of a Sampling of Foods

(Lower fat or nonfat versions exist for many of these products. Check labels.)

Food	Amount	Grams of fat
GRAIN PRODUCTS		
bread (French, Italian, mixed grain, raisin, pumpernickel, rye, wheat, white)	1 slice	trace-1
bagel, plain or water, 3½"	1	2
biscuit, baking-powder (from mix), 2"	1	3
English muffin	1	1
croissant, 2 oz. (4" x 4")	1	12
muffin (blueberry, corn, bran), 1.5 oz. (2½" x 1½")	1	5-6
roll (hamburger or hot dog)	1	2
cereal, most types (except granola)	1 oz.	trace-2
granola	¼-⅓ cup	4-5

Food	Amount	Grams of fat
oatmeal (regular or instant), cooked	½ cup	1
crackers		
Saltines	5	1-2
graham, 2½" square	2	1
cheese, 1" square	10	3
oyster	10	1
Nabisco Ritz	4	4
Nabisco Wheat Thins	8	3
Keebler Wheatables	12	3
Pepperidge Farm Goldfish	12	2
egg noodles (cooked)	1 cup	2
spaghetti or macaroni (cooked firm)	1 cup	1
rice (white), cooked	1 cup	**
pancake (homemade or mix), 1 oz. (4")	2	4
waffle (homemade), 2.5 oz. (7")	1	13
tortilla (corn, unfried), 1 oz. (about 6")	1	1
popcorn (popped in vegetable oil)	1 cup	3
FRUITS AND VEGETABLES		
fruits, fruit juices	*	**
vegetables	*	**
onion rings (breaded, partly fried, frozen)	2	5
French fries (fried in vegetable oil), 1¾ oz.	10	8
scalloped potatoes (homemade)	½ cup	5
potato salad (made with mayonnaise)	½ cup	11
potato chips	10	7
MILK PRODUCTS		
milk		
skim	1 cup	**
1% fat	1 cup	3
2% fat	1 cup	5
whole	1 cup	8
cheese		
American, blue, Cheddar, Swiss	1 oz.	8-9
feta	1 oz.	6
mozzarella, part-skim	1 oz.	5
Parmesan cheese (grated)	1 T.	2

Food	Amount	Grams of fat
cottage cheese		
1% fat	½ cup	1
2% fat	½ cup	2
4% fat	½ cup	5
ricotta cheese		
whole-milk	½ cup	16
part-skim	½ cup	10
yogurt (made with low-fat milk)		
fruit-flavored	8 oz.	2
plain	8 oz.	4
frozen (vanilla) soft-serve	4 oz.	4
ice cream (vanilla), about 11% fat	½ cup	7
ice milk (vanilla), about 4% fat	½ cup	3
ice milk (soft-serve), about 3% fat	½ cup	3
FISH, POULTRY, MEAT		
fish (skinless, flesh only, cooked without added fat or sauces)		
white-fleshed fish (cod, flounder, haddock, halibut, ocean perch, orange roughy, pollock, sole)	3 oz.	1-2
shellfish (except oysters)	3 oz.	1-2
oysters	12 medium	4
catfish	3 oz.	5
rainbow trout	3 oz.	4
salmon (Atlantic, coho)	3 oz.	7
mackerel (Atlantic, Pacific, Jack)	3 oz.	12
chicken (roasted, meat only, no skin)		
breast	3 oz.	3
leg	3 oz.	7
thigh	3 oz.	9
turkey (cooked, meat only, no skin)		
breast	3 oz.	**
dark meat	3 oz.	6
ground (broiled)	3 oz.	12
lean beef (cooked, meat only, trimmed of fat)		
eye-of-round	3 oz.	4
top round	3 oz.	4
top sirloin	3 oz.	6

Food	Amount	Grams of fat
tenderloin	3 oz.	9
flank	3 oz.	9
ground, 85% lean	3 oz.	12
ground, 80% lean	3 oz.	15
lean pork (cooked, meat only, trimmed of fat)		
tenderloin	3 oz.	4
chop (sirloin, loin, rib)	3 oz.	6-8
boneless loin roast	3 oz.	6
boneless rib roast	3 oz.	9
EGGS		
eggs (whole), large	1	5
egg white	1	0
NUTS AND LEGUMES		
nuts (almonds, cashews, peanuts, pistachios)	1 oz.	14-15
peanut butter	2 T.	16
legumes (cooked and drained)		
lentils, lima beans, pinto beans, kidney beans, black beans	½ cup	less than 1
chickpeas	½ cup	2
FATS AND OILS		
butter or margarine (regular, stick)	1 T.	11
reduced-calorie margarine	1 T.	6-7
oil (any type)	1 T.	14
shortening	1 T.	12-13
salad dressing (regular, commercial), blue cheese, Italian, French, ranch	1 T.	8-9
mayonnaise	1 T.	11
mayonnaise, reduced-fat	1 T.	5
cream cheese	1 oz.	10
cream cheese, Neufchâtel	1 oz.	7
sour cream	1 T.	3
cream, light	1 T.	5
cream, heavy	1 T.	6
half-and-half	1 T.	2

Food	Amount	Grams of fat
avocado		
California (about 2/pound)	¼	8
Florida (about 1/pound)	¼	7
olives (medium, green)	4	2
olives (small, ripe)	3	2
SWEETS		
sugar (white, brown, powdered)	1 cup	0
jam, jelly, preserves	1 T.	**
carbonated beverages	12-oz. can	0
syrup (maple)	2 T.	0
chocolate-flavored syrup (thin-type)	2 T.	**
chocolate-flavored syrup (fudge-type)	2 T.	5
milk chocolate	1 oz.	9
candy corn	30 pieces	1
caramels	1 oz.	3
licorice	1 oz.	**
marshmallows	1 oz.	0
gumdrops, jelly beans	1 oz.	**
sherbet	½ cup	1
coconut (dried, sweetened, shredded)	¼ cup	8
pie (9"; apple, blueberry, cherry, pumpkin)	⅙ (5.5 oz.)	17-18
cake (from mix; 2-layer 8" or 9" devil's food or yellow with chocolate frosting)	¹⁄₁₆ of cake	8
angel food cake	¹⁄₁₂ of 10"	**
pound cake (¹⁄₁₇ of loaf)	1-oz. slice	5
gingerbread, from 8" square cake (mix)	⅑ of cake	4
chocolate chip cookies, homemade (2⅓")	2	6
fig bars	2	2
sandwich-type cookies (1¾")	2	4
vanilla wafers (1¾")	5	4

T. = tablespoon

*For serving sizes, see the "6-Week Nondieting Weight-Control Plan," starting on page 109.

**Very small amount present; count as 0.

Note: Values are approximate. Brands vary.

Source: Primarily taken from U.S. Department of Agriculture data.

A Sampling of Helpful References for Low-Fat Eating and Cooking

(Newer editions of books may be available at time of publication.)

FAT COUNTERS

American Heart Association Fat and Cholesterol Counter by the American Heart Association. 1991. New York: Times Books.

Brand Name Guide (second edition) by Nutrition Coordinating Center. 1992. University of Minnesota, 2221 University Avenue SE, Suite 310, Minneapolis, Minnesota 55414-3076.

Eating Smart Fat Guide. 1991. Center for Science in the Public Interest, 1875 Connecticut Avenue, N.W. #300, Washington, D.C. 20009.

Complete & Up-to-Date Fat Book by Karen J. Bellerson. 1993. Garden City, New York: Avery Publishing Group.

Fat Counter by Annette Natow & Jo-Ann Heslin. 1993. New York: Pocket Books.

Fat Gram Counter (third edition) by Nutrition Coordinating Center. 1990. University of Minnesota, 2221 University Ave. SE, Suite 310, Minneapolis, Minnesota 55414-3076.

Living Heart Brand Name Shopper's Guide by Michael E. DeBakey. 1993. New York: Warner Books.

T-Factor Fat Gram Counter by Jamie Pope-Cordle and Martin Katahn. 1991. New York: W.W. Norton & Company.

MAGAZINES

Cooking Light. Southern Living, Inc., 2100 Lakeshore Drive, Birmingham, Alabama 35209.

Eating Well. Telemedia Communications, Inc., Ferry Road, Charlotte, Vermont 05445.

Fast and Healthy Magazine. The Pillsbury Company, 200 South 6th Street, Minneapolis, Minnesota 55402.

Weight Watchers Magazine. 20-First Corporation, 360 Lexington Avenue, New York, New York 10017.

COOKBOOKS

This list was compiled as the result of a mini-survey of food and nutrition editors and writers, as well as of registered dietitians. Fat levels and difficulty of recipes vary from book to book. Be sure to peruse books carefully to see that they meet your needs.

All-American Low-Fat Meals in Minutes by M. J. Smith. 1990. Minneapolis, Minnesota: Chronimed Publishing, Inc.

American Heart Association Cookbook (fifth edition) by the American Heart Association. 1991. New York: Times Books.

Controlling Your Fat Tooth by Joseph C. Piscatella. 1991. New York: Workman Publishing.

Cooking à la Heart (second edition) by Linda Hachfeld and Betsy Eykyn. 1992. Mankato, Minnesota: Appletree Press.

Cooking Light Cookbook by Oxmoor House Editors. 1993. Birmingham, Alabama: Oxmoor House.

Eat, Drink & Be Healthy by Janet M. Chiavetta. 1993. Raleigh, North Carolina: Piedmont Publishers.

Eat Fish, Live Better by Anne M. Fletcher. 1989. New York: HarperCollins.

Eat More: Weigh Less by Dean Ornish. 1993. New York: Harper-Collins.

Eating Well Cookbook edited by Rux Martin, Patricia Jamieson and Elizabeth Hiser. 1991. Charlotte, Vermont: Camden House Publishing.

Family Favorites Made Lighter by Better Homes and Garden Staff. 1992. Des Moines, Iowa: Meredith Books.

Four-Course, Four-Hundred-Calorie Meal Cookbook: Quick & Easy Recipes for Delicious Low-Calorie, Low-Fat Dinners by Nancy S. Hughes. 1991. Chicago: Contemporary Books.

Gourmet Light: Simple & Sophisticated Recipes for the Calorie-Conscious Cook, (2nd Ed.) by Greer Underwood. 1993. Old Saybrook, Connecticut: Globe Pequot.

Graham Kerr's Minimax Cookbook by Graham Kerr. 1992. New York: Doubleday.

Healthy Heart Cookbook by Sunset Publishing Staff. 1992. Birmingham, Alabama: Oxmoor House.

Jane Brody's Good Food Book: Living the High Carbohydrate Way by Jane Brody. 1985. New York: Norton.

Jane Brody's Good Food Gourmet: Recipes & Menus for Delicious Healthful Entertaining by Jane Brody. 1992. New York: Bantam.

Lean and Lovin' It: A Lean Cook's Book by Don Mauer. 1993. Glencoe, Illinois (P.O. Box 222): Don Mauer.

Light Touch Cookbook: All-Time Recipes Made Healthful and Delicious by Marie Simmons. 1992. Shelburne, Vermont: Chapters Publishing.

Live Longer Cookbook by Reader's Digest Editors. 1992. New York: Reader's Digest Association.

Low-Fat Microwave Cooking by Sharon Claessens. 1992. Emmaus, Pennsylvania: Rodale Press.

Low-Fat Way to Cook edited by Lisa Hooper. 1993. Birmingham, Alabama: Oxmoor House.

Mediterranean Light: Delicious Recipes from the World's Healthiest Cuisine by Martha Rose Shulman. 1989. New York: Bantam.

Microwaving Light and Healthy by Barbara Methven. 1989. Minnetonka, Minnesota: Cy De Cosse Inc.

Microwaving on a Diet by Barbara Methven. 1989. Minnetonka, Minnesota: Cy De Cosse Inc.

New American Diet by Sonja L. Connor & William E. Connor. 1986. New York: Simon & Schuster.

New Dieters Cookbook edited by Better Homes & Gardens Staff. 1992. Des Moines, Iowa: Meredith Books.

One Meal at a Time: The Only Low-Fat Diet You Need to Lose Weight and Lower Your Cholesterol by Martin Katahn. 1993. New York: Warner Books.

Prevention's Quick and Healthy Low-Fat Cooking by Jean Rogers. 1993. Emmaus, Pennsylvania: Rodale Press.

Prevention's Super Food Cookbook: Two Hundred Fifty Delicious Recipes Using Nature's Healthiest Foods by Prevention Magazine Editors. 1993. New York: St. Martin's Press.

Professional Chef Techniques of Healthy Cooking by Culinary Institute of America Staff. 1992. New York: Van Nostrand Reinhold Publishing.

Pyramid Cookbook: Pleasures of the Food Guide Pyramid by Pat Baird. 1993. New York: Henry Holt & Company.

Recipe Rescue Cookbook: Healthy New Approaches to Traditional Favorites edited by Patricia Jamieson and Cheryl Dorschner. 1993. Charlotte, Vermont: Camden House Publishing.

60 Days of Low-Fat, Low-Cost Meals in Minutes by M. J. Smith. 1992. Minneapolis, Minnesota: Chronimed Publishing, Inc.

Steven Raichlen's High-Flavor, Low-Fat Cooking by Steven Raichlen. 1992. Charlotte, Vermont: Camden House Publishing.

V

KEY TO SUCCESS # 5

Nip It in the Bud:
Break the Relapse Cycle

T LAST! You've lost the weight—you're finally at your goal. But soon you find yourself "slipping"—a few desserts here and there, a social situation that throws you, a bad day at work—and you decide a hot fudge sundae would soothe your soul. A few pounds return, then some more and before you know it, your weight's right back where you started. A familiar scenario? It doesn't have to be. The good news is that you can break the "relapse" cycle.

Without a doubt, the most striking similarity among the masters is that they have discovered a way to *nip weight gain in the bud.* That is, they monitor their weight closely, and if they gain just a small amount, they *immediately* take it off. Nearly every single master has a game plan for getting back down when a small amount of weight comes back.

Janice C.'s Story

WHEN I ASKED JANICE C. the three most important things she does to keep her weight down, her first reply was, "I have a weight range—the top being 118. Once I get beyond that, I decrease snacking and/or meal portions and moderately increase exercise." This method of nipping weight gain has enabled Janice to maintain a 50-pound loss. For the past 10 years, she has weighed 116, give or take a few pounds—no small feat for someone who is 5'2" tall.

Janice's weight problem began when she was about 12 years old, after her parents divorced and the family moved. "Before that, I lived in the country. If I wanted to play with a friend, I had to ride my bike for 45 minutes. But when we moved to the city, my best friend was two or three blocks away, and I had more access to food: the 7-Eleven store was right down the street. Also, my mother started working and going to school. We stopped having regular meals." By the time she was 14, when she stopped weighing herself, she was up to about 165. "It really was a combination of a change in activity and a change in eating habits that led to my weight problem."

People always told Janice that she "carried her weight well" and that she had a "pretty face." "Boys would befriend me, but they tended to have long-term relationships with thinner girls." As a teenager, she tried various diets but didn't get serious until she was 15, when a relative paid for her to go to a clinic where she got hormone shots and was placed on a 500-calorie diet. "I stuck to it like glue, and I got myself up to running 5 miles. When I woke up in the morning, I felt like I would pass out." Within several months, Janice was down to 109 pounds.

She gradually regained some but not all of the weight; for years, she stayed around 130. But she tried various schemes to recoup her losses: Ayds weight-loss candies, the Stillman diet and "crazy" diets. "I created my own things—always something drastic that I couldn't maintain. I'd eat fruit all day, only vegetables and salads or just two sandwiches a day. I was either running marathons or doing nothing. It was all or nothing." Janice adds, "I really had the good food/bad food mentality. I was good at restraining myself for a while. Then I'd go back to the 'bad' foods, gain the weight back, and the cycle would start again."

The turning point for Janice occurred about 12 years ago when she was a college student and her car broke down. "While I was waiting for my insurance company to settle, I had to ride my bicycle to work. As a result, I started to lose weight and noticed I felt better about myself. My self-esteem increased, my clothes fit better, and I had more energy, which, in turn, spurred me to continue on. I was also more careful about what I ate. I didn't deny myself anything—I just ate smaller portions, and I started eating breakfast."

Janice feels that this last time she lost weight, her goal shifted. "In high school, it was more for the external, social reward: to get the weight off and gain popularity. When I was older, I was doing it for myself. I had a more realistic view of what I wanted and lost weight for my own level of self-confidence and to feel better." She also believes that her new, sensible approach had to do with the fact that she was seriously dating, and the two of them ate out a lot and went to many family meals together. "I realized I had to learn to eat like a normal person. I knew I couldn't live the old way, with the crazy diets and the marathons." It took Janice about two years to stabilize at her current weight.

Now Janice starts her day with a small breakfast of toast, cereal or a granola bar. Her largest meal is lunch, which she usually eats in a restaurant. "I eat anything I want, but try to make it pretty nutritious. I might have fish tacos or a teriyaki bowl. I have a tendency to choose low-fat and nonfat products and still feel like I'm treating myself. I *enjoy* reduced-fat hot fudge and frozen yogurt." In the evening, she says, "I allow myself to graze on foods like salads and rice. If I do have chips or sweets, I watch the portions."

Janice's first means of monitoring her weight is going by the fit of her clothing. She also weighs herself once or twice a week, but not if she thinks it will be "bad news"; she knows weighing at that point will distress her and be of no benefit. "If I feel like I'm up to 118, judging by the fit of my clothes, I won't weigh for a few days to see if I can make some adjustments. I basically eat the same during the day, but I'm more careful about my grazing at night. I might exercise more, reduce portions and pay more attention to fat content. I know if I spend several days watching it, I'll be back down to 115 or 116."

As for exercise, Janice tries to do something three or four times a week—say, 20 minutes on a StairMaster, biking or walking, as well as some light hand weights. "My exercise can be sporadic, and it's easy for me to get into the habit of not exercising. But it *is* one of the most important things I do to control my weight."

Janice chose 116 as her goal because she knew she could maintain it without starving herself. "I learned from the past that 109 was ridiculous." It did take some time to feel confident about being able to maintain. Like other masters, she learned through trial and error that if she gains a few pounds, she can lose them by cutting back and not doing something extreme. "As time goes by, my confidence has built up. "

How does Janice think she's different from people who regain weight? "I'm obstinate. I never accepted myself as an overweight person, never perceived myself in the long run as being an overweight adult."

I asked Janice if it was difficult to continue to be motivated when there was no longer the reinforcement of watching the scale drop. "I continued to feel satisfaction because I knew where I had been. I consciously reminded myself of that. Now, I focus on how good I feel," she said. I also wondered what, after all this time, motivates her to prevent further weight gain immediately, and she replied, "I feel the reward every day when I put on my clothes. I concentrate on how good I feel about my body when I give a presentation, exercise, go to the pool and when men notice me."

Day-by-Day, Meal-by-Meal

L IKE JANICE, *the masters nip weight gain in the bud on a day-by-day basis and on a meal-by-meal basis.* Lorraine W. says that the most important steps she takes for keeping off her 37 pounds are: "I made a vow to myself never to let it get out of hand again," and "If I have a larger meal, I make the next one very light." (Lorraine is 5'2" tall and has kept her weight off for 5 years; she lost her weight when she was almost 60!) Lou Ann L., who's kept off 43 pounds for 15 years, says, "I try to eat until I'm full and then stop. But I'm loose in a lot of ways; for example, at a party, I'll eat whatever I want. But if I eat a lot, I'll eat less the next day or two."

The vast majority of masters stop gaining before they put on more than 5 pounds; most others allow themselves no more than 10 pounds. Indeed, more than 80 percent of the masters keep their weight within a 1-to-5-pound range; another 14 percent keep their weight within a 10-pound regain limit. According to Dr. Thomas Wadden, director of Syracuse University's Center for Health and Behavior, "Reversing small weight gains immediately, as they occur, is the single most important skill that patients fail to learn in conventional weight-loss programs."

Closely Monitor Your Weight

IF YOU'RE GOING TO KEEP small weight gains from getting out of hand, you have to have some means of monitoring your weight. Dr. Susan Ross found that of her successful patients, "Most realized the need for a 'red flag' or warning system to monitor weight fluctuations and prevent the fluctuations from going beyond a certain amount." When I asked the masters "How do you keep track of your weight?" I learned that nearly 9 out of 10 of them weigh themselves regularly. Like Janice, about a third of the masters weigh-in one to three times a week. About one-quarter consult the scale at least once a day. In fact, 15 people listed daily or regular weigh-ins among their top three maintenance strategies.

The high incidence of frequent weighing came as a surprise to me, since dieters are warned commonly not to weigh themselves any more often than once a week. It is likely that frequent weighing *is* unwise when you're trying to lose weight, because the scale doesn't always register small day-to-day losses, which can be discouraging. *But frequent weighing does seem to be an important checkpoint for many people after they've lost weight.*

As with most aspects of weight maintenance, how often you weigh yourself is up to you. Drs. Kelly Brownell and Judith Rodin point out in *The Weight Maintenance Survival Guide* that "people who have difficulty with maintenance do not have a set of guidelines. . . . They weigh themselves whenever they remember or feel like it." Since weight tends to fluctuate throughout the day, it is wise not to consult the scale more than once a day. Instead, weigh yourself at one particular time of day only. Note, too, that fluid retention (from menstrual changes or from eating salty foods on a particular day) can cause daily weight fluctuations that are not cause for panic, and the amount of clothing you're wearing can cause variations.

Not every master monitors weight by a scale. Carole C. "never" weighs herself but instead gauges her weight by the fit of her clothing. She adds, "I try to look great, not keep my weight down. It's a different perspective." Similarly, Tim H. says, "I rarely step on a scale. But I can tell when I gain 5 pounds because I can feel it: my clothes get tighter." About 4 out of 10 masters go by the fit of their clothes to keep tabs on their weight, some in combination with regular weighing. Doug S., who's kept off more than 100 pounds for 4 years, states, "When my pants get tight, I start dieting. I used to allow myself to buy bigger clothes. I had a range of pant sizes from 34 to 52. But I got rid of the big pants. Now, I won't buy bigger sizes."

Some masters say they keep a handle on their weight by noting how they look in a mirror. And Larry Z. monitors his 70-pound weight loss of 15 years by noting the fit of his belt, as well as by weighing himself. Joy B., who's kept 35 pounds off her tiny 5'1" frame for more than 4 years (20 of that off for 18 years), not only weighs herself once or twice weekly and checks how her clothes fit but looks at the size and shape of her legs, since that's where she tends to gain weight. "When my thighs touch, it means things are getting out of hand (and into mouth!)."

As always, pick one (or more) monitoring systems that are right for you. Be ready to experiment, and take into consideration your past experience of what did and didn't work. If you choose weighing, decide if you'll check the scale once a day, once a week or once a month. Maybe, like Janice, you're better off not consulting it if you suspect your weight is up a bit, or if you think you're retaining fluid. If you passionately hate to weigh yourself, then perhaps judging by your clothes is best, allowing yourself to go no higher than a certain size. You could also pick an item of clothing or two that you want to feel good in. Kim W., for instance, keeps track of her weight by how her jeans fit and how she looks in leotards. The important thing is to pick a monitoring system and use it faithfully.

Be Adamant About Establishing— and Keeping—a Weight Buffer Zone

NEARLY ALL THE MASTERS have a maximum upper limit for weight—a sort of "buffer zone"—and they are adamant about not exceeding it. Holly L. says, "I cut back if more than a pound or two stays with me for a week." (Her plan makes sense since some weight fluctuation is normal: you need only tackle the pounds that stay on for a week or so.) And Violet Y. says, "In 19-plus years, I have never let myself get over 4 pounds past my ideal weight."

A few male masters allow themselves more leeway with their weight, as do several women who were once extremely heavy. Larry Z. gives himself 15-pounds' grace, ranging from 185 to 200. "When I hit 200, I know it's time to stop." Tom J. fluctuates 10 to 20 pounds before he takes action. And Ann F., who once weighed close to 400 pounds, tends to fluctuate between 140 and 170 pounds.

Have a Set Plan of Action if You Hit Your Upper Limit

WHEN THE MASTERS hit the top of their zone, they do something about it. They don't harp on it, feel sorry for themselves or stall around, and within a short time, their weight is back down to the lower end of their comfortable range.

Here are some masters' plans of action:

• Don M. (111 pounds, 3 years): "If I'm up, I investigate why right away. I check my activity to see if it has changed and either raise that level or reduce overall calorie intake." He also says he stops all snacking.

• Steve S. (210 pounds, 13 years): "When my weight goes up, I do more of what I'm already doing." Specifically, he eats more fruits and vegetables and exercises more.

• Patsy Jean B. (73 pounds, 3 years): "I gain a few pounds at holiday time when I allow myself to eat fats and goodies. I get back on [my plan] and lose those few." She does this by following a diet, exercising more, giving up sweets and sometimes skipping meals.

♦ Tim H. (40 pounds, 6 years): When his clothes feel tighter: "I watch what I eat for a while. I won't buy peanut butter for several weeks, and I work out a little more."

♦ Larry Z. (70 pounds, 15 years): "If I feel heavy, I know what I have to do. I skip meals, quit snacking and stop drinking beer for a while."

♦ Tom J. (75 pounds, 27 years): "When my weight gets high, I balance it out with a 4-to-6-week period of stringency." He also keeps track of what he eats and exercises more.

None of this is to suggest that you have to do anything stringent if you gain a little weight. *The important thing is to be aware of small gains and do something about them right away—even if it's just returning to your normal way of eating and exercising and slowly letting that take care of the extra pounds.*

Following is a potpourri of strategies that masters use when their weight rises. (The first five were the top five responses.) Check off those that are most acceptable to you, and give them a try the next time you gain a few pounds:

____ exercise more
____ stop snacking
____ keep a food diary or count calories
____ give up or cut back on sweets
____ go on a diet
____ skip meals
____ go back to the person or group that helped you lose weight
____ apply techniques or food plan that helped you lose weight

____ weigh and measure food
____ eat carefully for 2 or 3 days
____ give up alcoholic beverages
____ don't allow yourself to feel guilty
____ eat smaller portions
____ increase fruits and vegetables
____ decrease fat intake
____ don't eat after supper
____ try inner reflection
____ drink more water

If your weight climbs, instead of viewing whatever action you decide to take as painful and punitive, paint it in a more positive light. Focus on how good you feel when you're eating healthfully and exercising. Ernie L., the master profiled in Chapter III, has learned to look on the bright side when he gains weight as a result of his frequent travels. "I've accepted the fact that when I go to Europe, I gain 5 to 10 pounds because I love the rich desserts and get less exercise." (He knows that he also has a tendency to gain over the winter holidays, as well as on business trips, when he's less in control of the food choices.) "The moment I have slight discomfort in the waist of my pants, I say, 'That's it.' I take a look at what got me there and try to reverse it." After Europe, for instance, he immediately returns to his four days per week of aerobics classes and cuts out desserts for a while.

If resuming his normal lifestyle doesn't get rid of the excess weight within several weeks, Ernie may step up the exercise and further decrease food consumption. (Since diets didn't work for him in the past, he does not think of himself as going on one.) Ernie is also patient with himself, giving himself time to shed the weight. "I used to want to get rid of it instantly and to punish myself. But I no longer say to myself, 'Three weeks of indulgence, now three weeks of punishment.' I realize that it may take 8 to 10 weeks."

When I asked Ernie if it was a hardship to resume his normal habits after a period of being away from them, he replied, "Oh, I suppose there's a moment of feeling sorry for myself. But I try to look at the positive rather than the negative. Since I do so much of my own cooking, I reward myself with tasty low-fat recipes—I'll think of the pasta dishes I like that are really great. Or I might buy some exotic fresh fruits or expensive leafy lettuce. Instead of spending $2.50 on a dessert, I'll spend it on a wonderful salad. And since exercise is such a part of my life, I look forward to it. Rather than dwell on the drudgery of an extra aerobics class, I might go cross-country skiing on the weekend—something that's fun."

As you experiment with the masters' tips for nipping weight gain in the bud, don't think of yourself as doing something punitive. Rather, be ecstatic that you're doing something about your weight before it gets out of hand. *Remind yourself that it's a lot less painful to deal with 5 or 10 pounds at a time than it is 30, 50 or 100 pounds.*

Don't Let Lapses Become Relapses

MOST OF THE MASTERS have broken away from the all-or-nothing attitude of either being "on" or "off" a certain food-and-exercise plan—of either following the rules or breaking them. *The masters give themselves permission to deviate from some preconceived ideal and recognize that there are no hard and fast rules when it comes to weight control. When they do "slip," they don't berate themselves, but they do take immediate action so the situation doesn't get out of hand. Thus, they prevent lapses from becoming full-blown relapses.*

Lapses are single events of "slipping," doing something *unplanned,* which is not ideal for weight control. A lapse might be impulsively downing a Danish from an enticing tray at work or eating a second or third piece of cake that you hadn't planned into your day's meals. It might be failing to exercise on a day you had intended to. A lapse could also be an evening of binge eating or indulging in a rich meal. In defining a lapse, I stress the word *unplanned,* because if you plan an indulgence, it's *not* slipping. I think it's healthy for most people to allow themselves treats occasionally, as long as they can learn to enjoy them and not feel guilty.

The problem when dieters view lapses as total losses of control is that the lapses often accumulate and become **relapses**, leading to significant weight gain. Relapse might occur after a month of following a low-calorie diet, then suddenly "giving in" at a party and having several snack foods or sweets. The next day, feeling that you've blown it, you skip breakfast but succumb to a grilled reuben sandwich and fries at lunch. This chain of events may go on for a week or so, and soon you find you've gained 5 pounds. *The trick of the masters is to stop it there—don't let the gain go any further.*

Eileen B. is a master who's certainly had room for potential relapse. About four years ago, she quit smoking and at the same time started on the course of losing about 45 pounds. She adds, "In the meantime, I became pregnant, gained exactly what my doctor specified and lost every pound of the pregnancy weight gain within four weeks of giving birth. I have had a weight problem all my life, and I now know, hey, it can be done! I never quit. Everyone slips. Ignore it, and carry on."

One of the keys to preventing lapses from becoming relapses is to view occasional slips as learning experiences. Think about what went awry, how you can prevent a similar situation in the future, and pick yourself up and say, "Oh well, everyone makes mistakes."

Another key to preventing relapse is to stop viewing slips as personal signs of weakness. Instead, recognize that lapses are unique responses to individual situations. In other words, giving in to a piece of chocolate cake at an office birthday party doesn't mean you are a weak person with no willpower. (If you'd looked around you, you'd have noticed lots of other people "giving in" to indulgence.) Rather, this was one highly tempting instance—one that would tempt almost anyone, not just you—in which you had unplanned food. No big deal!

Some people have even pointed out that the overweight may have a harder struggle overcoming their problem than smokers, alcoholics or drug addicts (and may be the most prone to relapse) because they cannot entirely give up the substance. Says one master who is also a recovering alcoholic, "At least with booze, you can give it up completely; not so with food."

A Plan for Preventing Relapse

BASED ON AN ARTICLE in the January/February 1993 issue of *The Weight Control Digest* by Dr. Kelly Brownell and fellow Yale psychologist Carlos M. Grilo, Ph.D., the following skills can help you to prevent relapse. *They should be used both while you're losing weight and at maintenance:*

SKILL #1
Identify your potential high-risk situations.

High-risk situations are times when you are likely to "slip" or have lapses from your weight-control plan. You can identify your areas of weakness by reflecting on your past weight-loss attempts and by using the following checklist:

I am at high-risk for unplanned eating or deviating from my exercise plan when I'm . . .

_____ alone	_____ celebrating
_____ lonely	_____ frustrated
_____ bored	_____ feeling rejected
_____ depressed	_____ avoiding a task
_____ very hungry	_____ in my car
_____ with others	_____ cooking
_____ at a party or social gathering	_____ around certain tempting foods
_____ at a restaurant	_____ walking in my door
_____ anxious	_____ clearing the table
_____ in a bad mood	_____ other

Ask yourself what it is about the situations that makes them troublesome for you. For instance, it may not be parties per se that pose the problem—they may only be risky when someone pushes food on you. Or eating in the car may only be a problem if you go grocery shopping right before dinner—and place the bags on the seat next to you.

SKILL #2
Prevent high-risk situations as best you can.

It's ideal if you can prevent high-risk situations in the first place. One way, according to Drs. Grilo and Brownell, is to write down several specific things you can do to prevent each of them. It's important to do this ahead of time, because if you wait until the moment, it's much easier to eat than to consider other options.

So if you can't resist reaching into grocery bags after you shop, try putting them in the trunk of the car. If you tend to overeat when you allow yourself to become starved, make it a point not to let yourself go any longer than three hours without eating something. Have someone else clear the table if you can't resist nibbling leftovers. Or if you eat out of loneliness and you just ended a relationship, consider signing up for a class or planning several get-togethers with special friends.

Janice knows that evenings with nothing to do are her high-risk times. "If I feel that I'm at the upper end of my weight range, I might consciously come home from work, eat some vegetables, then make sure that I'm busy. For instance, I might plan to do some chores or, better yet, go out shopping or visit a friend."

SKILL #3
Effectively deal with high-risk situations when they do occur.

You can't eliminate all high-risk situations, but you can learn to handle them more effectively when they happen. For, instance, if parties are your downfall, you probably don't want to stop going to them for the rest of your life. When you do go to a party, how can you avoid overeating? First, set a realistic goal. Is it reasonable to think that you'll eat nothing there, only drinking club soda with lime? It's more realistic to scope out the food situation when you first arrive at the party, select a few items that you'd really enjoy, load up from the vegetable and fruit platters, then station yourself some place other than next to the buffet. (For more on realistic goal setting, see page 147.)

For me, the act of coming home or walking in the door is high-risk: I automatically think of food. (I think it stems from childhood, when I'd get home from school and head right for the refrigerator.) Of course, I can't eliminate coming home, but I can bypass the kitchen door by going through my front door, grabbing the mail, then relaxing and sorting through it. Or I can plan ahead to have a low-fat food, like a juicy apple or fresh melon, waiting for me.

Is there any evidence that using these techniques in high-risk situations works? The answer is yes, according to a study by Dr. Grilo and colleagues, in which people in weight-loss programs were asked to describe two situations: one in which they overate (a lapse) and one in which they were highly tempted but did not overeat. For each situation, the people were asked about coping strategies they used: either *behavioral strategies* involving overt action like walking away from food, doing something else instead of eating, talking to someone, waiting until the urge to eat decreased or eating low-calorie foods instead; or *cognitive (mental) strategies,* like thinking about other things, encouraging themselves or thinking about the consequences of overeating.

When the dieters used either type of coping strategy, they almost always reported overcoming temptations. Better still, when they combined both behavioral and cognitive coping, they were even more likely to avoid a lapse. Combining a helpful behavior with a motivating thought may be the best defense yet against lapses. (For more on cognitive coping, see Chapter VI.)

Drs. Grilo and Brownell stress that you have to accept the fact that you cannot fix every situation or perform perfectly all the time: your goal should be to limit how much the situations influence you. In the weeks ahead, try to anticipate them, and apply the coping skills you find to be most helpful. But remember, as the masters do, that you'll still have slips.

SKILL #4
React constructively after high-risk situations.

So you were in a high-risk situation, and you wound up overeating or not handling it as you would have liked. The worst thing that you can do is to react with self-blame and guilt: both increase chances of relapse. Drs. Grilo and Brownell warn that negative emotional reactions pose a "greater threat to successful maintenance than do the few excess calories."

Here are some of the ways the masters handle high-risk situations after the fact:

- Tim H. (40 pounds, 6 years): "I don't berate myself when I eat less than healthily. I just eat better the next time."
- Ann Q. (49 pounds, 3 years): "One of the most important things I do to keep my weight down is to forgive myself for minor transgressions."
- Jean B. (45 pounds, 5 years): I don't feel guilty if I overeat one day. If you let yourself feel guilty, you will eat more."
- Bob W. (250 pounds, 21 years): "When I 'goof,' I just begin again."

If you handled a situation in a way that you were not entirely happy with, ask yourself the following questions:

• What went wrong? (Think about what you were thinking, feeling, expecting and what happened immediately preceding the lapse.)

• Could I have avoided the situation altogether? If not, how could I have handled it differently—what might I have done or said to myself to avoid overeating?

• How can I handle the same situation in a more constructive way the next time around?

• What can I do, in a nonpunitive way, to make up for the lapse? For a short time, can I exercise a little more or eat a bit less? Or should I just forget about it and go back to my healthful habits, which will eventually take care of the lapse?

Then congratulate yourself for your awareness of the lapse and make a pledge not to let it lead to another immediate lapse. Be aware that each time you use any of the relapse-prevention skills listed above, you are increasing your sense of self-efficacy—that is, your belief in your ability to control your weight forever. As you learn to prevent lapses and cope with them without panicking when they do occur, you will gain more confidence and likely be better able to handle the next challenging situation. Lou Ann L. has overcome enough lapses to know. "As the years have passed, I've grown more relaxed and confident about how I relate to food and how I look. I also know that if my clothes are getting tight, I can eat less for a week or two, and everything will fit again."

Learning to Set Realistic Goals

DID YOU EVER make a pledge to yourself that you'd never eat a piece of chocolate again—or, after starting a diet in May, say that you'd be a size 10 by mid-June? Maybe you've sworn yourself to not gaining a single pound over the holidays, when in fact you've never been able to accomplish the task. What about exercise: have you vowed to start running a mile a day, when you've done no exercise for the past six months? All of these vows and pledges are examples of unrealistic goals that are impossible or extremely difficult to achieve and will set you up for lapses and possibly relapse.

People who lose weight and keep it off have a tendency to set goals that are attainable. In the Kaiser Permanente study (page 66), maintainers reported setting small goals that they could meet. A Yale University study found that the women who had regained weight were either "very much on or off"; that is, for a while they would eat well and exercise, then they would go back to their old ways. In contrast, the maintainers in the same study were more realistic: they didn't feel they had to do everything all the time. For instance, they might exercise just three times a week, but they were consistent about it.

The following guidelines will help you set realistic goals:

◆ Steer clear of "never," "always" and "every day" goals.

They're too perfectionistic and reflect all-or-nothing thinking. What, after all, are the odds you'll never eat a piece of chocolate again? Or that you'll exercise every single day? In their book, *Permanent Weight Control*, Michael J. Mahoney, Ph.D., and Kathryn Mahoney, M.S.W., M.S., point out that all-or-nothing goals encourage all-or-nothing behavior. "You are asking yourself for perfect behavior, for errorless eating habits. You are leaving yourself no room for human error, for *gradual* improvement. You are constantly living *one* mistake away from failure, one error away from defeat." Thus, if your downfall is chocolate desserts, a far more reasonable goal than swearing off chocolate forever—one that you're likely to accomplish—would be to eat them no more than once a week or to allow yourself to have them only in controlled circumstances, such as when dining in a restaurant.

◆ Set "just for today" or "just for this week" goals.

In other words, work on short-term goals, rather than focus on your long-term desires. Ask yourself what small steps you can achieve today: Drink a cup of water before each meal? Have a serving of fruit with each meal? Use the stairs instead of the elevator at work? Master Lois M. makes this point well: "When you focus on having to lose 100 pounds, you think, 'What the hell; two more cookies isn't going to make a difference.' But you can do it if you learn to set your goals just for today or just for this meal. Then you don't have to think about having to lose 100 pounds." (Actually, an occasional "two more cookies" won't make much of a difference in the context of a day of low-calorie eating. But with a "what-the-hell" attitude, many people let those two cookies become 10 or 15—easy to do if you feel frustrated about a seemingly gargantuan task before you.)

◆ Replace "I will be" goals with "I will do" goals.

As the Mahoneys suggest, you may want to be thinner, be in shape or be a healthful eater. But what will you do to get yourself there? Make your goals action-oriented. For example, you might say, "I will walk three or four times a week" or "I will switch from a sugar-coated cereal to a high-fiber cereal."

◆ Set specific rather than vague goals.

Nebulous goals that don't describe a specific behavior tend not to work because you never know for sure if you've met them. So instead of vowing to "exercise more" or "not eat so many sweets," promise yourself to ride your exercise bike three times a week for 20 minutes or eat a sweet treat no more than three times a week.

◆ Base goals on where you are now, not where you want to be down the road.

The Mahoneys point out that reasonable goals are relative *only* to your past and current behavior. Thus, in setting a goal for a specific eating or exercise behavior, it's important to examine where you're coming from. If you've always gained over the holidays, it's more realistic to try to keep your weight stable than to lose weight. Maybe you're accustomed to eating a big bowl of ice cream in front of the television each night—after you've had dessert at supper. Instead of giving up the sweet bedtime snack altogether, you might try having fruit for dessert at suppertime and later having a measured cup of frozen low-fat yogurt in front of the TV.

◆ Avoid "should" and "have to" goals.

Goals like these tend to make people feel deprived and guilty. Let's say you're at a picnic, and you see a huge spread of mayonnaise-laden salads and desserts. Your tendency may be to feel you "shouldn't" have any of the high-fat items and "have to" eat only salad without dressing and a plain, broiled burger. Instead, ask yourself, "Who says I shouldn't? Who says I have to?" It's important to feel that you have the choice, and it's fine to have an item or two that's not a nutritional dream food—along with more healthful choices.

◆ Set flexible goals, and be ready to change them.

If your long-term goal is to cut your fat intake to 25 percent of your calories, but you've failed at the short-term goal of eating all bread, toast and potatoes dry, maybe you should use diet margarine instead of none. Or try cutting back on fat in some other way. None of this is to say that your goals should not be challenging. The Mahoneys add, "You should expect some difficulty in performing *new* behaviors in *old,* familiar situations." If you fail repeatedly, they say, you should "back up a step or two and try again."

Why is realistic goal-setting so helpful for long-term weight control? In the first place, it helps you experience numerous small successes, which in turn are highly likely to heighten your sense of self-efficacy, or belief in yourself. Your confidence is also raised by the fact that one success tends to breed another, as demonstrated by a number of the masters. After Janice discovered that moderate exercise could help her lose weight, she became motivated to start making reasonable changes in her diet. Similarly, Don C. found that success at exercise spurred him to tackle more goals. "Running made me feel considerably better. I lost some weight, and that made me want to change my diet. Success at one thing made me want to do more."

Linda W. gave me a more detailed description of her many small triumphs, stemming from reasonable goals. "I decided to start very easily because drastic plans had never worked for me. At the first meal, I decided to start cutting back by not using butter (or margarine) on my bread. I found that I could very easily get by without butter and still do not use it on anything. Then I started to walk, and that was when the weight really started to come off. Then I read an article in *Reader's Digest* about fat grams, and I cut back my fat intake. I also started doing toning exercises and kept that up for about 2 years. I joined an aerobics class three summers ago and love it." Indeed, one success led to another for Linda, who lost 39 pounds "slow and steady" and has kept it off for 6 years.

Drs. Robert Colvin and Susan Olson found, too, that the maintainers in their study had accumulated many "small wins," maintaining their weight losses despite personal crises, such as divorce and the death of loved ones. "It's not because their weight is more important than such catastrophes . . . but because the habits acquired through small wins are so deeply ingrained that they persist even when stressful events take the foreground."

Look at the Big Picture

WHEN YOUR SUCCESS at weight control is the result of meeting many small, achievable goals, it becomes more difficult for you to label any single "slip" or lapse as failure. One mistake can't undo all your positive changes.

Another way to look at it is that to lose weight—and especially to keep it off—you have to make multiple lifestyle changes. You're probably exercising, making an effort to be more active in your daily routine, developing a preference for lower-fat foods, keeping fewer tempting foods around the house, eating regular meals, making more nutritious snack choices, handling your feelings better and choosing restaurants with healthful food selections. How can one single act of overeating—or even several—undo all the other positive changes you've made? As Drs. Brownell and Rodin point out, "Even the worst eating binge is likely to add no more than 2 pounds of weight."

When I asked Janice what she does if she doesn't handle a food-related situation as she would have liked, she replied, "I don't berate myself, and I don't fixate on it. I get it in perspective: that one candy bar won't make me 20 pounds overweight. I look at the big picture. I remind myself that there are a multitude of things I do in a day, in a week, like eating breakfast, exercising and drinking water, that help me maintain my weight. That one candy bar is a drop in the bucket."

Experts suggest that you will be less likely to view a single instance of overeating as a catastrophe if you define success as more than reaching a goal weight. The turning point for a number of masters came when they decided to focus on *lifestyle change* and not just on weight loss. Janice, for one, feels that when she ultimately lost weight and kept it off, her perspective had shifted from the short-term goal of losing weight to a long-term vision of wanting to feel good about herself forever. So set *your* sights on the small goals that lead to positive lifestyle changes, such as healthful eating, more physical activity and feeling better about yourself, and always look at the big picture of the *many* favorable steps you've taken to control your weight.

Tim H. does just that to keep off his 40 pounds. "I love chocolate, and I believe in everything in moderation: there's nothing wrong with having one candy bar a day. But in the beginning, I was more punitive and beat myself up for having chocolate. Now, I see it as long-range planning—it's a lifetime routine. I give myself credit for my gains and try not to berate myself for my losses. Yeah, I'd like my diet to be better, but instead of saying, 'I'm doing it wrong,' I always feel I'm doing it 'more right' than I did before."

VI

Learn the Art of Positive Self-Talk

HAVE YOU EVER FOUND YOURSELF running late for an appointment, only to hit every red traffic light en route, make a wrong turn out of haste and get behind every slow-moving vehicle in town? At some level, you're probably thinking, "I'll never make it. I'm never on time for anything. Why don't these jerks get out of my way?" You find yourself tapping your foot, tailgating, driving too fast, blowing your horn and feeling like you might explode. What does it all accomplish?

What you say to yourself—your *self-talk*—about running late affects your actions and your feelings. You get yourself all worked up, run the risk of an accident and accomplish nothing other than getting to the appointment at the same time or later than if you hadn't gotten riled up.

Now, what if you had said more positive things to yourself like, "Oh, well. There's nothing I can do about running late now. It's not worth risking an accident, and sometimes it's just not possible to be on time. The worst thing that can happen is that I'll be 15 minutes late, and *that's* not the end of the world." More positive self-talk can lead to more positive behavior: you don't speed, you calm yourself down, you don't take a wrong turn, and you get to your destination just five minutes late.

You may not be aware of it, but a similar process goes on with food and weight control all the time. Many people engage in negative self-talk—destructive thoughts—that trigger them to overeat or eat foods that interfere with their goals. But the masters have learned to counter negative with positive self-talk—a technique that can help both as you're losing weight and as you maintain that loss.

Joanna M.'s Story

I SUSPECTED JOANNA M. WAS ADEPT at positive self-talk when she wrote me that she used a number of psychological "tricks" to control her weight. She doesn't know how she learned the art; she "stumbled onto it." No matter how she learned the skills, Joanna made it clear that positive thinking is a critical part of her everyday life. But it wasn't always so. Joanna struggled with her weight for many years before she ever really believed she could be successful. Intellectually, she knew that eating less could make you thinner. But up until about 15 years ago, that knowledge never influenced her food choices. At that time, she started to lose the weight, eventually dropping from 190 to 140 over an up-and-down course of about 5 years. Now, at a height of 5'8", she feels good at her weight of 143. And she should, for she's managed to keep off more than 40 pounds for 10 years.

Like many other masters, Joanna describes her early years as overweight years. "I was heavy as an infant, toddler and child." The problem was exacerbated when she was 5 and her mother died. "I was lonely and traumatized, and the person whose job it was to feed me had died. So food became very important to me." At some level, Joanna believes she was thinking, "As long as I'm eating, I'm coping without her."

Throughout her elementary-school years, she recalls her stepmother "locking up" tempting food, which she would "dole out" to Joanna's thinner sisters—but not to her. "My stepmother's intentions were good, but she only heightened my desire for those foods." So Joanna would sneak money from the house to buy candy, which she would eat secretly in her room.

"By the time I was 13, I weighed 147," Joanna recalls. Every year, her pediatrician would give her a lecture about her weight, and other children taunted her. Somehow, however, she was spared in high school when she slimmed down: "I was a little overweight, but not fat."

That period ended when Joanna went to college. "I started at a weight of 150 or 160. By the time I graduated, I weighed almost 200 pounds." She attributes the gain simply to overeating. "Those were happy years. It was just that food was constantly available in the college cafeteria, and I could have multiple helpings. Then, at night, a gang of us might order pizza, and sometimes there was drinking." Joanna wasn't a diet-hopper. "I only went on diets once or twice. I went on the Stillman diet for a week, but there were no serious attempts."

Joanna lost some weight again with her hectic graduate school schedule and stayed around 173 for a number of years. After graduating, she had problematic relationships with several men, which jogged her weight up and down because of the stress. A turning point in Joanna's weight battle came when a man with whom she had been living for two years left her for someone else. Although she describes herself as "devastated," a major goal in her life was finding a partner. "I needed to lose weight to attract someone new. So I began my first serious attempt at losing weight. I ate what I wanted, but in incredibly small amounts. If I ordered a hamburger and French fries, I would only eat part of them. I drank a lot of skim milk because it was soothing to me. For some reason, I snacked on liverwurst and crackers. And I ate a lot of vegetables." This was the first time Joanna saw that decisions she made throughout the day about whether or not to eat had a connection both with her weight *and* with her goal of having a romantic relationship. "Before that, I didn't really believe that if I ate properly, it would show up on my body."

At this point, Joanna also started to use positive self-talk. "I'd say to myself, 'I'm tempted to eat this, but it's more important to be thin.' I would think about how fleeting the enjoyment would be and remind myself of my goal, which was always a certain number of pounds or a time period. I would say, 'I'll do this for two weeks, or until I'm down to a certain weight.'" When she found herself starving for her next meal, and she still had hours to go, she would tell herself, " 'I may not be able to make it for three or four hours, but I can make it for one.' I planned between-meal snacks to look forward to."

In addition, she thought about a therapist she saw who also happened to struggle with her weight. "The woman ate such meager meals. I often thought to myself, 'If *she* can get through the day on lettuce and lemon juice, I can do it, too.'" To this day, Joanna will remind herself of the therapist's statement, "You and I are not the kind of women who can forget that we have a weight problem. That's just how it is." Rather than feel sorry for herself, Joanna finds strength in this matter-of-fact approach.

Between cutting back on food and using positive self-talk, Joanna got down to the low-140's. And soon, she found the success she had been looking for: a relationship with a man to whom she is now married. She did gain about 25 pounds after meeting him, but lost half of it in time for her wedding. Shortly thereafter, she became interested in nutrition and started eating a very low-fat diet. (Because of the risk of breast cancer, she has been conscientious about watching her fat intake for many years.) From 1983 to 1988, Joanna maintained her weight around 150 and also had a baby during that time. "I only gained 22 pounds, which I lost soon after the baby's birth." After she had her second child in 1988, Joanna dropped from 153 to 136, a weight she maintained until just recently. She did it in the space of about 6 months by eating about 1,000 calories a day during the week and 1,200 calories on the weekends.

Joanna's story isn't one of having a marked "attitude shift," then dropping all her weight and keeping it off. Her story is one of weight fluctuation, gaining and losing over the course of many years, but never gaining it all back. She doesn't present her tale as a horrible battle, nor did she seem to berate herself for her rocky history. Instead, her story comes across more as a process—one of learning what works for her and of speaking positively to herself. When she feels tempted to overeat, she talks to herself and uses visual imagery. "I picture how my stomach looks when my weight is down. Or I think about how I'll look in a new outfit or how my face looks when I'm thinner." She also remembers her maternal grandmother, who was important to her and who was careful about what she ate. "She ate very little, and she ate nutritious foods. Sometimes I think of her when I'm tempted."

Joanna does feel that all the years of watching the scale fluctuate, along with a chronically low calorie intake, lowered her metabolism. Yet in the past few months, she has revamped her eating habits and found a new peace with food and her weight. About a year ago, she consulted a registered dietitian about her diet and was told that, in order to step up her metabolism, she should consider increasing her daily calorie intake from 1,200 to 1,500 or more. But Joanna didn't follow the advice right away: she had to do it her way, on her terms and in her own time. Then, about 3 months ago, she realized how "tremendously difficult" it was to maintain her weight at 136. "My weight started creeping up for no apparent reason, and I was very resentful. So I decided to increase my calories to 1,500 a day. I said, 'Okay, we'll see what happens. I won't get on the scale for a month.'" She did, in fact, gain 7 pounds, then leveled off at 143. She says of her new way of eating, "It's great. I'm not hungry all the time. Before, I was cranky and miserable. My quality of life is much better now."

Accepting the change wasn't easy, and Joanna once again called positive self-talk into play. "It was stressful to gain the weight. In the past, if I gained a pound, it would ruin my day. I'd feel that I'd failed, that I was unattractive, and I would have to decrease my calories even more. Now if I gain a little, I say to myself, 'I know I'm eating the same amount and have the same amount of activity.' I know the weight gain is temporary, and I'm confident I'll go back down."

Along with her change in food intake came a change in body image and sense of personal value. She told me, "I used to hinge my sense of self-worth on my weight. Above a certain level, I saw myself as a failure; below it, I was a success. I told myself that if I maintained my weight, my life would change: all the clients at work would ask for me, or I'd walk into a party and be beautiful because I was so thin. But I got fed up with the struggle to weigh less than 140. I realized that my goal of 136 was somewhat arbitrary and that it really didn't matter if I weighed 7 pounds more. No one even notices."

Now, Joanna's day begins with "two breakfasts," totaling 300 to 400 calories. She's up very early and starts out having dry toast or toast with tofu cream cheese or jelly. Then at work, she will eat more of the same or have a bowl of high-fiber cereal with milk. Lunch is typically a big salad—like a Caesar salad or a salad with chicken—often eaten in a restaurant. (Since she's upped her calorie intake, she no longer "holds" the dressing.) After work comes the "high point" of her day— "decompression time"—before going home to deal with the demands of young children. She stops on the way and treats herself to frozen yogurt. "I make it a point not to come home ravenous."

Dinners are typically made from recipes from low-calorie cookbooks or magazines. "I carefully choose recipes or modify them to a lower fat content. And we eat huge salads with nonfat dressing, plus lots of vegetables. Between my husband and me, we might eat a pound and a half of asparagus!" While she's cooking, Joanna keeps a no-calorie beverage by her side. When she finds herself "looking around for more" after finishing meals and snacks, she begins to look forward to her next meal. She also finalizes each meal and snack with a hot drink, carbonated beverage or small mint.

Joanna adds that her kitchen is "full of junk food," but she rarely craves or eats it because she keeps her own special controllable treat foods on hand, like malted milk balls and special nonfat chocolate sauce from a mail-order house. "I'll eat the sauce on Fiber One cereal for an evening treat."

Joanna's exercise consists of jogging for half an hour (about 2½ miles) three or four times a week. She also rides horseback several times weekly. When I asked her if she uses self-talk to motivate herself to exercise, she responded, "Yes, when I get bored or lack motivation, I picture fat on the back of my thighs."

Her number one high-risk time is when her schedule is "all mixed up" or when she doesn't count calories. When I interviewed her, for instance, she had just returned from a business trip to Europe and was off her regime. "I came home and wanted to go on a 2,000-to-3,000-calorie excursion, but said to myself, 'The last thing you need when coping with jet lag is to go on a major binge.'"

I find Joanna's story to be enlightening not only because of her use of positive self-talk, but because it illustrates that maintenance is not static. When she hit a point of near intolerance for how she was eating, she made a change that enabled her to stay thin for life. She adds, "If you want to keep your weight down, you have to have fluid goals and motivations because life keeps changing."

What Is Self-Talk?

W HAT EXACTLY IS THIS "SELF-TALK" employed by masters like Joanna? It's that ongoing conversation—that mental dialogue—you constantly have with yourself. As Kelly S., who lists "positive self-talk" as one of her top strategies for keeping off 50 pounds for 6 years, puts it, "We all have these tapes running through our heads." Often, the "tapes" are recurring, and they determine how we eat in a given situation. In other words, self-talk can actually cause feelings and behavior that, if self-defeating, can lead to lapses. *But the masters have learned to make their self-talk positive, which, in turn, helps them control their eating and their weight.*

Psychologist Joyce D. Nash, Ph.D., notes in her book *Now That You've Lost It,* "People whose negative, self-defeating self-talk outweighs their positive, coping thoughts tend not to do well in their weight management efforts. . . . In general, the person who has a greater chance of achieving long-term weight management success will engage in more self-talk that reflects flexible thinking, how-to-cope thoughts, pats-on-the-back-thoughts, more self-confident thoughts and thoughts reflecting assertiveness and coping skills."

The "Now-I've-Blown-It" Phenomenon

I N MY EXPERIENCE, the most common example of negative self-talk is the "now-I've-blown-it" phenomenon: someone who has set an unrealistic goal, such as "I'm giving up desserts," has one cookie and decides, "I may as well eat the whole bag." *It isn't just the presence of sweets that triggers inappropriate eating—it's what an individual says to him- or herself about the sweets.*

What might happen if the person says something more positive and productive? "Oh well, one or two cookies won't make me gain weight, but eating the whole bag will. It's over and done, and I'll stop right here." The very act of changing that negative statement into this more positive self-talk can stop lapses from occurring.

Kelly S. recalls, "When I was in the ultimate hell of my weight problem, I knew that if I ate one cookie or candy, I was going to literally eat pounds of it." And so she did. But not anymore. "Now I tell myself there are no 'good' and 'bad' foods. I can eat a few bites of a dessert and be fine." By using such positive self-statements, she is now able to prevent lapses when she eats sweets.

How Negative Self-Talk Gets in the Way

NEGATIVE SELF-TALK INTERFERES with successful weight control in two ways. In the first place, it leads to "slips" in eating behavior. Joanna M. repeatedly struggles with negative self-talk after she's been out for the evening and anticipates coming home to leftover treats not eaten by her babysitter. She finds herself thinking, "I can't wait to get home and eat that," which can lead her to overeat. But she tries to counter this negative thought with, "Look, it's already midnight. I may as well go to bed, and soon it will be morning. It's silly to eat all this after having had such a good day."

Secondly, negative self-talk may produce feelings of depression and hopelessness, which in turn can cause more overeating. Peppi S., who has kept off 62 pounds, points out that negative self-talk "leads to giving up and the guilt and depression that go along with it. This leads to the vicious cycle that so many of us can get into: eating, guilt, depression and negative thoughts, overeating, guilt, etc."

She goes on: "To avoid slipping, I am always trying to 'talk to myself.' I feel maintenance is all about *consciously* making choices. If I choose to have a dessert that I haven't had in a while, I don't bash myself for making that decision. I made the choice, I deal with the choice and make the necessary sacrifices for choosing it. None of this 'all-or-nothing' thinking, where you say, 'Well, I blew it by eating this, so the rest of the day doesn't count.' Not that we don't all have better days than others. You've got to see these as warning signals; if you don't stop it soon, you can very easily get back into old habits."

When Is Positive Self-Talk Helpful?

POSITIVE SELF-TALK *can work to your advantage at all stages of weight control: when the "attitude shift" is taking place, while you're losing weight and at maintenance.* When you're in the midst of the attitude shift—or as Stanton Peele and Archie Brodsky put it in *The Truth About Addiction and Recovery,* "when you are moving from being 'on the fence' or 'thinking about' changing your habits to a firm determination to change"—you can use your reasons for wanting to lose weight as "internal pep talks." When Joanna M. was finally ready to lose weight permanently, she told herself, "I want to look good more than I want to eat." In making the decision to lose her 50 pounds once and for all, Kelly S. psyched herself with, "The weight is no longer going to be a barrier to feeling good about myself and pursuing my goals."

When you're losing weight and at maintenance, positive self-talk is particularly helpful in high-risk situations. *Positive self-talk can work at moments of choice.* When Joanna M. felt tempted to overeat as she was losing weight, she reminded herself about her end goal, "and that was more important than the immediate gratification of food." At maintenance, one of her high-risk situations comes when she's very tired. She talks herself out of indulging by asking herself, "How am I going to feel after I eat this? I remember how it used to feel."

As Kelly S. was losing weight, she realized that one of her difficult times was studying for college exams. Her recurring negative self-talk was, "I need the M&M's to get through this test. I'll diet tomorrow." But when she was ready to lose weight, her self-talk became, "I can get through this test without binge eating."

Positive self-talk can work after the fact. If Joanna M. winds up eating some of the food left over from the babysitter, she tells herself, "I'm usually so disciplined. I can have some momentary lapses. If it shows up tomorrow, I know I'll lose it."

Peppi S. sums up the benefits of positive self-talk with, "I listen to myself. [I ask myself] why I want a certain food, how that certain food tastes, what my expectations are and how I'm going to deal with the emotions if I choose to eat it. Then, if I choose to eat the food, I sit back and think about what I'm feeling. If the food was a letdown, I register this in my mind so the next time I get a craving or desire for that food (or any other food for that matter), I will remember that the last time I tried it, it wasn't all that great, and I might be more inclined not to want it."

Learning the Art of Positive Self-Talk

A PROBLEM MANY OVERWEIGHT PEOPLE HAVE is that the negative self-talk is so deeply ingrained that they're not even in touch with their mental dialogues with themselves. Indeed, a number of my patients used to tell me, "I don't think before I eat. I just do it." Peppi S. admits that before she lost her 62-plus pounds, "I never sat down to figure out why I overate. I just thought it was because I liked to eat too much. *Au contraire!* It was because I had lots of emotions or stressful situations bombarding me, causing me to satisfy them the easiest way I knew how. And the thing I was really good at was eating."

But there are techniques—psychologists call them "cognitive restructuring"—that you can learn to get in touch with your negative self-talk and turn it around to positive thinking, making it less likely that you'll eat in ways that interfere with weight management.

In their book *Permanent Weight Control,* Michael J. Mahoney and Kathryn Mahoney popularized the following cognitive restructuring techniques to help people struggling with their weight. These steps are based on their suggestions:

◆ Detect your self-statements.

This is the most difficult step: getting in touch with what you say to yourself. As the Mahoneys point out, "If you're like many people, you may go through an entire day without monitoring what you say to yourself. This doesn't mean that your thoughts are unconscious—only that you seldom make an effort to listen in on them." They suggest performing a "mental inventory" anytime you feel tempted, discouraged or depressed. That is, when you feel the urge to engage in behavior that is inconsistent with weight control, don't just tough it out—ask yourself what is going on inside your head. If you can't come up with anything, try completing the sentence "I am acting as if . . . " For instance, if you feel you can't resist the urge to eat a candy bar, you might say, "I'm acting as if I'll die or the world will end if I don't have a candy bar."

Some people find it helpful to keep a diary of their thoughts throughout the day, asking themselves what they are thinking before, during and after they eat or feel tempted to eat. The Mahoneys suggest placing small reminders or prompts, such as stickers (Kelly S. finds Post-its to be useful), in or on highly visible places like your watch, wallet, clock, mirror and scale. Each time you see a sticker, pause and review your thoughts for the preceding few minutes. Can you find any negative self-talk?

Judy F. is both a master at weight loss and a registered dietitian who specializes in counseling overweight people. She helps them get in touch with their negative self-talk by having them list 12 reasons they want to change their behavior. Then, when they want to eat something, she advises that they reread their list so they're forced to think about what they're doing.

◆ Evaluate your self-talk.

Is what you say to yourself in any given situation true, rational, sensible, helpful? As San Francisco-area psychologist Silas M. Wesley, Ph.D., points out, "The mind *lies* (as well as tells the truth *some* of the time). It's important to catch the mind in one of these all-too-frequent lies, overgeneralizations and gross exaggerations. . . . The discovery needs to be made that you don't have to believe everything that your mind says!"

When evaluating self-talk, sometimes it helps to ask yourself what you'd say to someone else in the same situation. For instance, how would you respond to someone who said, "I blew it, I may as well pig-out for the rest of the day?" You probably would tell him or her, "That doesn't make any sense."

◆ Turn the negative self-talk to positive self-talk.

After recognizing the irrational nature of notions like "the world will end," you might say, "No, I won't die if I don't have candy. And the short-term pleasure of eating it now is not worth it when I see how great I look in my new jeans."

Another way of challenging negative self-talk is with a technique called "thought-stopping." Dr. Joyce Nash suggests that whenever you have negative self-talk, you think to yourself "Stop!" and immediately dismiss the negative thought, focusing your attention on a counter-argument or positive thought. She finds that it helps some people to refocus their attention when they wear rubber bands on their wrists and snap them at the same time they think "Stop!"

It Takes Time and Practice

I T TAKES TIME to learn the art of cognitive restructuring, to actually believe in your new, positive self-talk and to be able to act in ways that are consistent with long-term weight control. As the Mahoneys put it, "Appropriate self-talk *typically* takes months, even years, to develop . . . there is frequently a lag between changed self-talk and changed feelings." Joanna M., for instance, wasn't always able to forgive herself so easily when she slipped. She admits, "It took a long time. It used to be that gaining one pound would drive me crazy. But that didn't stop me; it gave me renewed determination."

Dr. Wesley suggests that, rather than deal with the notion of having to change your whole life and way of thinking, you take things one thought at a time. In essence, that's what Joanna M. did when she was faced with the prospect of having to wait for another meal: she told herself if she could just make it through the next hour, she'd be okay.

In taking thoughts and events one at a time, concentrate on your ability to overcome unpleasant or challenging situations or feelings. Use self-statements like, "I've made it through similar situations before" or "It's only as bad as I tell myself it is. I know I can make it." *Your ability to use positive self-talk to manage individual situations will boost your belief in your weight-management abilities.*

Dr. Nash emphasizes that it is not possible to wipe out all negative self-statements: "To attain success, the objective is to get the positive self-talk to outweigh the negative, aiming for a ratio of about 2 to 1, positive to negative."

In all honesty, some masters find certain rather negative self-statements to be helpful—for example, Joanna M.'s comment about picturing fat on her thighs to motivate herself to exercise. And when she's tempted to indulge, she sometimes recalls how disgusted she felt after once stuffing herself with fruitcake. Alyce C. has "a picture of a very fat person" posted on the door of her refrigerator. In her book, *Alyce's Fat Chance*, she adds, "Some people put a skinny person on their door . . . that didn't work for me. Call it the Power of Negative Thinking."

As always, you have to find what works for you. But most psychologists would agree that positive self-talk is more productive than negative.

How the Masters Put Positive Self-Talk to Work

FOLLOWING ARE SOME OF THE CATEGORIES of self-talk that dieters commonly use. Take from the masters the positive self-talk statements that will work for you:

• **Self-fulfilling prophecies**—setting yourself up for something by telling yourself that it will or won't happen. Says master and registered dietitian Judy F., "If my patients are talking negatively, they are almost destined to eat negatively." In other words, if you tell yourself you'll never be able to lose weight and keep it off, you'll probably see to it that you never will. Peppi S. used to say, "I can't." *Now, she uses positive self-talk to create a productive self-fulfilling prophecy:* "The greatest thing I learned from Nutri/System is to say, I can; I can do anything I set my mind to do." Similarly, Doris M., who was "desperate after 30 years of diets," became inspired when she went to Weight Watchers and saw "thin, healthy people maintaining 50-to-100-pound weight losses." She adds, "I could do, and I *did*!"

• **All-or-nothing self-talk**—black-and-white thinking. Unrealistic goals that establish rigid rules set you up for failure. Low-calorie diets and rules about foods he should "never" eat used to trigger all-or-nothing thinking in Don M., who, after one small deviation, would say to himself, "I'm off it. I've been bad—I've fallen off the tightrope." The next day, he'd give up. Now, with his new low-fat way of life, he still feels he needs to stay away from certain foods, but instead of being negative, he focuses on treats he *can* have.

• **Body size or weight-related self-talk**—bemoaning your rate of weight loss or having an unrealistic goal for your body. This kind of negative self-talk might say, "I only lost half a pound this week. Why bother?" But instead of being impatient about weight loss, Rosetta F. says, "I tell myself that if there are 3,500 calories to a pound, I can lose about a pound a month by just not eating 100 calories a day that I am now eating. A pound a month times 12 months is 12 pounds, times 3 years is 36 pounds lost." Jennifer P., who's 5'5" and weighs 142, down 44 pounds from her maximum weight, says, "I wanted to weigh 123, but my recommended weight is higher. Also, I don't want to deprive myself and be obsessive about exercise in order to lose. I'm a size 10, and that's okay." Don M.'s body-related negative self-talk can be, "I'm still not normal; I weigh 20 pounds more than I ultimately want to." His positive refrain is, "The difference between what I was and where I am is so vast that I can now wear 'drop-dead' clothes! I haven't been this thin since I was 13 years old."

• **Catastrophic self-talk**—always thinking the worst will happen or feeling things are worse than they are. For example, I frequently heard my patients make comments like, "I'm up a pound this week. I'll probably gain all the weight back." But it helps to ask yourself, "What's the worst thing that could happen?" For example, if you overeat for a weekend, the worst that could happen is that you might gain a pound or two. As Lynn M. states, "If I gain a pound, I don't panic. If it takes a week or two to take it off, I have enough confidence in myself that I will lose it." When faced with a high-risk situation, like going to a party, Joanna M. doesn't panic, but instead "blocks out" 400 to 500 calories she can spend. She uses positive self-talk: "I think of women I have known who control their weight and imagine what they would eat in this setting." She also focuses on socializing and thinks about how good she looks when her weight is down.

• **Rationalizing self-talk**—making excuses in order to allow yourself to overeat. When she was heavy, Joanna M. made excuses by telling herself she "was going to go on a diet sometime." But at some level, she thought, "It won't work." When she was successful, she told herself (and believed it), "If I don't eat that, I *will* lose weight." After a lapse, Peppi S. used to rationalize by saying, "What's one more day of overeating?" Now, if she slips, she says to herself, "Okay, so I ate it!" and she stops right there. After dieting and regaining weight, Don M., who once had clothes in multiple sizes, used to say, "Oh well. I've got clothes that fit me." When he lost weight once and for all, however, he put all his big clothes in a "fat box" and donated them to the homeless. "Now, when I desire a short-term 'high' from a sundae, I remind myself that I no longer have to shop in a big men's store. I say, 'Yeah, you did it!' " Then his desire for the sundae passes. Lydia R. described her self-talk at a recent dessert buffet: "I had one thing I really wanted. I told myself that all those desserts don't really taste that good anyway. Besides, they're all sugar and fat." In the past, she would have said to herself, " 'They all look so good. I may as well have what I want tonight. I won't have the chance again.' So I'd have a taste of everything and wind up with the equivalent of four pieces. I used to talk myself into it instead of out of it."

• **Self-deprecation**—putting yourself down for human tendencies or calling yourself demeaning names. People who see themselves as "bad" because they sometimes stray from their goals or who call themselves names like "fat pig" and "slob" set themselves up for relapse. Mindy B. used to say, "I'm fat. Who cares? I'm going to eat it anyway." Now, if she gains a few pounds, she thinks, "I like myself here. I don't ever want to be that fat person again," and she immediately takes the weight off. When Don M. was heavy, his recurring disparaging thought was, "I'm an outcast because of my size—I'm not likable." He's turned that statement around: "Everyone, including me, is special and unique. I like who I am."

• **Punishing self-statements**—chastising yourself for lapses. Remember Ernie L.'s past tendency to feel he had to punish himself with stringent dieting when he gained some weight after traveling? Now, his positive self-talk is, "I have come to accept the weight gain when I travel, and I no longer feel I have to get it off instantly. I realize that it may take some time, so I focus on the positive instead of on drudgery." Similarly, Dorothy C. comments, "Rather than flagellate myself and vow to fast or cut back drastically the day or week after a mini-binge, I have learned to accept setbacks and move on."

• **"Should" self-statements**—beliefs about obligations that have little or no basis in fact. Peppi S. was full of shoulds: "You should always clean your plate. You should eat what's available before someone else does. You should not let anything go to waste, so you should finish it off. You should eat now so you won't be hungry later." She adds, "These are beliefs that you have to be willing to rethink into new ideas." *So when you feel "shoulds" about foods, ask yourself, "Who says I should? Does this make any sense?"* I used to tell my patients who couldn't bear to waste food to ask themselves, "Is the 'wasted' food better off in the trash can or as excess on my body?" When Joanna M. feels the urge to "eat it now before the kids finish it up," she takes a piece of the item and tucks it away so she doesn't feel she has to down it immediately.

• **Have-to-have food thoughts**—feeling you can't delay immediate gratification for a particular food: "I'm dying for a __" or "I can't stop thinking about __; I have to have one." But the masters use positive statements to talk themselves out of certain situations and foods. Margie M. uses the popular statement "Nothing tastes as good as being thin feels!" Joanna M. asks herself, "Which means more: eating this or losing fat?" She adds, "When I'm hungry, I remind myself that it's only a short time until my next meal or snack, and I can stand anything for that amount of time." When Mindy B. was losing weight, she told herself, "Whatever I want to eat that is fattening, I can have next month. It will still be in the store." A similar statement helped some of my former patients who found themselves obsessing about a food when they were trying to lose weight: "I know what it tastes like, I've had it before, I'll eventually have it again. I'm just choosing not to have it right now." Peppi S. reflects, "So often, it's the built-up anticipation for a food. I often find that when I have it, it isn't so great."

• **Dealing-with-saboteurs self-talk**—telling yourself you have to give in to someone else's attempts to sabotage your weight loss or maintenance efforts. So often, well-intentioned (and sometimes ill-intentioned) friends or relatives get in the way of weight control. Don M. occasionally hears, "You're too thin" and is sometimes offered high-fat food gifts. "In the past, I would have thought, 'Oh, they're right—it's time to stop losing weight. I can't refuse food that's given to me.'" Now he can say to himself, "I know in my heart that I'm not too thin, and they don't understand what I'm trying to accomplish." So he graciously accepts the food and then gives it away. Joanna M. is also occasionally admonished by jealous relatives that she should be eating more. "But I don't cave in; I remind myself I'm not the sort of person who can be talked into anything. It makes me more determined." (For more on social pressure and sabotage, see Chapter X.)

• **Poor-me self-talk**—believing that your lot in life is horrible because you have to watch your weight or feeling that weight control should be easy. A number of masters had encouraging words about coping with such feelings. When Lydia R. gets through a high-risk situation without overeating, she tells herself, "It feels good to nurture myself with healthy food; it's not torture. I feel proud of myself." Peppi S. accepts that she is more susceptible to gaining weight than other people. But she doesn't feel sorry for herself; she sees herself as making conscious choices that she feels good about. She goes on, "I look at maintenance as a life-long commitment and not as a self-defeating punishment. Maintenance is a way of life for me; it's all about making choices: I choose to read food labels, I choose to eat what I used to consider forbidden foods when I feel the urge to eat them. But I am also very careful to register in my mind what that food tastes like, how I'm feeling when I eat it and how I feel after eating it." In short, for Peppi, maintenance is not a plight, it's a choice. Instead of feeling that maintenance is a struggle, Doris M. defines her years of "carelessness, making poor food choices and feeling like a failure" as "struggling." Mindy B. uses positive self-talk to avoid "poor-me" thoughts about chocolate, a food she feels she cannot control. "I tell myself this is one thing you cannot have. Some people can't have milk, and this is a fact of life for me."

Focusing on Where You've Been

A S I TALKED WITH THE MASTERS about their positive self-talk, a recurring theme was their focus on where they have been. *When they feel tempted to eat in ways that interfere with weight control, they habitually think about their past and compare it with the present.* "I think about my body—the way it used to be and the way it is now—and all the money I've spent on clothes," states Joanna M. "It makes me not want to eat." Similarly, Fern C. admits, "It hasn't been easy; I feel like quitting every so often. But when I remember what I looked like fat, I work harder at it."

Peppi S. motivates herself by occasionally trying on a pair of her old, large jeans. She adds, "I have to remind myself every day by looking at my body in the mirror or weighing myself that I have come a long way and know the positive feelings far outweigh the negative feelings. And when I exercise, I remember what it was like when I was heavy, that I couldn't even walk a block, much less do a step class for one solid hour! I constantly think of how it used to be, how far I've come, and how I am a happy, healthy and energetic person."

Don M. stays on track, not only by recalling "the extraordinary moment" when he found that the clothes in the big men's shop were too big for him, but when he was able to purchase health insurance at a normal rate. "Right after I lost weight, I applied for health insurance, and they still charged me higher rates because they bet I'd gain the weight back. The next year, they dropped the rates, but not all the way. Now, I'm charged the normal rate for life insurance. Thinking of that keeps me motivated when I'm tempted to overeat."

The clear message from the masters is: Challenge your negative, defeating self-talk with thoughts about your accomplishments. You'll come to believe in yourself more and more.

VII

Move It to Lose It

EXPERTS SAY WITHOUT HESITATION that a critical difference between maintainers and regainers is their commitment to exercise. As Mary Ann K., who managed an 84-pound weight loss, says of her maintenance method, "Exercise is a big part: you have to move it to lose it."

"In the complex and often uncertain world of obesity research," note Yale University's Carlos M. Grilo and his colleagues in a recent review, "one fact can be stated with authority: exercise is associated with weight loss." Moreover, increased physical activity is probably the best single predictor of who will *keep off* weight.

What may come as a surprise is that most masters are *not* exercise fanatics—people who work out arduously every day or for hours at a time. *Indeed, experts suggest that what's most important about exercise is consistency and enjoyment—and less so the amount or type of activity.*

I'm not going to talk about how to get your heart rate up or tell you the best way to stoke your metabolic fire. Instead, this chapter provides information from the masters for getting hooked and staying hooked on exercise by designing your own personal fitness plan—one that you can live with and tailor to your needs as your circumstances change.

Jim V.'s Story

JIM V. IS A MASTER AT WEIGHT CONTROL *and* at exercise. In fact, he considers exercise to be the most important thing that he does to keep off his 250 pounds. Jim has lost more than half of his former 475-pound self. When he was losing, he found, "It came off so much faster and I felt so much better when I exercised." But Jim is the kind of guy who doesn't believe things until he sees them. "I had to put it to the test, so I stopped walking for a month. My weight loss decreased immediately. I said to myself, '*This is going to be the key.*'"

As with so many masters, it took years before Jim was ready to take control of his weight problem. He told me, "I was overweight as far back as I can remember. From about ages 5 to 10, I was chubby; I was obese through high school and college." Fortunately, Jim had a number of things going for him that made him feel good about himself despite his weight. He was very active in the drum and bugle corps, he ranked high in academics, and he always managed to have a group of supportive friends who accepted him as he was. He endured the "typical name-calling" by peers, particularly at the all-boys high school he attended, "where 75 percent of the guys were into sports. I had to stay away from that crowd because they mocked me."

Jim maintains he didn't really become uncomfortable about his weight until he was in college. "I felt misplaced. I couldn't get involved in activities as much as other people. I wanted to be in theater, but I couldn't because of my size." What really did Jim in when he was in college was his embarrassment at his inability to fit comfortably in the chairs. "It was the main reason I left college and got a job."

When he was about 19, with his weight in the "high-300s," Jim made his first and second-to-last attempt at losing weight. He went to a dietitian at an outpatient hospital clinic and lost about 90 pounds on a sensible, low-calorie diet. "I went because my parents forced me. I did it to please them. But I went right back to my old habits." Within 2 years, Jim had gained all the weight back.

For the next 7 or 8 years, Jim's weight problem got worse. He had a clerical job that was sedentary, as was his social life. "I'd go to work, go home, go out to the movies. My reason to go out with friends was to go out to eat. I always ate on the run, ate lots of fast foods and ate more than three times a day. I was never satisfied."

Jim's discomfort grew, as did his size: he hit his all-time high of 475 when he was 29. (He's 6'3" tall.) His readiness to take control of his weight increased when, as the teacher of a prominent drum and bugle corps, he had to do a lot of traveling. "I was so uncomfortable and embarrassed, squishing into airplane seats." He also found himself be-coming complacent about his daytime job.

It took a critical, life-threatening incident for Jim to finally take ac-tion. "It was the Fourth of July, 1989. I was out in a boat with an in-ner tube tied behind it. I stepped in, and the tube flipped. I got caught under it, and my pants hooked onto the boat. My brother-in-law jumped in to save me, but he practically killed himself doing it." That was Jim's turning point. "I said to myself, 'If I can't save myself because of my weight . . . ' Right away, I went to my doctor, who re-ferred me to Dr. Blackburn. I went the next day and said, 'I'll do any-thing.' " (George Blackburn, M.D., is a weight-control expert at New England Deaconess Hospital in Boston.)

Jim then went on the Optifast all-liquid "fasting" diet for 18 weeks. He had five specially formulated "shake" meals a day and no solid foods. When I asked him if that was difficult, he replied, "The first three weeks were torture, then it was a breeze. I didn't want to stop." Jim also went to behavior-modification group meetings and special meetings for people on the fast, while seeing a dietitian/nurse for indi-vidual counseling. "I just sucked in the information—the things to change my habits. I saw the situations I had placed myself in. Even though I was just drinking shakes, I was practicing for maintenance."

Over the 4½-month course, his weight plummeted to 350 pounds. Then it was time for a break: slow refeeding, easing him onto a low-calorie diet with real food that still allowed him to lose about 3 pounds a week. "The difficulty was the choices. I knew intellectually about fat, but I had to read labels and weigh things."

Jim began to exercise toward the end of the fast: he chose walking. "I probably pushed myself too hard in the beginning. I started with an hour, but the pace was slower [than now]. I found a place where I en-joyed walking around a pond. It was peaceful, and a lot of people were doing the same thing. There was lots of encouragement. The feeling I got from it was so wonderful, and it was something I was doing for myself."

After two months on the low-calorie plan, Jim still had a lot of weight to lose, so Dr. Blackburn offered him the opportunity to go back on the liquid fast for 16 weeks. Once again, the first three weeks were rough. "It was a shock, it was brutal, but the results were amaz-

ing. I went through four different wardrobes by the time I was done."
(Jim admitted that if he had it to do over again, he would not have
gone on the second fast because the choices he was allowed on the
low-calorie diet made him feel empowered, and he didn't want to give
that up.)

Again, there came a 6-week period of weaning off the liquid for-
mula and onto regular food. Then came a year and a half of "maintenance," which meant eating three meals a day and no more than 30
grams of fat, as well as attending weekly group meetings with a dietitian. Jim never missed a meeting, and to this day, chooses to go back
to see his dietitian about once every three months. "When I feel I'm
getting lackadaisical, and I need a jump start, I go back for a shot in
the arm. I need to hear, 'You've been through this before, and you've
done all this work. You know how you feel when you're in control.' "
(All together, it took Jim about 18 months to get down to his current
weight of 225. He has done so well that he now runs some weight-loss
groups for the program that helped him.)

"Now, I can identify when I hit 'that' point, like when I'm busy
teaching drum and bugle corps, and there's lots of food around.
Usually, I look and think before eating. But if there's too much pressure, I stop thinking. I reach and eat without thinking. But I sense
when it's happening. Before, I would let it go out of control."

Jim described his longest lapse, which occurred this past winter. He
gained 10 pounds (the upper limit of his "buffer zone") when he was
under extreme pressure, traveling with the drum and bugle corps, on
top of a full-time job. "All my thoughts were consumed by the kids [I
was teaching]. But I decided not to let things like that become as important as my health. I identified the problem immediately and went
to see Marty [his dietitian] and got back on the track."

When I asked Jim about the transition from the fast to maintenance, he admitted it was "scary." "Your mind-set is that you don't
want to stop losing weight or that sense of accomplishment. It's a real
downer for a while." How did he get his sense of accomplishment
when the fast was over? He told me, "By getting through every day,
doing my food and exercise plan, doing the things to take care of myself. In the past, I always took care of others. It was a day-by-day
process, and it still is." Also, like most other masters, Jim now sees

that he couldn't conquer his weight problem until he accepted full responsibility for it. "When I finally realized that I wasn't doing it for my parents but for me—that's when I felt successful."

Today, Jim says the process is much easier. And he has little fear of regaining the weight. However, he didn't start to see himself as a thinner person until two years ago, after he went through the painful process of having cosmetic surgery to remove the excess folds of skin on his chest, legs and stomach. "Now, I feel like a typical, normal human being." For motivation, Jim will sometimes recall his surgeon's warnings about how important it is to maintain his weight loss. "If I think of myself regaining, I think I might explode!" A somewhat punitive self-talk strategy, but it works for him.

Now, Jim religiously eats three meals a day. A typical breakfast consists of cereal with 1 percent milk and a bagel, plain or with jelly. For variety, so he doesn't get bored, Jim occasionally has an egg or low-fat frozen waffles. Lunch might be a bowl of soup, a large salad with dressing on the side (usually low-fat dressing, but once in a while regular, when he "has a taste for something"), or a "light" sandwich like turkey with mustard instead of mayonnaise. Then dinner is a "good-sized meal"—usually pasta with plenty of vegetables. "Lots of chicken" is in his repertoire; he rarely eats red meat. He tries to make it a rule not to eat anything past 7:00 p.m.; if he does, it's a handful of pretzels. He also eats three pieces of fruit, spread throughout the day. Jim has a good sense of how many calories he needs to maintain (he's had his metabolic rate measured) and figures he eats between 2,300 and 2,800 calories a day—hardly a starvation level!

Since he has quite a sweet tooth, Jim tries to stay away from sugary foods. "On special occasions, like holidays, I will allow myself a treat. I choose the one thing I like best." Although he makes it a practice to avoid fast-food restaurants, Jim has not given up eating out with his friends. "I did lose a lot of friends who felt I wasn't going to be 'the happy-go-lucky, let's-go-out-to-eat-dinner person.' But I still have a core of friends who will go to restaurants where you can make [healthful] choices."

Jim says his impetus to keep his weight down is more health-related rather than a "look" he's after. "I do it because I feel better. I'm motivated by the health benefits—better sleeping and breathing." And the exercise helps him "stand taller, feel stronger and have better endurance."

As for his exercise during maintenance, Jim says, "When I stop for a bit, my weight goes up. When I increase my activity, I go back to normal." His exercise routine now consists of 60-minute walks along a river each day on his lunch hour. (He figures he covers three to four miles.) "It re-energizes me for the afternoon. I'm ready to go for another four hours. I'm not as hungry, and it's improved my job performance drastically." Jim goes on his walk every week day, unless it's extremely cold or "very crazy" at work. If it's cold, Jim walks at a mall "without my credit cards and my wallet. I don't need another bad habit." Not long ago, Jim added working out at a health club three nights a week with a personal trainer to his exercise routine. He goes on a treadmill for 15 minutes, a rowing machine for 10 minutes, followed by 40 to 50 minutes of weight-lifting. (Jim is a smoker, which is his next habit to tackle.)

Since the health-club routine added to the walking sounds like a rather intimidating amount of activity, I asked him how he responds when people in his weight-loss groups say they can't begin to have time for all that exercise. He replied, "I tell them there are 24 hours in a day, and you have to be able to find one hour a day for yourself. If people exercise 3 times a week for 20 to 45 minutes, that's a great start. You have to set reasonable goals. Even I would feel satisfied spending an hour 3 times a week walking." (Recall, too, that Jim lost weight quickly and maintained his losses just fine by walking 5 days a week.)

To make exercise enjoyable, he uses headphones, occasionally walks with a friend at work and purposely chooses pleasant surroundings. (Sometimes he walks along the beach.) He also thinks it's motivating to exercise at places where other people are doing so. At his health club, he finds it helpful to work out around "accomplished athletes," whom he fondly refers to as "muscle heads." He finds, "They constantly encourage you. They are the most tolerant people because they want you to feel the way they do."

Ultimately, Jim's secret to maintaining a 250-pound weight loss is "planning my meal pattern and exercise." He stays hooked on exercise by "experiencing how pleasing and stress-reducing it can be."

How the Masters Move It to Lose It— and Keep It Off

W HEN I ASKED THE MASTERS to tell me how they were finally successful at *losing* weight, their most consistent response was "exercise." Although the question was open-ended, and many masters gave multiple responses, exercise was mentioned more frequently than any other *specific* method of weight loss.

When I asked them to list the three most important things they do to *maintain* weight loss, their most frequent specific response was, again, "exercise." Approximately three-quarters of them included exercise in their top three.

And when I asked the masters to tell me what they do if they *gain* weight, the most common answer was "exercise more." In fact, they're more likely to step up exercise in order to deal with small gains in weight than they are to go on a diet, omit sweets, stop snacking or keep a food diary. (Again, multiple responses were possible, and many masters did all or a number of the above, including exercise.)

The masters' commitment to exercise is striking when you consider that less than 10 percent of the U.S. population is physically active for at least 3 one-hour sessions each week. In contrast, the overwhelming majority of masters exercise from 3 to 7 times a week; a third of them say they do so 5 or 6 times weekly, while about 20 percent exercise 3 or 4 times.

At the high end, about 16 percent exercise daily. There's Steve S., who's gone from 435 pounds to 225 and has maintained that loss for 13 years; he holds the world record for marathon stair climbing. And Donna C. keeps 108 pounds at bay, in large part by walking 3 miles each morning *and* night, as well as by using the stair stepper or ski machine for 30 minutes, 4 to 5 days a week. At the other extreme, about 22 percent work out very little—0 to 2 times weekly. Larry Z., for example, maintains a 70-pound loss without any formal exercise. And Jeffrey B., master of 55 pounds for 22 years, exercises only when his weight rises. (See page 185 for more typical exercise regimes of masters.)

Most successful weight controllers *do* exercise on a regular basis, as revealed by the Kaiser Permanente Medical Center study (page 66) that compared women who successfully maintained their weight loss with those who had regained. In the same study, 90 percent of the women who had lost weight and kept it off reported exercising regularly—at least 3 times a week for 30 minutes or longer—while only about a third of regainers said they exercised regularly. Moreover, regainers who did exercise said they did so less often and less vigorously than maintainers. Finally, maintainers reported more activity in their leisure and daily work time than did regainers.

Similarly, Drs. Robert Colvin and Susan Olson found that most of the maintainers in their study were committed to exercise. They noted that 11 out of 13 men—and 32 of 41 women—reported exercising regularly to maintain their losses. Another study in which overweight people lost weight on four different diets revealed that, regardless of the diet followed, those who exercised maintained weight losses far better than did those who did not exercise. In addition, people who *stopped* exercising at the end of their diets regained, while those who *began* exercising at the end tended to keep off their lost pounds.

Exercise will not necessarily make you lose a lot more weight when you first start your weight-loss effort. But in the long run, people who exercise are likely to lose more weight and keep it off than those who do not.

A number of masters told me that they see a clear connection between periods of weight gain and lack of exercise. Suzanne T., for instance, recently gained 10 of her 80 lost pounds back after she was in a wedding, went on vacation and her "exercise time diminished." But, she adds, "I'm currently losing those 10 pounds." Similarly, when Nancy R. stopped exercising for a period of 6 to 8 months (she also stopped watching her diet), her weight shot up about 25 pounds. Now that she's exercising again, her weight is back down to 145—55 pounds shy of her one-time maximum of 200 pounds.

While some experts are adamant that exercise is mandatory for successful weight management, I did locate 15 masters (about 9 percent) who say they don't exercise at all—other than engaging in daily activities—and a number of them maintain more than 50-pound losses. Moreover, only about half of the successful weight losers in Dr. Ross's study described exercise as important to their weight-control efforts.

Quite frankly, I don't know how these people do it! Perhaps they are more physically active in their daily routines than when they were heavy, or perhaps they eat less food than other masters, or their metabolic rates may be higher.

Master Molly A. is living proof that weight loss can be done without exercise. She told me, "I was heavy all my life, from age 18 on; I was a size 20 for years." At her heaviest, Molly weighed 227. More than 8 years ago at the age of 55, she started to lose her 63 pounds. "All without exercise. People can't say they can't lose weight because they can't get out of a chair. I did it." (She doesn't exercise because she needs knee replacements.)

For the vast majority of people who want to lose weight and keep it off, exercise is important. But for those who refuse to or can't exercise for medical reasons, it should be reassuring to know that weight loss and maintenance are still possible.

The Wonders of Exercise

WHY IS EXERCISE CRITICAL to so many of the masters? Because it combines a number of metabolic, medical and psychological advantages.

♦ Exercise burns calories.

The table on the following pages illustrates how many calories various forms of exercise expend. The number of calories *you* burn for any one activity depends on how often, how intensely and how long you do it, as well as on your weight. (Generally speaking, it takes more calories to move around a 175-pound body than a 125-pound body.)

It can be discouraging to see how few calories on a day-to-day basis even fairly rigorous exercise like running burns off. If a 175-pound man, for instance, were to go out for 20 minutes and run at a rate of 5.5 miles per hour—quite a lot for most people—he'd use about 250 calories, which may not sound like much for a strenuous workout. But the critical difference with exercise is in its cumulative effects: if that same man were to run for 20 minutes 4 days a week, in a year's time he'd burn off an extra 52,000 calories, or about 15 pounds.

What does it all add up to? When you're losing, you'll lose faster if you exercise. At maintenance, you'll be able to eat more food yet maintain your weight: that 20-minute runner could eat two or three hot fudge sundaes a week without gaining. Moreover, the amount of weight people lose by exercising is generally greater than would be expected from the number of calories the exercise alone expends.

Calorie Values for 10 Minutes of Activity

Activity	Body Weight (in pounds)		
	125	175	250
Sleeping	10	14	20
Sitting (watching TV)	10	14	18
Standing	12	16	24
Walking downstairs	56	78	111
Walking upstairs	146	202	288
Walking at 2 mph	29	40	58
Walking at 4 mph	52	72	102
Running at 5.5 mph	90	125	178
Running at 7 mph	118	164	232
Cycling at 5.5 mph	42	58	83
Cycling at 13 mph	89	124	178
Shoveling snow	65	89	130
Badminton	43	65	94
Baseball	39	54	78
Basketball	58	82	117
Bowling (nonstop)	56	78	111
Canoeing (4 mph)	90	128	182
Dancing (moderately)	35	48	69
Dancing (vigorously)	48	66	94
Football	69	96	137
Golfing	33	48	68
Horseback riding	56	78	112
Ping-pong	32	45	64
Racquetball	75	104	144
Skiing (Alpine)	80	112	160

Activity	Body Weight (in pounds)		
	125	175	250
Skiing (water)	60	88	130
Skiing (cross-country)	98	138	194
Squash	75	104	144
Swimming (backstroke)	32	45	64
Swimming (crawl)	40	56	80
Tennis	56	80	115
Volleyball	43	65	94

◆ Exercise likely has metabolic benefits.

Studies suggest that moderate exercise tends to increase resting metabolic rate (see page 78), which, in turn, may help offset the drop in metabolism that can occur when you diet. As you lose weight, you tend to lose some muscle along with the fat, but evidence suggests that regular, aerobic exercise can slow the loss of muscle tissue, at the same time that it promotes body-fat loss. Since muscle tissue burns more calories than does fat tissue, it's reasonable to expect that your conditioned body would burn more calories than when it was out of shape. However, because muscle tissue weighs more than fat tissue of the same volume, weight loss can be less than expected for some people, at least when they first start exercising.

◆ Exercise may suppress your appetite.

Contrary to the common notion that it's a waste of time to exercise because it will only make you hungrier, studies suggest that the extra activity suppresses appetite in some people. The effects of exercise on the desire to eat are complicated, however, and seem to depend on the intensity of the activity and on your gender. In general, when physical activity is increased moderately, it tends to decrease appetite, food intake and body weight; vigorous exercise tends to increase appetite but hold weight stable. Women appear to benefit less than men from the appetite-squelching impact of exercise. Studies suggest that normal-weight women tend to eat more when they boost physical activity, but not enough to make them gain weight, so that the net effect of exercise is that they are able to eat more without ill effects. Overweight women do not appear to eat more when they exercise, and thus they lose weight.

◆ Exercise is good for your body and psyche.

Exercise has been shown to have preventive health benefits, lowering blood pressure and cholesterol and helping to decrease the risk of diseases like diabetes and osteoporosis. According to a number of experts, exercise also has important psychological benefits for weight control. Studies have shown an association between higher fitness levels and better mental health. Specifically, there is evidence that exercise improves mood and psychological well-being and enhances self-esteem, while at the same time decreasing stress, anxiety and depression. Psychologists feel that these mental boosts come together to bring about greater commitment to weight control.

Exercise can be a means of preventing relapse: it can replace problem eating and alleviate stresses that make people want to eat. You can put exercise to work for you during high-risk times, such as when you're lonely, blue or bored. In fact, it may help to exercise at a time of day when emotional eating is likely to occur. (It's not easy to work out on a StairMaster or do "power" walking and eat at the same time!)

Exercise can also pick you back up after the fact. If you've had a "slip," you can counteract it by working out, which not only offsets some of the calories you've eaten, but helps you feel recommitted and in control. Jim V., who used to eat when under stress, is well-aware of the psychological bonuses of exercise. "I do it because it makes me feel better. It's the greatest reliever of stress I've ever known."

Here's what some other masters have to say about what exercise does for them:

◆ Dorothy C. (32 pounds, 8 years): "Regular exercise helped burn calories *and* reduce stress that triggers overeating. It became its own motivation: I was able to gradually 'replace' my food 'addiction' with physical activity. Exercise has helped me feel better physically, get control over my life and feel good about myself."

♦ Kelly D. (54 pounds, 4½ years): "I think, in my life, the most important part is exercise. It has become a way to live healthier and a secret to relieving stress as well."

♦ Ernest L. (45 pounds, 12½ years): "Exercise, exercise, exercise," he wrote, when asked to list the three most important things he does to keep his weight down.

♦ Ann F. (220 pounds, 10 years): "I exercise every day, which seems to have done wonders not only for weight maintenance and toning, but also for general well-being. It's helped enormously in controlling stress and in my general health."

♦ Tim H. (40 pounds, 6 years): "It forces you to pay attention to your body and therefore take care of it."

♦ Kevin C. (45 pounds, 7 years): "Exercise allows you to eat that much more on maintenance; because of exercise, I can be a lot less concerned when I do overeat."

How Much Is Enough?

SHOULD YOU WORK OUT 3 days a week or 5? Is 15 minutes long enough? How intense should your workouts be? What's the best time of day to exercise? One problem with minimum exercise "prescriptions" is that they contribute to that old "all-or-nothing" thinking: if you can't meet the goal, even for one day, you may as well not bother. The truth is that *any exercise is better than no exercise*, and even modest exercise can bring about significant psychological and health benefits. In one recent study, for instance, 27 women who walked 4 nights a week for 10 weeks (beginning with 20-minute walks and working up to 40-minute ones) experienced a loss of body fat and an increase in muscle, even though they didn't go on diets. By the end of the study, their pulse rates had dropped, indicating that their hearts were taxed less than before. In another study, women who walked for 1 hour, 5 days a week, at a relatively leisurely pace of just under 3 miles an hour had as much increase in their good (HDL) cholesterol as did women who walked at a rate of 5 miles an hour.

In addition, there is evidence that you're more likely to stick with exercise if it's less intense: the drop-out rate for vigorous programs has been reported to be as much as twice as high as for moderate-intensity exercise programs. Moreover, while moderate exercise tends to improve psychological well-being, high-intensity exercise can actually raise levels of tension, anxiety and fatigue in certain people.

The bottom line is that you don't have to run marathons, become a body builder or do daily step-aerobics classes to reap the benefits of exercise. As *Washington Post* columnist Ellen Goodman recently put it, " . . . we don't have to be fully regimented, highly aerobic and thigh-mastered athletes in order to be fit. It appears that all we have to do is put one foot in front of the other. Up the stairs. Down the block. Around the corner. In the garden. To and from work."

Finding What's Right for You

A S WITH FINDING THE RIGHT WAY TO LOSE WEIGHT, the word from the masters when it comes to exercise is, *you have to find what's right for you.* The table below shows the many forms of activity chosen by the masters.

Approximate numbers of masters who engage in various forms of exercise:

Walking	72
Bicycling (regular and stationary)	34
Aerobics (includes jazzercize and step)	31
Nautilus/weight lifting	21
Step climbing	21
Running, jogging (includes treadmill)	19
Calisthenics	14
Swimming	11
Ski machine	7
Dancing	6
Racquetball	4
Horseback riding	4

Note: Many masters engage in multiple forms of exercise. Some other forms of exercise were mentioned, but fewer than four times each.

Some typical exercise routines described by the masters include:

• Cindy B. (38 pounds, 3 years): 4 to 5 times a week, she walks briskly (2 miles in ½ hour) at noontime. Sometimes she rides a stationary bike.

• Carole C. (39 pounds, 20 years): 5 to 6 times a week, she either "power walks" 2½ miles or bicycles. On weekends, she bicycles 15 to 30 miles.

• Cathy C. (38 pounds, 11 years): 3 to 4 times a week, she swims or uses a total workout bike (for arms and legs) for 30 minutes at a time.

• Chuck F. (62 pounds, 10 years): 1 to 3 times a week, he uses a stationary bike for 15 to 30 minutes and does mat work followed by free weights.

• Judy F. (40 pounds, 27 years): 5 to 6 times a week, she walks 2 miles.

• Don M. (111 pounds, 3 years): 3 to 4 times a week, he walks briskly for 40 to 45 minutes.

• Becky M. (40 pounds, 12 years): 5 times a week, she walks briskly for ½ hour.

• Thalia P. (32 pounds, 4 years): 3 to 4 times a week, she does an aerobic class or the step machine for 30 to 60 minutes.

Granted, all of these masters exercise far more than most Americans, but they are *not* fanatics. *My sense from most masters is that exercise is a healthy obligation—part of the routine of life—not a rigid obsession.*

How do you find what's right for you?

In considering any one form of exercise, ask yourself the following:

• Is the form of exercise enjoyable or at least not unenjoyable? The odds are that if you hate what you're doing, you'll give it up quickly.

• Will you do it on a regular basis—not just today, but month after month?

• Is there a financial cost involved, and can you afford it? You may not be able to swing a fancy health club, but a YMCA, YWCA or community center may offer what you're looking for at a reasonable price.

◆ If you have to travel to an exercise facility, how conveniently is it located? How will you get there? (The greater the effort, the less likely you are to stay with it.)

◆ Does the type of exercise you're considering suit your schedule? If, for example, you work 60 hours a week, it may not be realistic to have a fitness instructor plan an hour-long exercise regime 5 days a week. If you're not a morning person, you may not relish getting up every day at 5:00 a.m. to go swimming.

◆ Is privacy important to you? If you are self-conscious about exercising in front of others, you might want to consider (at least initially) a solitary activity or joining a club or class specifically for overweight people.

◆ If you choose to go to an exercise facility, is it clean and pleasant-looking? Is the emphasis on enjoyment rather than on a "no-pain, no-gain" philosophy? Is the equipment well maintained and is there only a short wait for it? "Yes" answers to questions like these help to increase exercise adherence.

◆ Is it safe to perform the type of exercise that interests you? Perhaps your neighborhood is not safe for walking after work, so you may want to find an indoor track or do mall walking.

◆ If you need childcare, is it available, and do you feel comfortable with the arrangement?

◆ Do you prefer exercising alone or in a group? Would you be more motivated if you could find a friend or relative to exercise with you? Are you more likely to stay with it if you have a leader? If so, then a class situation may be best. But if you hate classes and the "hype" of some aerobics instructors, some form of home exercise may be ideal if you have the discipline to stick with it. (See page 263 for more on social support and exercise.)

◆ Does your climate suit the form of exercise you're considering? For example, if you live in Arizona or southern Texas—and you're not an early-morning person—perhaps jogging is not the best idea—at least for the many months of the year that the temperature soars above 90 degrees F.

The masters at weight loss went through a trial-and-error process before finding the form of exercise that was right for them. For Donna

C., "It was between walking and swimming. I don't like to get wet, so I picked walking. I also had a dog to walk—he lost several pounds, too!" Sam E. goes to a 50-minute aerobics class 3 times a week, but only stays for 30 minutes "because that's what the American Heart Association says is minimum. I can live with that." Holly L. tried exercise tapes and found she was too uncoordinated for aerobics: "This was a bit frustrating. Then I began walking. This I liked but found it hard to make time for until I decided it *had* to become part of my day. Now, on weekends, when I cannot fit it in, I quite often find myself looking forward to Mondays when I will be able to."

If you're considering buying home exercise equipment, which, if you stick with it, may wind up being cheaper than yearly membership fees at a club, make sure you're familiar with the machine before you take the plunge. You might want to try a friend's machine several times or join a club for a short time, just to familiarize yourself with various forms of equipment. Note, too, that activities you may not think of as exercise "count," like bowling, ping-pong, golf, leisurely walks and gardening. *What's critical is that you start defining yourself as being physically active and that you do whatever you choose consistently.*

Weighing the Exercise Options

S HOULD YOU WALK, RUN, SWIM OR STEP? The following guide gives you some of the pros and cons of a number of popular forms of aerobic exercise—that is, the type of exercise that gets your heart rate up and gets you huffing, puffing and burning fat.

• **Walking:** As you saw in the table on page 184, the most popular form of exercise among the masters is walking, mentioned by nearly half of them. In my opinion, walking is the most doable form of exercise, particularly for individuals who need to lose 30 or more pounds. It costs no money, requires no special equipment or clothing (other than a decent pair of walking shoes), can be done alone or in a group almost anytime and anywhere and is relatively easy for people who are overweight and/or out of shape. The *Tufts University Diet & Nutrition Letter* (April 1992) points out that, for the purpose of building endurance, 40 to 50 minutes of fast walking brings about the same benefits as 20 to 30 minutes of jogging. Moreover, if a walker and a runner of the same size cover the same distance—say, 2 miles—they'll each burn approximately the same number of calories. Not only is the risk of injury lower with walking since it is less stressful to weight-bearing joints, but you may be more likely to stick with it because it is lower intensity and less likely to cause exhaustion. People who have hip, knee or back problems may want to consider walking in a pool. If interested in group walking, you can contact a local walking club through your YMCA or mall.

◆ **Jogging:** Jogging has just about all of the conveniences of walking, and it burns more calories than does walking for the time invested. Yet jogging can be hard on the joints, especially in overweight people, and can lead to discomfort and injuries.

◆ **Cycling:** Either on an indoor stationary bicycle or an outdoor bike, you can get a good workout by cycling. Some people find it more enjoyable than jogging, and it is less hard on the knees, ankles and feet. With an indoor cycle, you have the option of purchasing one with pumping handlebars for arms and shoulders, so you get both an upper- and lower-body workout.

◆ **Aerobic dancing:** A lot of people like aerobics because of the variety of exercises, music and group interaction. More vigorous types of aerobics tend to involve jumping or running in place, however, and the wear and tear on the joints can be considerable, especially for heavy people. Furthermore, step aerobics that require stepping on and off a platform can worsen knee problems. (The higher the platform, the greater the risk of injury.) Low-impact workouts, in which one foot is always on the ground, eliminate most of the jumpy, jerky movements that can cause injury. Be aware that some aerobics movements require coordination and can be difficult to perform. According to the *Tufts University Diet & Nutrition Letter*, ½ hour of aerobic dancing burns roughly 183 calories for a 130-pound woman and 237 calories for a 170-pound man.

It's wise to shop around for an aerobics class that suits your level of fitness. Try to find a class with a certified instructor who is more concerned with meeting the group's needs than with getting a personal workout. If you prefer solitary exercise and going at your own pace, purchase an aerobics videotape.

• **Stair climbing:** If you choose stair climbing as your regular form of exercise, it's best to do it on a machine, such as a StairMaster or Lifesteps, because going up and down real steps can be harder on your joints. You can get a great aerobic workout on these machines, but blood pressure and heart rate can rise very quickly, so beginners should be careful not to overdo it. In fact, StairMasters offer a tough workout and may best be reserved for after you have a good fitness base—for instance, in walking. Be aware that you can't necessarily go by the caloric-expenditure reading on the machine, because leaning on the rails reduces expenditure: an estimated 7 percent fewer calories are burned for every 10 pounds you support by leaning.

• **Rowing:** A rowing machine affects more parts of the body than most other forms of exercise mentioned thus far: it works out your arms, legs, abdomen, shoulders and back. Rowing is also easier on joints than running or aerobic dancing. But if you have a back problem, you should definitely get your physician's okay before choosing this routine.

• **Skiing:** Cross-country ski machines do more than tone your legs, they exercise most major muscle groups, but mainly the arms and legs. A workout on a ski machine is considered one of the best overall forms of exercise. Although it takes some practice to coordinate the arm and leg movements, skiing puts little strain on the body and affords a low risk of injury. Like stair equipment, however, ski machines are quite taxing and may be best saved for when you've achieved an initial level of fitness some easier way.

• **Swimming:** Swimming exercises all major muscle groups and carries a low risk of injury. Because water cushions the body, swimming is especially suitable for pregnant women, people with arthritis and those recovering from injuries. The buoyancy of water can be advantageous for obese individuals because it reduces stress on joints. Aquatic exercise—perhaps with other overweight people—is also a possibility.

Is Strength Training for You?

WHEN I WAS IN MY TWENTIES, I jogged 5 miles a day, 5 days a week. (Up until that point, I was a real slug: I had trouble passing the President's Physical Fitness tests they give to kids. It literally took years for me to work up to 5 miles of jogging.) But it started to become torturous, and I began asking myself, "Am I going to be able to do this—from both a physical and mental standpoint—for the rest of my life?" Truth is, I was sick of it. Then I read an article that talked about how the ideal exercise regime is one that combines aerobic exercise with strength training—lifting weights—and I made the switch to a combination of the two.

Some overweight people prefer weight training to other types of exercise requiring more skill or coordination. It's noncompetitive and easy to learn. Beginners can see results quickly, which keeps them going. You don't need to knock yourself out to get the benefits: lifting light weights 2 or 3 times a week for 30 to 40 minutes per session is adequate.

The real advantage of strength training is that, by increasing the size of your muscles, you may be increasing your body's metabolic rate. In other words, because muscle tissue burns more calories than fat tissue, strength training may help you burn more calories. One interesting study revealed that people who did weight training plus aerobic exercise (cycling) for ½ hour, 3 times a week, lost more weight and more body fat than did those who cycled alone for the same amount of time. (Note, however, that not all studies have shown this effect of weight training.)

Another major advantage of strength training is that it can slow down or prevent the loss of muscle tissue that naturally occurs as you age. Between the ages of 20 and 70, the typical sedentary American loses about 30 percent of the total number of body muscle cells, resulting in a depressing loss of about 6 to 7 pounds of muscle per decade. Not only do the remaining muscle cells begin to shrink, but the pounds lost in the form of muscle tend to be replaced by fat. Strength training can, to a large degree, reverse this trend by building up the muscle cells that remain.

Strength training, however, does not turn fat into muscle: there's no such phenomenon. Muscle and fat cells are completely different and cannot be changed from one to the other. But you may lose some fat because of increased calorie expenditure related to strength training, while at the same time, you look better because you've firmed up and developed muscles.

Strength training can benefit anyone, regardless of age. Take the case of master Celia G., who didn't lose her 36 pounds until she was 64. (She's maintained that loss for 5 years.) About 3 months into her dietitian-supervised weight-loss plan, she started doing "body toning" with special-resistance machines because she "didn't want flabby arms." The results? "I took off a total of 12 inches in my upper arms and thighs and enjoyed the work." (Similarly, when I started doing strength training, I found that I went down a size, even though I gained several pounds from the increase in muscle mass.)

Getting Started

SINCE ABOUT HALF OF ALL PEOPLE who begin an exercise program drop out within 6 months, it's important to get off to the right start. Before jumping in with exercise, *first and foremost, get your physician's okay,* particularly if you are overweight or have/had any of the following: heart disease or heart problems of any sort, chest pain, high blood pressure or other risk factors for heart disease (such as high cholesterol), stroke, diabetes, back problems, orthopedic or musculoskeletal problems, kidney or liver disease, arthritis, osteoporosis or metabolic problems. You should also get medical approval if you have not engaged in vigorous activity for a long time or are a 40-plus-year-old man or a woman age 50 or above. If you have medical problems, it may also be wise to consult with an exercise physiologist or physical therapist. Finally, you should talk with your physician about whether a medically supervised exercise stress test is appropriate for you.

Do away with the anti-exercise excuses.

"I've been inactive for too long." If you think you're so out of shape that you'll never be able to stay with it, take heart. Most studies on the subject suggest that when you compare the initial fitness levels of people who stick with exercise with those of individuals who drop out, there are no differences. If you're a beginner, however, be forewarned that exercise is unlikely to make you feel better right away. In fact, you're likely to experience some initial soreness and stiffness that usually goes away after a week or two. *With time, exercise will make you feel good,* but it may take as long as a few months before the fitness benefits set in; the psychological boost may be evident within 2 to 3 weeks.

"Exercise is for young, slim people." Recall the many masters who started their journey to maintenance after the age of 40. At 70, Fern C. (she has kept off 28 pounds for 21 years) exercises every day. She walks and does 20 minutes of different exercises, including some for stretching and some for muscular tone. She also square dances. August J. (47 pounds, 11 years), who is 85 years old, walks every day; he tries to cover approximately 10 blocks "on an empty stomach." Jennie C. (25 pounds, 4½ years) is 84 and walks every day, weather permitting. She also gets exercise raking leaves and gardening.

"It's too risky to exercise." Your chance of developing diseases caused by lack of exercise is much greater than the risks from exercise itself, note Drs. John Foreyt and G. Ken Goodrick in *Living Without Dieting.* The probability of injury is minimal if you use a gradual approach. Even some masters who have chronic medical problems find a way to "move it." Mary S. (71 pounds, 4 years) doesn't let arthritis stop her from walking 3 to 4 miles daily. When she can't walk, she uses her exercycle, which, she says, "I hate, but it fills in the gaps." Holly L. became motivated to lose her 97 pounds 3 years ago, when, at age 69, her "legs gave out." Now she exercises 5 to 6 times a week. Although she once could barely walk "half a block," she now does power walking—"1½ miles at a fast clip" plus 80 "step-ups" and bend-and-stretch exercises. If the weather is bad, she uses an exercise bike.

"I'd look awful in those skimpy leotards or tank tops." Who says you have to wear them? In fact, most people I see working out at my local Y have on big, baggy T-shirts that cover all the less-than-perfect parts. You're actually better off wearing loose, comfortable clothing that you feel good in. However, it can give you a boost to buy attractive warm-up suits and colorful T-shirts and shoes. Stay away from heavy sweats for indoor or warm-weather exercise—they don't make you lose weight any faster and only serve to overheat you.

"At my size, I'm too self-conscious." Instead of focusing on the two or three beautiful bodies in a gym or exercise class, look at the many people who are far from perfect. In order to feel more comfortable, you may want to shop around to select an exercise facility catering to larger people. You could also start your exercise program at a slow time of day or year, so you feel less self-conscious. "Since the health-club business is slower during the summer months, there was time for me to get into the aerobics room relatively unnoticed," says Kim W. of the time when she hit her peak weight of 162 pounds. It was then that she started working out at the health club she managed.

Jim V. points out that slimmer people often give heavier individuals credit for exercising. "When I first started walking, people were *more* encouraging because I was overweight. I never encountered problems because of my appearance. If anything, people were more helpful."

"I don't have time." The truth is that you have to make exercise a top priority and schedule it into your life—just like dental flossing, styling your hair and putting on your seat belt. Although he didn't think it was possible, Jim V. found the time. He says, "I used to feel like my life was so active that I had no time to do it, but it's not the truth." Now he tells himself that he "works all day for someone else," and that hour and a half at night is for him alone. No one's schedule could be busier than that of Stephan P., a chef, author, consultant and frequent traveler, who was, until recently, involved in running four restaurants. He's managed to keep off 25 pounds (he's 5'7" tall) in large part by exercising for an hour, 5 or 6 times a week.

Finally, try asking yourself, "If Presidents Clinton and Bush can find time to exercise, why can't I?" Once you get past the point of discomfort and into the routine, you will likely find you really miss exercise on your days off, as does master Tim H. "Exercise is number one. You have to develop it as a habit. It's so much a part of my life that I don't feel right without it."

"My family and friends are not supportive." There's no question that a commitment to exercise changes your lifestyle, which can pose threats to your inactive partner, make friends jealous or frustrate children who aren't accustomed to your taking time for yourself. Awareness of the issue can help, as can your sensitivity to their feelings. But sometimes you just have to state, "This is how it is." It may be of value to try to get the nonsupportive person to exercise with you. (For more on support, see Chapter X.)

"I don't have the money." Several forms of exercise cost little or nothing. There's no reason to invest in fancy equipment or clothing unless you want to. Walking is free. However, some people who spend money on exercise equipment or a health-club membership find that the financial investment makes them more committed. You also have to think about priorities: how much do you spend each year on restaurant meals, compact disks and going to movies?

"I'm too tired." Actually, you'll likely find that regular exercise gives you more—not less—energy. Many people who feel "beat" at certain times of the day feel refreshed after exercising. Jim V.'s noontime exercise "reenergizes" him for an afternoon of productivity.

"It's too hot/it's too cold." Once you get hooked on exercise, weather will not deter you. It's important to dress comfortably and go at the time of day when the temperature is most favorable. (Or find an indoor, temperature-controlled place to walk, like a mall or indoor track.)

Whatever form of exercise you choose, start small and set realistic goals. Your short-term goal should be to start doing something—anything—to get yourself moving. Ernie L., profiled in Chapter III, started "small" by running 1 minute a day, slowly working upward. If you decide to walk for 15 minutes every other day and find you can do more, you'll feel very accomplished. But if you decide to exercise every day for an hour and end up doing it only 2 days for 20 minutes, you may feel like a failure. After you have accomplished your minimum goal, then you can add on another day of exercise and/or another 5 minutes to your routine.

It's important that your goals have some flexibility, not rigidity. One study showed that people who set their goals according to how they felt on any given day were less likely to drop out of an exercise program and more likely to continue exercise in the long run. So if your normal walk takes 45 minutes, but you have a slight headache or an extremely busy day ahead of you, figure it's better to walk for 20 minutes than not at all.

According to the American College of Sports Medicine, a long-term goal for fat loss would be to exercise at least 3 days a week for a minimum of 20 minutes and at sufficient intensity to expend approximately 300 calories per workout session. Since that goal is very rigorous, it would also be adequate to exercise at least 4 times a week, burning off 200 calories per session. (Going by the chart on page 180, you can see that, for a 175-pound person, walking at a pace of 4 miles per hour for 30 minutes, about 4 times a week would do it.) *But give yourself plenty of time to reach that goal.* When former marathon runner Tom F., the master profiled in Chapter VIII, first started running, it took 3 to 4 months before he was able to run a continuous mile.

In the beginning, keep your exercise plan simple. Even if you have professional guidance, you should play a major role in developing your program so, like your weight-loss plan, it becomes your own. No matter what form of exercise you choose, cut back if you feel tired or overly taxed. You're better off staying at a lower level of intensity than risking discouragement and giving up. With time, you should be able to move on.

Little Things Mean a Lot

IN YOUR DAILY ROUTINE, you can perform many little activities that add up: like taking stairs instead of elevators and parking your car way out in a parking lot, rather than right next to a store. Indeed, experts estimate that walking up and down two flights of stairs a day instead of using an elevator would allow a 176-pound man to lose about 6 pounds each year.

Unfortunately, as a society, we've gotten lazier and lazier physically. From 1965 to 1977 alone, estimated average calorie expenditure in individuals declined by 200 calories a day, in part thanks to labor-saving devices from electric juice squeezers to sit-down lawn mowers to remote-control garage-door openers.

Moreover, a study conducted by Yale University's Dr. Kelly Brownell and colleagues in several public places where stairs and escalators were next to each other found that only 5 percent of 40,000 people used the stairs. For every 5 normal-weight people who used them, only 1 overweight person did.

The trick to increasing "routine activity" is to undo our sedentary habits. Here are some ways masters "move it" in their day-to-day lives:

• Jim V.: "When I go to a mall, I park my car far away from the entrance. I always take the stairs at work."

• Graham Kerr: "I get up every hour and move around. I think it's good to have an alarm or an hour glass as a reminder."

• Lou Ann L.: "I always do stairs rather than elevators."

• Ernie L.: "I'm not a jittery person; I'm a sitter, a leaner. So I force myself to expend energy. I walk at work and take stairs."

To reverse the nonmovement trend, try to come up with as many ways as possible to increase your exercise in your day-to-day activities, starting with the morning:

• Use a bathroom on a different floor to brush your teeth before leaving for work.

• Get off the bus or have the cab drop you off two blocks before your destination.

• Upon arrival at your place of work, take stairs at least part of the way to your floor.

• Move your wastebasket to a side of your office that forces you to get up when something has to be discarded. (No shooting baskets!)

• When in airports, don't use moving walkways.

• Take the steps to use the water fountain on a different floor.

• Walk to co-workers' offices to give them messages rather than calling them on the phone or using an intercom.

• Walk your dog instead of letting him run in the back yard.

• Get up to switch TV channels rather than use a remote control.

• Walk across the room rather than ask the nearest person to hand an item to you.

• Sit in a rocking chair and rock as you watch TV.

Sticking With It

HOW DO THE MASTERS STICK WITH IT? How do they make a life-time commitment to exercise? As always, their approaches vary, but many of them use techniques suggested by experts.

• **Make it fun.** Ann B., who switches from rollerblading to cross-country skiing to stair stepping, says, "I found things to do that I enjoyed, so exercise wasn't a chore." Tami B. does a similar array of exercises and states, "I try to play at exercise. It makes it more like fun than drudgery." Kim W., a master who now teaches aerobics classes, told me, "I try to bring the playfulness back [to the people in my classes]. If they enjoy what they're doing, they'll stick with it and be successful." Ernie L. has fun with aerobic dance. "My mother was a dance teacher, and I have always loved dance. I find it relaxing, almost spiritual." But, unlike running, which he could do alone, Ernie finds he needs the camaraderie of group members for aerobics. He adds, "At first, I was the only man; now I have three friends with me."

In addition to finding enjoyable forms of exercise, it helps to have pleasurable accompaniments for exercise, like watching soaps or the news on TV, exercising with a partner, reading the tabloids or listening to music. (There is evidence that people tend to perceive exercising with music as being easier than without.)

◆ **Make changes.** A number of masters have switched from their initial exercise routines—either for physical or mental reasons. Ernie L. gave up running when he developed knee problems. Then, for a long time, he did aerobic circuit training (a combination of weight lifting, running in place, bicycling and treadmill running), but got bored with it. "I'll probably change again in the future," he says. "You have to keep looking at what's right for you." In the words of Dorothy C., "One of the keys to sticking with exercise is to vary the routine. It helps that I enjoy aerobics, but after 11 years, I do need to use all kinds of 'tricks' to stay motivated: special music tapes; new classes, gyms and machines; new clothing; running with my husband." Finally, some masters change their form of exercise with the season. Wendy M. runs in the summer and does the stair stepper and bike in the wintertime. And Ann Q. walks more in summer and spring, yet uses a NordicTrack and bike in the winter.

◆ **Give yourself a break.** Most masters take days off from exercise. As much as he exercises during the week, Jim V. relaxes every weekend and does "fun things" like traveling and going to the beach.

◆ **Use positive mind games.** Instead of dwelling on how much more you have to do, how far you have to go and how much a stitch in your side hurts, focus on the beautiful day, the nice neighborhood and landscaping and the smell of spring. Like some masters, you can also use inspirational thoughts to spur you on. Dorothy C. fantasizes about being an Olympic athlete. While Kim W. was getting hooked on exercise, she fantasized about being a dancer: "The movie *Flashdance* had been really popular around that period of time, and I knew that I wanted to move like her."

Jim V. uses positive self-talk to overcome his distaste for working out when it's hot. He says to himself, "Okay, so it's hot. It's no different than a cool night. Go out and work out. You'll feel all the better for it." He adds, "When it's over, I'm glad I did."

◆ **Focus on the pay-off.** As Donna C. puts it, "The pay-off is so great. Walking is a good mind-clearer. I feel great. I have stamina. I'm rarely sick. I have two grown daughters who marvel at me. They always used to find me at home in front of the TV. Now they may call and not find me there." Since exercise doesn't necessarily show up on the scale right away, try, as Jim V. does, to focus on other measures of success, like sleeping and breathing better, standing taller and feeling stronger. Also take note of lower blood pressure and pulse rate, as well as stress reduction. Some people find it motivating to keep records of how much they exercise, along with related improvements.

• **Be realistic about what exercise will and won't do for you.** Let's face it: walking for ½ hour, 5 times a week is not going to turn you into a Cindy Crawford look-alike. Even Tim H., who both lifts weights and works out on a ski machine, states, "I could spend my whole life never being satisfied with my body. When I was more over-weight, I'd look in the mirror and think about how I wanted to be. Now, I look at how I am." Realize, too, that not everyone falls in love with exercise. "I *hate* to work out, but it feels so great after," confesses Sam E., who has kept off 35 pounds for 10 years. Even people who like to exercise sometimes go through periods when they seem to lose interest: that may be the signal that it's time for a change.

• **Don't make it a catastrophe when you fall short of your goal.** As with eating, relapse-prevention strategies can help with exercise. Start by setting realistic exercise goals. Since all people fall short at times, try to anticipate potential high-risk situations that increase the odds you'll skip out on exercise. Is it when you're overtired, stressed out or when you have waited until too late in the day? Develop some sort of plan for coping.

If you do miss a day of planned exercise, don't let it throw you. When Jim V. can't get out to exercise, he doesn't feel guilty, as he did in the beginning. "I say, 'There are seven days in a week—I can make up the time elsewhere.' So I may go dancing that night." Similarly, Tami B. says, "I try to do some form of exercise daily, but I don't fret if I don't." A day of missed exercise here and there doesn't even amount to a pound of weight gain.

• **Give yourself time to get to the point of pleasure.** Jim V. agrees that one reason why so many people give up on exercise is that they don't stick with it long enough to be able to enjoy it. For him, it took nearly a year. "You have to try it—suffer it through at first. You get there faster than most people think. You have to set that time aside for yourself. It's not being selfish, it's being wise."

SOME RECOMMENDED EXERCISE REFERENCES

The American College of Sports Medicine's ACSM Fitness Book. 1993. Champaign, Illinois: Leisure Press.

Biomarkers: The 10 Determinants of Aging You Can Control, by William Evans and Irwin Rosenberg. 1992. New York: Simon & Schuster.

The Exercise Habit by James Gavin. 1992. Champaign, Illinois: Leisure Press.

VIII

Face Life Head-On

L ET'S BE HONEST. For most people—whether they are slim or overweight—food provides great enjoyment. From day one, food is associated with affection and nurturing. Many of us have learned that food is at least temporarily comforting when problems arise. But for some adults, food becomes life's *only* pleasure.

A number of masters reported that, in the past, they had used food to obliterate their emotions rather than confront their feelings. Research does suggest that overweight individuals tend to eat more than those who are of normal weight in response to negative emotions, particularly if tasty foods are available.

There's little question that the short-term effect of stuffing yourself with food can be anesthetizing, bringing temporary relief from anxiety and frustration. Food provides immediate gratification, and overeating can lead to feelings of sluggishness, drowsiness and calmness. In the long run, however, the pay-off diminishes, and the person who overeats is left with feelings of guilt and remorse, a worsening weight problem and the unresolved problems that precipitated the eating in the first place.

The masters have put an end to this vicious cycle: they've learned to face life head-on. They've learned to deal with life's problems in constructive ways, without turning to food.

Tom F.'s Story

TOM USED TO DO all the "wrong" things: he smoked, drank too much and was too heavy. When his physicians called him to task at the age of 28, Tom decided to quit smoking and lose weight. He has been successful for 17 years. At a height of 6', he now holds his weight at about 185, down 50 pounds from his all-time high.

Tom's weight problem didn't begin until he was in his mid-twenties. "Up until that time I was trim, and weight was not an issue. I weighed about 160 when I graduated from high school. My first inkling of a problem was when I was getting out of the Navy, and none of my dress uniforms fit." After he left the service, Tom dropped the excess weight because he was more physically active, playing tennis and swimming.

But that was temporary. When Tom started his career as a field engineer, he began to gain weight once again. "I'm the kind of person who tends to have a singular focus; if I'm going to work, I really work." He threw himself into his career. As an escape, he sought refuge in alcohol. "My eating habits were atrocious. Dinner might be a 12-pack of beer, a pizza, and then I would keep on working. Exercise was completely out. Eventually, my weight shot up to 230." Tom was also smoking two to three packs of cigarettes a day.

Within a few years, there were physical and psychological manifestations of Tom's lifestyle: he had lower-back problems and many frustrations with work. After seeking the counsel of several physicians, he was told that nothing was wrong—that is, nothing that losing his "gut" and cleaning up his lifestyle wouldn't cure. "I decided either to prove the doctors wrong or find out if they were right." All at once, he quit smoking and joined the local YMCA.

"I experimented with various forms of exercise, but nothing seemed too exciting." Then Tom discovered running: "I liked the challenge and the way it made me feel. It took me three to four months to be able to run a continuous mile. When I did, I became motivated, so I started to run more." With time, Tom worked his way up to running 70 miles a week. He even ran 10 marathons.

As he got into running, Tom became more interested in diet. He went back to basics: whole grains, more vegetables, less meat and less food. Within 2 years' time, he was down to 150, which proved too scanty for his 6' frame. He finally leveled off at a weight of 160 to 165. Eventually, Tom also swore off alcohol.

Then, 6 years ago, Tom developed a heel spur and couldn't run for about a year. That's when emotional eating set in. "I had become addicted to the running, and it was an escape from my problems. When I had to give up running, I had no substitute, and I felt sorry for myself. So I reacted by turning to 'eats.' In the middle of the day, I would make myself a sandwich and say, 'That tasted good, I'll have another.' Then I might make a batch of chocolate chip cookies and eat half of them."

Tom eventually came to the realization that he had been avoiding many issues in his life related to past family relationships. "I had been using running, then it became food." He came to grips with his problems—and his eating—and his weight settled in at 175 to 185.

Today, Tom's exercise consists of about five hours a week of some combination of running, stretching, StairMaster workouts and weight training. He is excited about his decision to start competitive running once again. "Exercise is one of the greatest joys in life, particularly running," he says.

In his eating habits, Tom tries to avoid caffeine, most white flour, salt and fat. He tries to keep tempting items out of the house. He loves to bake and prides himself on his homemade breads. Typically, breakfast is his largest meal of the day, consisting of foods like fruit, yogurt, cereal and bagels. (He may eat all of these in one meal.) Tom usually skips lunch, then eats a light supper of, for example, baked potato, soup or spaghetti.

Of his relationship with food, Tom says, "For me, concern about diet comes and goes. When I'm stressed, diet is the first thing to go: I 'pick' more and buy more high-calorie foods at the grocery store. I might stop at the store, buy a box of cookies and eat the whole thing. Food is easy: I can do it alone, and it works in a hurry. But when I accept whatever the problem is and do something about it, the overeating disappears."

Tom is well aware that his main emotional trigger for eating is fear: for example, if he is worried that he may lose a major business client. "At first, I think, 'I'm inferior; I'm no good,' " he says. "So I have to fight that. I've started to write down my problems, write about the fear and anguish that can build. With brutal honesty, I list the fears as well as the bright side. The fear doesn't go away, but I can then make a decision to do something, to take action. This prevents my turning to food. As things come up, I'm able to deal with them."

Tom continues about his problem-solving philosophy: "My problems are all within, and that's where the solution lies. I used to delude myself by saying things were outside of me, so they weren't my problems. Now, I feel the key is accepting responsibility—once I accept the problem *and* the responsibility, it eases. I say to myself, 'What can I do about that?' Then I'm working on a solution so it doesn't happen again. That way, I'm building my personal integrity, instead of getting out of my worries by eating. I'm looking the problem right in the eye." He adds, "You know, life is full of obstacles. You have to take the deaths and disappointments and move on. The solution to all of life's problems is within you. It's simply a matter of self-talk to do something."

Tom is not a "touchy-feely" kind of guy. It's not always easy for him to identify his feelings, let alone express them. I mention this because some studies suggest that overweight men are less prone to emotional eating than women. Perhaps the truth is that men are less aware of the emotional side of eating, as well as have trouble admitting difficulty in handling their problems.

Like so many of the masters, Tom has identified the connection between eating and his emotions. He uses problem-solving skills to put an end to temporary lapses in eating habits, and his positive self-talk allows him to manage life's stresses without turning to food: *he's learned how to face life head-on.*

Maintainers vs. Regainers: How They Cope

MASTERS AT WEIGHT LOSS appear to handle stressful events in their lives very differently from people who regain weight. In the Kaiser Permanente study comparing women who successfully maintained weight loss with those who regained (page 66), researchers found, "Maintainers believed themselves capable of handling their problems and used problem-solving skills to cope with their difficulties. In contrast, relapsers did not deal with their problems directly (perhaps because they lacked effective problem-solving skills) and reported that they used food to make themselves feel better when upset."

When asked "How are you dealing with this?" concerning a troubling issue, few regainers in the study used "confrontive" ways of coping. Compared with maintainers, regainers were more likely to try to escape from or avoid their problems by eating, sleeping, drinking or wishing the problem would go away. Maintainers were more inclined to "talk out their feelings" or seek professional help than were regainers.

A striking 95 percent of maintainers used "planful problem-solving" skills or confronted issues; in contrast, just 10 percent of the regainers used these skills. And the difference wasn't that the relapsers had more serious problems; aside from weight-related and health issues, there were no significant differences in their types of difficulties, including those related to relationships, self-fulfillment and job or career.

Most of the masters I interviewed were once regainers themselves, who at that time handled problems and emotions ineffectually. Before she lost her 43 pounds, master Lou Ann L. recalls, "When I was fat, food was a kind of 'forbidden fruit.' I always felt guilty about eating sweets. But they were also a reward and a way to push down negative feelings." And Peppi S. states, "I never realized that the emotions or situations were causing me to fall back on eating blindly, without any thought. Then I would feel guilty and guess what? Overeat some more. I never got in touch with my emotions." (That was before she lost 62 pounds.)

But the masters have shifted their behavior from that of the regainers to that of the maintainers. They have not only learned to identify emotional situations that make them want to eat, but to deal with their feelings *and* problems more constructively.

Bob W. recognizes that, starting in grade school, he used food to comfort himself, "to make a difficult family situation more bearable." He goes on, "I heard voices in my head [saying], 'Ah, have some food—it will make it all better.' I used to use food to 'fix' my life and emotions." By the time he was in eighth grade, Bob's "voices" had spurred him all the way up to 400 pounds. Now, having been at a weight of about 150 for 21 years, Bob says, "I have changed my life and found other ways to cope with emotions. I finally arrived at a place where I no longer wanted to hide my feelings with excess food."

Quite a few thin-for-life masters, like Tom F., still find themselves slipping into emotional eating from time to time. As he puts it aptly, "Just because you know how to do something doesn't mean you're going to do it all the time." Doug S., who keeps more than 100 pounds at bay, admits, "If I have a bad day at work, I will come home and eat constantly. Sometimes I have good command of it, and sometimes I don't." Still, Doug has made progress in recognizing the connection between tension and overeating.

Similarly, Ann F. finds, "During periods of stress or fatigue, I still struggle with overeating and will go back to my comfort foods, such as potato chips and candy (in lesser amounts)." But like Tom F., Ann has gone one step further in dealing with emotional eating. She adds, "When I want to overeat, I try to figure out if it's fatigue, anxiety or if I need comfort; I try to figure out what I really need. Then I might go out for a swim."

Alisa S. notes that she sees a link between periods of depression and weight gain. But like many masters, she finds strength in adversity: after 7 years of keeping off 64 pounds, Alisa finds, "I do struggle at times with feeling fat and defeated, but I feel the gratification of regaining control over my emotions and my weight."

"The key to successful living is to figure out what emotions trigger you to want to overeat, find an effective strategy [for coping] and recognize the satisfaction gained by your strategies and, last, a sense that YOU are in control," says Peppi S.

Labeling Your Emotions

How can *you* LEARN to handle your emotions more effectively, so you turn to food with less frequency? As Peppi states, *the critical first step is getting in touch with what you're feeling—labeling your emotions.* When you have a burning desire to eat or to continue eating and eating—but you know in your heart of hearts that you're not even hungry—ask yourself what's going on. (See page 100 for suggestions on determining hunger.) Are you angry, lonely, bored, depressed, anxious or using food to relax or celebrate?

Some people find it helpful to make themselves wait for a set amount of time—say, 20 minutes—when they have a desire to eat or find themselves craving a particular food. Indeed, in the University of Iowa study on 82 people who had kept off more than 50 pounds for an average of 4½ years (page 26), the most commonly mentioned strategy for dealing with cravings was to wait them out. The delay provides an opportunity to focus on what you're really feeling and to talk yourself out of eating.

Sometimes, however, emotional eating has gone on for so long that it's become automatic: you're so used to stuffing yourself when you're upset or bored that, like a robot, you turn to food and feel you *can't* sort out your emotions. Says Ann B., "My feelings were vague—I didn't know what I felt." Wendy M. had her "heart broken" as a teenager, so she used food as a shield to protect herself from being hurt again by men. "I was afraid to look at the hurt, so I turned to food. It helped for a while. Then I said, 'I've got a long life ahead of me; I'm gonna get hurt a lot.' " Now, Wendy sees that she held on to her weight because she wanted people to like her for her personality, not her appearance. "I realized that I didn't need to be heavy to have people like me for me." Wendy is now 40 pounds lighter and has maintained her loss for 8 years.

Similarly, Ann B. used to hide behind her weight. Then, in her weight-loss program, she tried to confront and visualize her fears of becoming thin. "I had to deal with being more sexually attractive to men. Realizing that helped me move on."

How can you get in touch with emotions that trigger eating? If your emotional eating has become automatic, you may find there are signals that the problem is about to occur. All through college, for example, whenever I was under tension, I had a habit of wandering into the kitchen and searching through the cupboards or refrigerator. It almost always happened in the evening after supper, so I wasn't really hungry. I have since come to realize that when the uncontrollable urge to snoop through the kitchen comes over me, it usually means that I'm tense or that something is bothering me. For you, the signals may be different: perhaps craving something salty or sweet or simply thinking about food when you know you're not hungry.

Another way of tuning in to your feelings is to write them down, as Tom F. does. Or like Aileen Y., who says, "When I feel a lot bombarding me, I write how I feel; it's stream-of-consciousness writing." Just the act of putting it down on paper helps Aileen get in touch with her emotions. Recently, for instance, within the space of three weeks, her grandmother, father and dog died. "Writing saved me because I wasn't keeping it bottled up. If I hadn't dealt with those feelings, I believe I would have gained a whole lot of weight." Writing her feelings out has been a major tool for Aileen in keeping off 115 pounds for more than 11 years.

Putting a Lid on Emotional Eating

ONCE YOU'VE LABELED the emotions that trigger you to overeat, and when you're ready to stop dealing with your problems by eating and come to terms with your feelings, the next step is to find another way to cope. Claudia B. says of her final effort to lose 115 pounds, "I was ready to deal with the feelings that came up when I put the food down."

You need to ask yourself if emotional eating actually accomplishes anything. Does it truly cure your boredom? Does it make the loneliness go away? Does it cheer you up in the long run? Most masters would agree that the answer to each of these questions is "No."

Master Bob W. has developed a "problem checklist" for the people he now counsels at Kaiser Permanente's "Freedom From Fat" weight-management program. He suggests first asking yourself, "Am I really hungry? Why am I in this place with this food in my hand? Do I need it?" He advises gently reminding yourself that food is not a "cure-all" for life's problems, then thinking, "What do I need right now? To talk to someone? Rest? A hug? A pleasant activity? A cup of tea shared with a friend? Will food help me out? Has it ever really made me feel better? Maybe food isn't the solution."

Mindy B., who has lost and kept off 84 pounds for 7 years, is aware that she has a tendency to rummage through the cupboards when she's upset with her husband or herself. Her self-talk is, "Look, you're just hurting yourself." Then, if it's nice outside, she goes and works in the yard, which "mellows" her out.

Ann B. states, "Exercise helps—it's empowering." Tami B., who finds boredom to be a sore spot in her struggle to maintain her 38-pound loss, says, "I find other things to do when I'm bored, like exercising."

Some masters find that interpersonal communication helps them deal with their issues more constructively. Compared with when she was heavy, Ann B. finds, "I talk to people more about my emotions." Tom F. sometimes works out his problems by talking them over with another person. "If I keep that problem to myself, it just goes around in my mind—say, at a rate of 800 words per minute. But when I verbalize the problem, it comes out at a rate of 150 words a minute and helps me see what the issue is. It shines an honesty spotlight on the situation, and I become more rational about dealing with it."

Certainly positive self-talk has an important place in learning to face life head-on. As you read through this chapter on how masters cope with emotional eating, you'll find example after example of positive self-talk. When Ann B. coped with loneliness by eating, she used to say to herself, "Oh well, it doesn't matter what my body looks like anyway. It's inevitable to be heavy." In the next breath, she shared her new self-talk (at her weight of 115), "I really, really like having a healthy, strong body and the way people react to me. Having this body outweighs whatever comfort I got from food. It's not worth sedating myself with food."

Finally, since food is often used to release tension, just learning to relax may help prevent emotional eating. The psychology section of a good bookstore is filled with guides for relaxation. Some people take courses in yoga or transcendental meditation. Another technique, called "progressive muscle relaxation," involves tensing and relaxing certain muscle groups, paying close attention to the relaxation phase. Or you might choose a simple home remedy like reading, going for a bike ride or having sex—the "grab-your-mate-instead-of-your-plate" solution!

"The quickest relaxation technique is deep breathing," according to *The Truth About Addiction and Recovery*, by Stanton Peele and Archie Brodsky. They suggest leaning back, closing your eyes, picturing a pleasant scene in great detail, taking as much air as you comfortably can into your lungs, then breathing out slowly. Repeat at least several times. The idea is to practice the technique so you can call it quickly into play at tense moments.

Dealing With Specific Emotions

S PECIAL WORDS ARE IN ORDER about the emotions overweight people are likely to "stifle" with food: anger, loneliness, boredom and depression. (See page 222 to determine if professional counseling is in order.)

◆ **Anger.** Says master Aileen Y.: "I used anger and angry behavior as a buffer to keep me from having an honest relationship with people. If I was angry, I didn't have to be intimate. I could keep people at a distance. Instead of being honest with myself, I used food to sate my feelings." Now, Aileen, who is an active Overeaters Anonymous member, deals with her anger by sharing it—either with her OA sponsor (support person) or by writing about it. "Now, I look at my part of the situation and am honest about my feelings. I make peace, accept the situation and move forward."

Of course, the way you deal with anger depends on the circumstance and the individual. You may find it useful to make a list of appropriate ways to handle anger, as well as other emotions that trigger overeating. For anger, your list might include:
  ◆ Talk to myself to see if it's really worth being angry.
  ◆ Walk away from the person or situation.
  ◆ Tell the person how I feel.
  ◆ Use relaxation techniques.

• Go for a walk or bike ride.
• Buy a book on dealing with anger and assertiveness.

• **Loneliness.** "I started to gain weight when I was a senior in high school," recalls Kelly S. "A lot of my friends had steady boyfriends, and I didn't. So on weekends, I'd volunteer to work at a homemade ice cream shop. I learned to pacify how hurt I was with food . . . [and tell myself] that an ice cream sundae at the moment would make me feel better. I would wake up in a 'drugged' state. I was dulling the pain. In a short period of time, I gained 30 to 40 pounds." But at some level, she recognized what she was doing. "I knew it made me feel worse. I gained weight, couldn't fit in my clothes; it was self-imposed isolation. I realized that I had to start reaching out." As Kelly saw more clearly the connection between her emotions and overeating, she was able to channel her energy into her career goal: becoming a registered dietitian. Now, 50 pounds lighter for 6 years, she specializes in counseling people with weight problems.

Your list of appropriate ways to cope with day-to-day loneliness might include:
  • Call a friend or relative.
  • Go shopping.
  • Join an adult-education class.
  • Go to a support group or club.
  • Rent a movie.
  • Get a pet.

• **Boredom.** In the process of losing her 62 pounds, Peppi S. figured out that she is likely to overeat when she first comes home from work and is bored. Now, when she finds herself searching through the cabinets, she asks herself, "What am I doing? Am I bored, hungry? I try to figure out why I'm doing what I'm doing. In the past, when I came home from work, I wouldn't know if I was hungry or bored. Now I might try some other activity or drink water."

• **Depression.** Before Ann B. lost her 35 pounds, she was in the habit of "anesthetizing" her feelings of vague depression and loneliness by eating. After going through a Shaklee group weight-loss program that helped participants identify the triggers for eating, she stopped using food "as a drug." Ann said to herself, "Whatever is going on with me, it isn't worth being overweight." In fact, Ann's number one strategy for keeping her weight down is, "Don't eat for emotional reasons . . . I think it's most important to find out why you're using food." Now, Ann sorts out her emotions on paper. "I keep a personal journal of my thoughts and feelings to identify them. When I write it down, I can figure out what's bugging me."

Some ways to cheer yourself up when feeling blue:
- Get a new haircut or a facial.
- Exercise.
- Buy yourself something special.
- Get together with a friend.
- Take a day off from work just for you.
- Forget the chores and play with your kids.
- Go to a play, movie or sports event.

Unpleasant emotions and problems are part of life. They will be there whether or not you turn to food. Sometimes, you just have to accept what you are feeling. Master and weight-control counselor Kelly S. says, "I think sometimes people need to be 'there' for that feeling—or just to feel something and do nothing. You can choose to use food one more time, but you know what the consequences will be."

A Primer on Problem Solving

PSYCHOLOGISTS HAVE DEVELOPED some strategies for helping people cope with life's stresses more effectively, and the techniques can be applied to weight-related problems, as well as to day-to-day issues. I've combined several strategies for problem solving in the following six-step process:

STEP #1
Define the problem.

What is getting in the way of losing weight? Look for patterns: the time of day that your problem occurs, what precedes it, what follows it, whether it happens when you're alone or with certain people. It's important to be honest with yourself. As psychologists Daniel Wheeler and Irving Janis advise, if the problem is genuine, do not ignore it, rationalize, procrastinate, bypass or panic.

Weight-related example: You have no trouble sticking to your low-fat food plan all day long, but you find yourself thinking about food and picking all evening. What precedes the problem? You've finished supper and are full. At about 8:00, your skinny husband starts getting out chips and sweets, leaves them on the counter and marches in and out to munch on them as you both watch TV. You tell yourself, "I'm not going to have any snacks after supper." What happens? You always give in, and once you start snacking, you have trouble stopping. What's the upshot? You go to bed feeling fat, defeated and guilty.

Nonweight example: You feel overwhelmed because, once again, your babysitter has canceled at the last minute, forcing you to take another vacation day from work to care for your kids. The problem is that you have an unreliable babysitter and may have to find a new one.

STEP #2
Come up with alternatives.

What can you do about the problem? Psychologists believe that by coming up with many alternatives, you increase the odds of finding effective solutions. Think about your past experiences with similar problems and evaluate what worked and what didn't. Ask yourself how a friend who is a good problem-solver might handle the situation. Or, as Tom F. does, talk with a friend about the problem. Use the information to generate additional strategies for yourself.

Weight-related example: What are other possibilities for handling the nighttime snacking problem? Get out of the house: go shopping or join an exercise class. Ask your husband to snack on low-calorie foods or quit snacking altogether. Ask him to put open packages of food away. Buy snack foods you're not particularly fond of. Watch television in a different part of the house. Try to engage your husband romantically. Plan your own after-dinner snack and wait until a specific time to have it. Start a new hobby to take your mind off food. Go to bed at 8:00.

Nonweight example: What to do about the unreliable babysitter? Have a long talk to find out what's going on. Confront the sitter, saying that if she cancels again, you'll fire her. Quit your job and stay home with the kids. Place your children in a daycare facility. Ask a relative or friend to care for the children.

STEP #3
Evaluate the alternatives, listing pros and cons for each.

In essence, Tom F. does this when he writes down his fears as well as "the bright side" of a problem. Mentally picture yourself engaging in each possible solution for the problem. Think about how feasible each option is: consider time and effort, financial implications, your likelihood of succeeding in the short run *and* long run, emotional costs and gains, consistency with your values and possible impact on others in your life.

Weight-related example: Evaluate whether it's realistic to think you'll go out every night: what would the impact be on your marriage? Are you likely to engage in nighttime exercise on a long-term basis? (On the plus side, it would get you out of the house and make you come home feeling refreshed; on the downside, you may be a morning person who knows that you've never been able to stick with evening exercise.) Is it reasonable to expect your thin spouse to quit snacking or switch to low-calorie foods? Is he likely to put food away if you ask nicely? Is it realistic to think you'll go to bed early each night? If you're more romantic, will it change the snacking? Can you envision yourself looking forward to a treat that you've saved for an evening snack?

Nonweight example: You know that talking to your sitter will have little impact because you've tried it before. Are you prepared to follow through if you have to fire her? Can you afford to stay home with the kids? What are the pros and cons of group daycare versus having a sitter in your home? If you ask your relative or friend to help, are their views of child rearing consistent with yours?

STEP #4
Make a decision and a commitment.

Choose the alternatives that give you the greatest benefits at the least cost.

Weight-related example: You decide that the most viable options are to ask your husband to put packages away and to save a snack for yourself for later in the evening. And although evening exercise is not realistic for you, you decide that you can go out with a friend or go shopping one or two nights a week.

Nonweight example: You decide to try childcare outside of the home since it will give your children exposure to other kids their age and is less expensive than having a sitter.

STEP #5
Implement the strategy.

Develop a plan to actually carry out your decision(s).

Weight-related example: Buy some low-fat treat foods for yourself and plan what, when and how much you'll have each night. Put out some individual bowls for your husband to serve himself, and remind him to put packages away after he has a helping. Call a friend and "make a date."

Nonweight example: Call friends and neighbors for day-care recommendations, prepare interview questions, do some preliminary phone screening, then check out the best ones in person. After you make a choice, give your current sitter notice and prepare your children for the change.

STEP #6
Evaluate the plan and switch gears if necessary.

Compare the actual outcome with the desired outcome. "Your problem behavior doesn't have to be totally eliminated for your experiment to be a success," point out Michael J. Mahoney and Kathryn Mahoney in *Permanent Weight Control.* If the plan was partially successful, how could it be improved? If it didn't work, consider the possible reasons. Did you give it your best effort? Did you try the plan for a long enough period of time? Were your goals realistic? Was your strategy too ambitious? What other tactic can you try? (Go back to your list of alternatives, or come up with some new strategies.) Finally, if the plan didn't work, ask yourself what you can learn from it.

Weight-related example: Are you snacking less at night than you did before? Are you able to avoid free-for-all snacking by saving a low-fat treat for later? Do you go to bed feeling better about yourself? If your husband refuses to put packages away, perhaps *you* can do it so they're not constantly staring at you. You also might try buying treat foods for him that are not your favorites or engage in some new evening activities that remove you from television and food.

Nonweight example: Is your new daycare provider more reliable? Do you like her/him, and are your philosophies compatible? If your children still cry every morning when you drop them off, have you given the situation enough time? If the daycare is not working out, do you want to consider your second choice or a relative for childcare?

Are You a Binge Eater?

THERE'S A DIFFERENCE between occasional emotional overeating and serious binge eating, which is often called "compulsive eating." Not all people with weight problems are binge eaters: studies indicate that the problem occurs in a quarter to half of obese people who seek treatment in hospital- and university-based weight-control programs. There is some evidence that the problem is less common in people who don't seek treatment. If you are a binge eater, it can be psychologically devastating and medically harmful. The good news is that a number of masters at weight control have overcome the problem. (See page 220.)

If you answer yes to a number of the following questions, you are probably a binge eater:

• Do you have a habit of consuming unusually large amounts of food—several thousand calories' worth (say, a quart of ice cream, 6 brownies and 16 chocolate chip cookies)—in a relatively short period of time, usually in less than 2 hours?

• Are the foods you choose for such binges calorie-laden "forbidden" foods?

• Do you often keep on eating, even though you are full to the point of being uncomfortable?

• Do you commonly eat alone because you're ashamed of how much you eat?

• Are such periods of overeating followed by feelings of loss of control? Severe physical discomfort? Despair? Guilt? Disgust? Self-condemnation?

• Are periods of overeating followed by attempts at strict dieting and/or stringent exercise?

• Do you ever use laxatives, diuretics or make yourself vomit to "get rid of" the food you've eaten? (If you answer yes to this question, you should be evaluated by your physician and a psychologist or psychiatrist because any such practices can have serious health consequences.)

In *Now That You've Lost It*, Dr. Joyce Nash points out, "All binges are episodes of overeating, but not all overeating episodes qualify as binges." When overeating happens only occasionally and "is accompanied by few or mild emotional reactions, it falls into the category of simple overeating," which may or may not be triggered by emotional stress. Dr. Nash emphasizes that all people, both heavy and thin, overeat from time to time, but those who engage in simple overeating do not feel out of control, while a true binge eater does.

Finding a way to overcome binge eating is important because research suggests that binge eaters are more likely to drop out of behavioral weight-loss programs, and they appear to do less well than non-bingers when it comes to long-term weight loss. In addition, binge eaters tend to experience more depression, anxiety and low self-esteem than do other overweight people who do not binge. It is not known whether their psychological problems contribute to the abnormal eating or result from it. Whatever the case, there is evidence that depression lessens when binge eating declines. (See page 223 for advice on finding a reliable counselor.)

Overcoming Binge Eating

A LTHOUGH THERE ARE AT PRESENT no tried-and-true remedies for binge eating, there is some preliminary evidence that use of anti-depressant drugs, as well as positive self-talk and behavioral approaches, may help some binge eaters. (You may want to talk about the possibility of antidepressants with a physician or psychiatrist.)

Many of the techniques used by the masters are likely to be of value to binge eaters. In particular, Susan J. Bartlett, M.Ed., a psychologist who specializes in obesity and compulsive eating at the Eating Disorders Program at the Graduate Hospital in Philadelphia, Pennsylvania, advises in a recent issue of the *Weight Control Digest* that binge eaters regain control by returning to the basics of sensible eating, such as structured meals and mealtimes, menu planning and portion control. Since many binge eaters tend to consume little or nothing, then overeat all at once, having three scheduled meals may help prevent excessive hunger by spreading the calories throughout the day.

Several binge eaters I worked with had some success by planning a "controlled minibinge": they planned to have a set amount of a treat food at their usual time of bingeing, and they experienced some success in controlling and enjoying the food without remorse.

Dr. Nash suggests that until binges are under control, it is wise to focus on stabilizing weight, not trying to lose. She also suggests that if you decide to binge, you should wait 15 minutes then "go ahead and binge, but do it in a particular way: Give yourself permission to eat without guilt. Eat slowly and savor each bite." Dr. Nash also stresses the value of exercise because it can help with feelings of calmness and relaxation. She cautions, however, that exercise should be reasonable and not become a compulsive habit in itself.

Binge eaters tend to have rigid rules about dieting, weight goals and how they should perform. Thus they are likely to benefit from learning how to set realistic goals, as well as from relapse-prevention strategies (see Chapter V). In addition, problem-solving techniques may help binge eaters.

Whatever time of day a binge is most likely to occur is a good time to get out of the house and away from food. Ms. Bartlett helps her clients reduce the temptation to binge by encouraging them to plan evening activities with family or friends or go to exercise classes. A telephone buddy may also be helpful for difficult moments.

Drs. Foreyt and Goodrick in *Living Without Dieting* suggest considering Overeaters Anonymous (OA), a free, nonprofit self-help group for compulsive overeaters based on the 12 Steps and spiritual underpinnings of Alcoholics Anonymous. The steps involve admitting that you are powerless over food and turning your life over to a "higher power." (OA does not espouse any particular diet; the goal is not weight loss per se, but to break free from compulsive overeating.)

OA is by no means the solution for every binge eater. Before going to OA, I recommend first seeing a psychologist or psychiatrist who has experience with food-related problems.

How Some Masters Conquered Binge Eating

ANN F., WHO ONCE WEIGHED 380 pounds and has kept her weight in a range of 135 to 170 pounds for 10 years, overcame her problem in large part by telling herself that there are no "good" and "bad" foods and by recognizing the value of exercise. (She tried OA but found the approach to be too restrictive.) She states, "Probably the biggest changes in my eating behavior are that I basically eat what I want (in moderation), do not go on stringent diets or fasts (I had a long history of this), and rarely 'binge' since I eat what I want. In other words, I might have a piece of cake or two but never the whole cake anymore (thank goodness)! I may overeat at a party on Saturday night, but rarely wake up Sunday wanting to overeat. I usually feel lousy from the excess and will make it a point to exercise and eat really well the following day." It's worth noting that Ann had gastric bypass surgery, which puts a mechanical limit on the volume of food she can eat. But if she hadn't overcome her habit of binge eating, she could have undone the benefits of the procedure.

• Aileen Y., who has kept off 115 pounds for more than 11 years, once "had to be eating all the time." There were times when I didn't know what I wanted—[it was] that 'insatiable hunger.' " She recalls "going through boxes of cereal, loaves of bread, quarts of milk, half gallons of ice cream"—all in one day and in secret. Of the time when she lost weight once and for all, she told me, "I recognized that my eating—of any kind of foods—was out of control. I felt suicidal and depressed. I was desperate. When I started [going to] OA, it was such a relief to find support and a solution!" She gained control of her binge eating by "living and working my OA recovery program, which includes prayer, meditation, calling a sponsor [OA member], attending meetings, writing my feelings out, using the OA Steps and tools." She also plans in writing the foods that she will eat each day, which include "three moderate, nutritionally balanced meals with a snack of fruit." She "chooses not to include" sugar or red meat, alcoholic beverages or caffeine. Aileen has become more realistic about what she "should" weigh. "I thought 125 to 130 was to be my weight." Now, with age and after some health problems, she accepts herself at 145 (she's 5'5"). "I'm being reasonable now!"

• Dorothy C., who has weighed 123 for 8 years (down 32 pounds from her all-time high), remembers eating an entire frozen Sara Lee pie after a large quantity of granola cookies. "At my worst, I did it every day." She also used to make herself vomit. When I asked her how she solved her problem, she told me, "One day I decided to leave two cookies in the box. I thought, 'This feels like I'm more in control, like a normal person.' Before, it was always all or nothing: eat everything in sight so it doesn't torment me until it is gone." She adds that in conquering binge eating, "There was no one epiphany; it was gradual. For a number of years, I channeled my compulsive energy into exercise, which provides structure: psychologically, it gives a sense of control. Now I'm less compulsive." Since she realized that she did a lot of binge eating out of boredom, stress and depression, Dorothy learned to fill her time with other activities, like reading, calling friends, shopping, using delay techniques (waiting out her urges to eat), as well as exercising. Dorothy admits that she occasionally has lapses. "I still turn to my favorite foods out of boredom or stress, but less frequently. And now my definition of a binge is gobbling a bagel with butter or five or six cookies—before it was the whole bag. It's a victory to learn that you can cut it off." She also tries to satisfy sweet cravings with no-fat hard candy or jelly beans (rather than with chocolate) and usually eats some kind of dessert with meals, such as yogurt, a Weight Watchers brownie or fruit, "so as not to feel deprived."

◆ Nancy K. has conquered binge eating for 12 years, which has enabled her to maintain a 60-pound weight loss. In the midst of her problem, she might have eaten "a dozen doughnuts and three Hostess fruit pies" secretly within the space of an hour. Then she'd feel guilty, so she'd go and buy a salad because she felt she needed "something good." She'd go through this routine at least once a week, then say to herself, "What a jerk. How stupid. You're fat and ugly, and now you make it worse." That commonly led to another day of binge eating, followed by a several days of starvation: "just Tab and salads." Nancy attributes her triumph over binge eating to her becoming a born-again Christian. "I decided I couldn't continue life eating the way I was. I believed that faith in Jesus would give me the strength to overcome it." From then on, she told me, "I quit dieting, quit saying 'I cannot have this, this and this. I tried eating in a more reasonable, consistent manner: three meals and a snack. I never said, 'No, this is not allowed.' There were no weight-loss goals and no rules. My goal was to quit binging and be a better eater." She lost her weight very slowly, at a rate of about 10 pounds a year. She said to herself, "Hey, it's better than gaining." Now, at a weight of 135 (she's 5'7"), Nancy says she still struggles to be a "good eater. If I eat four cookies, that's a lot for me." Sometimes, she finds herself skipping meals and grabbing snack foods. But when she hits her upper weight limit of 139, she says, "Okay, start back to healthy eating." She adds, "Sure, I wish I could eat whatever I want, but I've accepted that I can't. This is something that I'm going to deal with for the rest of my life; I'm thankful for where I am."

Is Professional Counseling a Good Idea?

IF YOUR WEIGHT SERVES AS A SHIELD or a way to hide from psychological issues, you may need professional help, both in uncovering the issues as well as in dealing with them. For instance, some women who are seriously overweight may have backgrounds of sexual, emotional and/or physical abuse that require counseling. And, as indicated earlier, some overweight people have higher than normal levels of depression and anxiety, as well as low self-esteem—all of which often go along with binge eating.

Professional counseling not only can help you deal with these issues, but it can also help you anticipate how life will be when you slim down. As master Nancy K. states, "People blame all their problems on their weight, but the problems don't go away when you're thin." And sometimes, without the weight to hide behind, the problems become magnified. A number of masters told me that new issues arose because they had never been of normal weight before. Some, for instance, had problems in relationships, while others had (and still have) a difficult time seeing themselves as thin.

How do you go about finding professional help? First, you want to make sure that a counselor has respectable credentials. Be aware that in most states, anyone can call him- or herself a "psychotherapist," so the title does not assure acceptable training. Most states, however, require psychologists to be licensed in order to practice, which means that they must have a sound educational background and credentials. Other legitimate mental-health providers for your consideration include psychiatrists, licensed social workers and pastoral counselors.

Dr. Joyce Nash advises that the best way to choose a counselor is to ask for a referral from someone you trust, such as a physician, other counselors, religious leader or nurse. It's best if the counselor you choose is not someone whom you know socially or whose personal life you know a great deal about.

There is no guarantee that working through your problems will lead you to become thin for life, but it may increase your odds of becoming a master. Indeed, one recent study on overweight people in a professional weight-loss program revealed that those with the fewest psychological problems lost about twice as much weight as those who had the most problems. The more resources you have, the more likely you are to succeed at permanent weight control.

IX

Get More Out of Life

How's the balance in your life? Are your days filled with "shoulds" as opposed to desires? In other words, how much time do you spend doing things you feel you *have* to do versus things you *want* to do? Do you put everyone else's needs first, always leaving your own concerns for last? Do you ever reward yourself with anything other than food? Are you happy in life? Does your weight keep you from activities you'd really like to take part in? Are you satisfied with the way you spend your time? How about your relationships: are they what you want them to be?

En route to becoming successful maintainers, many masters sorted through these questions and found they weren't satisfied with the answers. Somewhere along the way, they decided they weren't getting enough out of life and were spurred to develop more fulfilled, balanced and happy lives. Many also made positive changes in relationships and found ways to get their own needs met. They learned to feel better about themselves as well. *In short, these masters found a way to get more out of life.*

Jennifer P.'s Story

After struggling with her weight most of her life, food and weight control are now "almost nonissues," Jennifer P. told me. Why? "A stable environment and a healthy family life" are among her major keys to success. After sorting through some serious emotional traumas of childhood, Jennifer has developed a rich and rewarding life—one that doesn't revolve around food or force her to hide behind her weight anymore. At a height of 5'5", she feels happy with herself at 142 pounds. She's stabilized at around that weight for the better part of 7 years—down more than 40 pounds from her maximum of 186. "I've had two children since losing and still maintain this 140ish weight."

Jennifer remembers herself as a "chubby" child, whose weight first became an issue around second grade, when she heard her parents comment, "We have to watch Jennifer." By the time she was in sixth grade, her weight was up to 115 (her height was 5'3")—certainly not obese, but heavier than most other children her age. She attributes her weight gain around this time to two incidents of sexual molestation, one by a relative, the other by a boy at a party. She recalls saying to herself, "If I just get fat, then boys will leave me alone." The abuse by the relative occurred for about two years, every two to three months at family gatherings. Years later, Jennifer realized, "The real issue was hiding my sexuality behind my weight."

Jennifer steadily got heavier, gaining 10 pounds each year around the time of the holidays, which marked the anniversary of the first incident of sexual abuse. "In seventh grade, I went from 115 to 125, in eighth grade from 125 to 135. At the same time, I would roller-coaster: diet and eat, diet and eat. I was an all-or-nothing kind of person. By the time I graduated from high school, I weighed 175." She continued to gain weight until the end of her freshman year in college.

Her weight-loss efforts included the usual methods: most often calorie-counting, but sometimes liquid diets, over-the-counter diet pills and fasting. She also went to Weight Watchers as a teenager, which she found to be helpful. Her typical "reward" for her dieting efforts was a 5- to 10-pound loss, which she would quickly regain. She attributes her weight problem to the diet-binge cycle: "I'd do 1,000 calories [a day] for weeks, then I'd lose control and go for it. After having three meals, I might eat a Dairy Queen parfait, then two or three doughnuts. A few hours later, my friends and I might go to a 7-Eleven store and get some candy bars. I'd say to myself, 'I'll start over tomorrow.' But it always took me a few weeks to get back on track."

Jennifer's triumph over her weight problem was a long, slow process that began the summer after her freshman year of college. That June, she started dating a man who told her she'd be a "10" if only she lost some weight. Angry at his lack of acceptance, she refused to do so until he was out of the picture. After he went away that August, she somewhat sheepishly admits, she fasted for 7 days and lost 15 pounds. That started her pattern of losing weight during the summer and gaining some—but not all—back during the school year when she was around the boyfriend. "After the first summer, I gained back 5 pounds. The next summer I lost 22 and regained about 10 pounds. The summer of my junior year, I lost another 12."

Jennifer certainly did it her way. How? "I got addicted to exercise. I would run about 30 miles a week." (She is no longer an exercise "addict.") When I asked her about how she ate, Jennifer replied, "I figured out the low-fat thing. But I didn't know what to call it back then. My plan was semimodeled after Weight Watchers'. I always liked healthful eating and found new treats like frozen yogurt and diet ice cream." (She figures she consumed about 1,500 calories per day.) During the school year, she was able to maintain some of her losses by continuing running. She refused to diet, although she continued to watch her fat intake. "I just ate a lot, so I would gain some weight back."

When I asked Jennifer how, without therapy, she was able to stop hiding behind her weight, she replied, "I got distracted from the need to keep men at bay by my anger at my boyfriend. My need to show him I was okay overpowered my need to hide behind the weight. Otherwise, I might have kept the weight on." She added, "Somewhere along the way, I also learned to like myself: all of me, my body included, as I was. I felt my weight was mine, and I was going to do it my way." (Jennifer did undergo therapy about two years ago. She told me, "I had to deal with why I put the weight on, and I had to learn to deal with the way men look at me, now that I'm thinner.")

During the summer of her junior year, Jennifer met another man, one who loved her unconditionally. "He was someone who liked me for me. It was healing. Then the weight really became *my* issue." At first she regained 10 pounds, but she took it off in time for her wedding the following year. At that point, Jennifer was down to 152.

Jennifer made the break from the "all-or-nothing attitude" during the first two years of her marriage after deciding, "I'm just going to be normal. I asked myself, 'What would a normal person without a weight problem eat?' One bowl of cereal. One sandwich. One or two cookies. And that's what I would eat. I let the weight thing be whatever it was." Slowly, over the course of the next 5 years, Jennifer lost the last 10 pounds. Toward the end of that time, she learned a great deal from a registered dietitian. "I wanted to make sure my weight was down before I started a family because I was afraid of ballooning. The dietitian taught me about low-fat eating. I learned you can eat a lot and stay full." The dietitian also taught Jennifer to stop depriving herself. "Sometimes, I'd eat everything but the food I really wanted. So once a day, if I had an urge, I'd eat the food that I wanted.

"The long, drawn-out process of losing and maintaining taught me that sometimes my body is ready to lose weight, and sometimes it's not." She learned that, for her, a good time to lose weight was when stress was low and she could focus on losing. When she hit a plateau, she would accept it and slowly increase her calorie intake until she "felt comfortable again."

Jennifer believes that in order to lose weight permanently, she had to put herself first. Her parents were missionaries, and Jennifer had been taught that her own desires were secondary to those of others. "I was always trying to meet everyone else's needs, please everyone else. The message was that I should always be perfect, nice, godly and unselfish—that I shouldn't feel better than others. When I was trying to meet everyone else's needs, there was a big hole inside me. And I filled it up with food. We had a family rule that no one should be better than anyone else. But I knew I was my dad's favorite and that I was the prettiest of my three sisters. My sisters' boyfriends were attracted to me. I had to play myself down so I wouldn't be hated by my sisters. My weight equalized things."

Eventually, Jennifer was "able to push others' needs aside and let weight loss happen." Today, one of Jennifer's "shoulds" is, "Be selfish when you need to." When I interviewed her, for instance, she had just had a birthday. "My family and I were at a lake, and my husband was taking care of the kids. I told myself, 'It's okay to sit here selfishly, relax, read a book and let him take care of them.'"

Another important part of her success, Jennifer believes, is developing a calmer lifestyle. "I think a lot of my eating was because of family stress and chaos. Having a calm husband has helped me. I also do some meditation and journal writing to let out anger and anxiety and to explore my emotions. And I enjoy quietness." Jennifer admits that for the first 5 years after losing the weight, maintenance was "really tough, but now it's easier. I think it's emotional. My life is more peaceful. I think about food less."

Jennifer also makes a conscious effort to stay "internally aware" of why she's eating. "I try not to eat because of emotions. When I want to eat for reasons other than hunger, I stop and think, 'What is really going on here? What's the real issue creating this anxiety?' Sometimes I figure it out and choose to eat anyway. But I try, instead, to take time out and be by myself to determine what's going on. I write in my journal or go jogging. When I run, I can obsess in my own space. Then I tend to be okay." Jennifer is pleased to say she is no longer a compulsive exerciser. Her exercise frequency varies from "not at all" to three or four times a week, depending on the season and her schedule. When she does exercise, she either jogs for three miles, does a circuit-training program for ½ hour or does aerobics for 30 to 45 minutes.

Jennifer's maintenance food plan consists mainly of low-fat healthful foods. "It's habit to me to find fun things that are low-fat." A bowl of cereal (low-fat granola) with skim milk constitutes breakfast. Lunch is usually a yogurt, wheat muffin or plain bagel, fruit and diet soda. Supper might be chicken, tuna or other fish with pasta or rice, a vegetable and a roll; sometimes it's beans and rice or soup. She treats herself to sweets once a day: a handful of chocolate chips, several cookies, licorice or some low-fat treat. Her other snacks include fruit, unbuttered bread, pretzels or diet soda. Jennifer doesn't feel deprived. "I eat what I want. If everyone else is eating nachos with cheese, I have them too. Sometimes when people see me eating like this, they ask, 'Do you eat like this all the time?' They don't realize that I then watch what I eat for the rest of the day."

Jennifer weighs herself about once a week. She used to do so every day until recently. But after her scale broke, she realized she was "addicted" to weighing herself and decided to change. If she gains between 1 and 5 pounds, she cuts back on sweets and makes an effort to stop and think about what she's eating. She also consciously lowers her fat intake.

What, for Jennifer, is the secret to long-term weight control? "Determine what eating does for you. You need to start figuring out what your weight keeps you from. Consider getting some therapy. You need to sort out your issues and your eating."

What's "Getting More Out of Life" Got to Do With Maintenance?

J ENNIFER'S PAST HISTORY of putting her own needs last fits with a pattern observed by G. Alan Marlatt, Ph.D., a relapse-prevention expert from the University of Washington. He believes that a number of overweight people have unbalanced lifestyles bogged down with a multitude of "shoulds." Their lives have little room for pleasure. If your life is unbalanced in this fashion, he says, you may feel deprived and seek immediate gratification from food as a payoff for your martyrdom. I often saw this behavior in my overweight clients who gave to others so much that the only "nice" thing they did for themselves was to indulge in food.

To remedy the situation, Dr. Marlatt advises, "Balance your lifestyle, and your sense of craving and deprivation likely will be less." In a review article on long-term weight loss, obesity experts Kelly Brownell and Robert Jeffery note that people who succeed at weight control tend to develop new hobbies, interests, friendships and job skills.

Jennifer P.'s story illustrates how strongly her ability to maintain weight loss is connected with establishing a stable environment, sorting through personal issues, taking care of her own needs and finding career satisfaction. Many of the other masters I spoke with also donned protective armor against weight regain by developing more fulfilled and interesting lives and, at some point, starting to feel better about themselves. Losing weight was just part of an unfolding process including many positive changes that seemingly had little or nothing to do with food and eating. *For some masters, the changes happened beforehand.* It was as if certain aspects of their lives had to be in place before they could be ready to take on permanent weight loss. Ann F. told me, "Some people make changes in crisis, but I needed to feel good about myself outside of my weight before I lost it. At that point, I had a good job, stable friendships, and I liked myself, despite my weight."

For other masters, lifestyle changes happened along the way, as they gained confidence because of their initial weight loss. For instance, as Charlotte O. was losing her 96 pounds, she started to branch out by becoming more involved in community organizations. *For a third group of masters, certain aspects of their lives changed and motivated them to begin losing weight, and their newfound confidence helped them make more changes that, in turn, reinforced their weight loss.* Take the case of Vicki B., who wasn't ready to lose her 60-plus pounds until her three sons were in school, when she had time to herself. "I went to work and started to lose." After she lost the weight (nearly 9 years ago), Vicki achieved her dream of becoming an actress: she's landed parts in local productions, TV shows and commercials. She admits that the "frequent scrutiny" she's under is a powerful incentive to keep her weight down and creates high stress levels. "But," she adds, "I'd rather be 139 pounds with high stress than 200 pounds with high stress from being overweight."

When her weight approached 200 pounds, Peppi S. says she did not want to go out, felt sorry for herself, stayed at home and ate. Now, her 62-pound weight loss has given her the confidence to become "a happy, healthy and energetic person. That's who I always dreamed of being and now that I am here, I will never go back. If I can be an example of how one can go from being depressed, overweight and a bitter person to one who is willing to take risks, try new things, get the most out of life and be happy and comfortable with myself, then I am truly successful."

Tom F., the master featured in Chapter VIII, got more out of life by making a career change. When he first decided to do something about his weight, he was "fundamentally dissatisfied with life." He was no longer happy in his work as a field engineer, so he had a talk with "the little boy inside. One of the things that I always wanted to be was a fireman." That's what Tom became for 14 years. He's moved on now and owns a software engineering business.

Dr. Ross found in about half of her maintainers a connection between being in control of losing weight and how they felt about the rest of their lives. She stated, "It appears that food intake could be the result of being in control in general or that it can be the means of getting control."

The Self-Esteem Connection

NOT ONLY DOES HAVING A HEALTHY LIFESTYLE appear to be related to long-term weight control, but some studies suggest that having a good concept of self and a positive attitude are associated with losing and maintaining weight. It makes sense that improved self-esteem and developing a more fulfilled life go hand-in-hand. If you feel better about yourself, you are likely to have confidence to make other changes in your life.

For some masters, their improved self image came *before* the weight loss, while for others it took place *as a result* of becoming thinner. Before Vicki B. began losing weight, she decided, "If I'm going to be this way, I'm going to look nice. I finally started buying some nice 'fat' clothes for myself and began to accept and like myself; then the changes began." Within a year, she started to lose weight. Similarly, Ann B. stated, "I accepted that I could like my body even if it *never* changed. There was a tremendous power for me in simply accepting myself as I was. Not 'I'll like myself when I lose weight,' which is what I said to myself for *years,* but 'I like myself, period.' " (Ironically, for some masters, accepting themselves as heavy was the precipitant for losing weight!)

Self-esteem played a role in weight loss for Tami B. too. "As I was gaining weight, I wouldn't go out because someone might see me," she says. "So I stayed home and ate and felt sorry for myself. I was in a failure cycle. Once I figured out what was happening, I decided to break out. Having fun and feeling good was more important!"

As for the boost in self-esteem that often takes place *as a result* of losing weight, Charlotte O. says, "I finished losing the weight [96 pounds] and gained enough self-esteem to get a job, leave an unhappy marriage and raise my two children alone. That happened 13 years ago; now at age 39, I feel better, and I look better than ever." Glenda L. told me, "After losing [45 pounds], I had a better sense of myself and self-esteem. I was the same person, just a better one." And Irene S. says of her 77-pound loss, "It has changed my life with high self-esteem and confidence."

Similarly, Dr. Ross's maintainers all mentioned positive changes in self-esteem, which, in turn, enabled them to project a more self-confident image. Some people then felt they could take on more responsibility at work or make job changes, while others reported no longer feeling they had to give in to or be dependent on others. "They could now be more self-directed and 'lean and mean.' There was no more need to do things that would compensate for being fat." Likewise, Drs. Colvin and Olson found that 18 months after the initial interviews with their successful maintainers, "The most important personal change, as perceived by 68 percent of the subjects, was a powerful positive increase in self-image, self-esteem and confidence." Losing weight won't automatically cure a long-standing self-esteem problem. That's why you have to develop other incentives and reinforcements in your life to protect against weight regain.

So how can *you* start feeling better about yourself? Psychological counseling can be of great help. Like Jennifer P., quite a few of the masters mentioned in this chapter told me they had counseling at some point in their lives. But there are also some steps you can take on your own. For starters, a number of psychologists suggest that you *stop living your life for the day when you will be thin*. Don't wait until you're thin to start looking nice, buying new clothes and exercising. Buy some great clothes that fit you as you are right now. Get a new hairstyle, a facial, a beauty makeover. Start thinking of yourself as an attractive person.

If you begin seeing yourself in a more positive light, it can enable you to be treated in ways that reinforce feeling good about yourself, which, in turn, may ready you for weight loss. Ann F. recalls, "About two years before I lost the weight, I spent a lot of money on nice clothes, and I let my nails grow. (I had always taken care of my hair and my face.) Before that, I went through a period of only wearing black slacks and overblouses. But I changed that completely. People started reacting to me differently. They didn't look down on me. It made me feel that it was possible to lose weight."

Dr. Joyce Nash told me that another way to improve self-esteem is to close the gap between the person you are and the person you think you should be, your ideal. (The greater the gap, she points out, the lower your self-esteem.) The problem for many people is that the ideal is unrealistic, based on perfectionistic goals. Dr. Nash recommends closing the gap by reevaluating your goals and working on day-to-day behavior and successes. She states, "We've learned to evaluate ourselves in negative ways. We tend to look for where we've failed instead of how we've improved. You need to acknowledge little positive steps, day by day." She suggests that, at the beginning of each day, you make a pledge to be successful at one small task. Then, in the evening, focus on the small things that went right that day.

Psychologists Stanton Peele and Archie Brodsky advise making a list of your personal resources. Itemize the things you like about yourself, what you're good at, your accomplishments, what others like or respect about you. You might list your conversational ability or friendliness, skill at playing an instrument or fixing broken household items, graduating as a top student in your high school class, or your parenting skills. The authors stress that in so doing, you focus on your assets and are reminded of your own worth. They add, "Being the first to recognize your own successes will help provide you with the strength to do better." The idea is to focus on your positive attributes, all of which are tools to fight your weight problem.

I must stress that there is no guarantee that boosting your self-esteem will ensure permanent weight loss. In interviewing experts, I found that a number of them said that, all by itself, developing a positive self-image is not likely to lead to losing weight for good. It's my hunch that, in order for it to be helpful, improved self-esteem must be coupled with a number of the Keys to Success, such as "taking the reins," "doing it your way," "accepting the food facts" and "facing life head-on."

Beyond Weight Loss

A FTER STUDYING SUCCESSFUL MAINTAINERS, Drs. Colvin and Olson drew the following conclusion: "Weight loss is not an end in itself; it is the means to an end. . . . It is a means to more important goals." In fact, they suggest that weight loss as a goal in itself is a guarantee for failure.

The masters have, indeed, found far more success than simple weight loss. Their newfound lifestyles and improved self-esteem now extend to other areas of their lives:

• Peppi S. (62 pounds): "The how-to's of maintaining my weight spilled over into other aspects of my life. I've become a more assertive person and am willing to take risks now—be it speaking up for myself or trying things I would never try before. Losing weight has not only rid me of my fat shell, but it also stripped me of some of my inhibitions and fears. I can handle almost anything now because of all the things I've learned."

• Charlotte O. (96 pounds, 13 years): "I'm not afraid to stand up for myself. When I was heavy, I took what people handed me. Now, I figure if I could take enough control of my life to lose weight, I can take enough control not to let people treat me badly anymore." She adds that another big step for her is getting on an airplane by herself. "When I was heavy, I would not have done that. I was always so self-conscious about my appearance. Now, I know I can walk in anywhere."

• Glenda L. (45 pounds, 4 years): "Part of it is physical: I look good and have more confidence. But part of it is mental: you know you can overcome a problem and translate that to other problems. If I can do this, I can do something else. You want to do more things." When I asked Glenda what weight loss enabled her to accomplish, she replied, "Get a divorce. Things that were bad became less tolerable. I felt better about myself and felt I didn't have to put up with it anymore. I knew I could make it. I also got back into opera, which I had neglected. I knew I could do it because of the discipline of weight loss."

• Thalia P. (32 pounds, 4 years): "I started waking up. I had more confidence to tell others where my limits were. I began to get more respect by taking risks to be assertive. This has come very hard to me, but with continual practice, I've become more free." She admits that her career as a research and development scientist at a chocolate company presents somewhat of a problem in her struggle to maintain her weight, but adds that it is "very, very minor compared to the other changes I had to make and struggles I had to overcome in my personal growth to achieve permanent weight loss."

Once weight loss is started or completed, people gain new confidence, like themselves better and tackle new challenges. These, in turn, become powerful reinforcements for keeping the weight off.

Developing a More Fulfilled Life

T WO OF THE STUDIES on successful maintainers have made a similar observation: the women who lost weight and kept it off were more likely to have developed lives outside of their families. In the Kaiser Permanente study comparing female maintainers with regainers (page 66), the researchers found that significantly more maintainers had salaried positions in addition to their jobs as homemakers.

Researchers Drs. Robert Colvin and Susan Olson found that well over half of their female maintainers, while heavy, had been full-time homemakers. "The years between the ages of 18 and 35 were characterized by marriage, childbearing and rearing, semi-reclusion in the home . . . and weight gain." After mastering weight loss, however, Drs. Colvin and Olson reported the women had "moved out of the home into the outside world." After losing weight, more than 60 percent were full-time business and professional women. And many of the maintainers who didn't work had substantially increased the amount of time they spent outside the home.

None of this is to say that being a traditional homemaker leads to obesity, or that if you choose to remain one, you can't reduce your weight. It suggests, however, that some individuals predisposed to a weight problem may find more success in losing and maintaining weight loss if they cultivate a life outside of the home. Here's what some of the masters have to say:

• Vicki B. was primarily a homemaker and a mother when she was heavy. "I was happy being a stay-at-home mom, but I wasn't fulfilled.

It wasn't a horrible life, but I didn't have the courage to do things because of my weight. I didn't have confidence." Now, Vicki does a lot of volunteer work and public speaking in addition to acting and professional writing. She also finds herself doing more physical activities, now that she feels "good enough to wear Levis."

♦ Jennifer P., who established her career before starting a family, partially attributes her ability to make food and weight "nonissues" to career satisfaction: "I love my job. I'm too busy to think about food." Jennifer hasn't gained weight during the summers she's been off from her college job. She's enjoyed having that time with her two young sons. (Jennifer got a master's degree in psychology and works as a counselor.)

♦ Tami B. gained weight when she was in college, raising a small child by herself. "I couldn't get out of the house. I'd come home, watch TV and eat. I was bored. I didn't want to do anything that would put me in the public eye. Then, once I started to lose weight, I developed interests in physical activities I never would have done before, like rollerblading and aerobics. Now, I keep busy; I have an active lifestyle." (Tami completed college and is now a registered dietitian.)

♦ Charlotte O. says the biggest change in her life since losing weight has been getting a job. "When I was heavy, I was a homemaker. I baked bread, cooked for the kids and ate it all. I was happy staying at home and taking care of the kids. But I wouldn't have had the confidence to get a job. When you're heavy, you sit back and envy people who do what you want to do." Not only has Charlotte gone to work, but she has made major changes in her outside activities. "I go camping, hiking, boating, swimming. But when I was heavy, I didn't do even minor things, like play games at a family picnic. I didn't want to make a fool of myself. Now [my attitude] is, 'Okay, let's go.'"

♦ Lorene N. became very involved in a food and clothing bank as she was first losing her 61 pounds. By keeping busy, she has less time to dwell on herself and food. "I also got reinvolved with church so I have less time think about poor little me."

♦ Cindy P., the master in Chapter II, lists "staying social" as one of her top three maintenance strategies. "Being with people makes me want to stay thin." She adds, "Now, I go dancing or horseback riding instead of going out to dinner."

By now, you may have noticed the near-absence of men in this chapter. I found that few men divulged information about "getting more out of life." It may be that men are less likely to share their feelings about this subject. *Whatever the case, the techniques and advice suggested in this chapter are meant for women and men alike.*

Developing a more fulfilled life doesn't mean you have to go out and get a master's degree or have a full-time career. It simply means finding new interests, hobbies, pleasures and activities, some of which take you outside of your home. Irene S. says, "I used to play tennis, but I quit because I was fat. (I'm thinking about going back.) Now I hit golf balls with my husband, jump off the diving board and slide down a slide at the pool." Mary Ann K. is "into physical, fun activities like volleyball and bike riding. Before, I would come home, watch TV or go to the mall."

Here are some activities you can try in order to help yourself develop a more fulfilled lifestyle:

• **20 Small Pleasures.** Make a list of 20 things you enjoy doing and post it in a prominent place. (Think about activities that you used to like to do, perhaps before you had a family.) My patients used to find it helpful to consult their lists when they had an urge for "nonhunger" eating. Master Bob W.'s list of "simple things" that make him happy includes sharing a cup of tea with a friend, singing songs, sitting looking at the stars, watching his garden grow and playing with a neighborhood cat or dog

• **The Three-List Strategy.** Each day, make three separate lists: things I *absolutely* have to do, things I want to do for me and things that can wait. The idea is to cull out the necessities and get them done promptly. Then be certain to move on to at least one or two activities that you want to do for yourself, and postpone the other stuff.

• **Things I've Always Wanted to Do.** Make a list of activities that you've thought about doing. Then rate their feasibility on a scale of 1 to 5, with 1 being "possible" and 5 being "impossible." (My list might include running in a marathon and taking singing lessons. I'd have to rate the marathon as "4," in part because I don't think my knees could take it, in part because I wouldn't want to take the time to train away from my family and my career. Singing lessons would be a "1": I could find a way to work them into my life.) After you develop your list and ratings, choose one or two activities that received a "1" or "2" and make a step-by-step plan of action.

Learning to Reward Yourself—Without Food

MANY OF THE ITEMS on your lists above can be used as rewards—bonuses you can give yourself for meeting certain goals when you feel good about yourself, or to boost yourself when you're feeling down. Finding ways to reward yourself is important long after you've reached your weight goal, when you no longer have the reinforcement of watching the scale go down and attention from others has waned.

As Jennifer P. was losing, she "allowed herself to do anything but eat as a reward. I'd get a haircut or new clothes. Today, I treat myself with movies, clothes, activities with the kids, going to a women's group once a month. I also see exercise as my time, my treat." When Charlotte O. went down several sizes en route to her 96-pound loss, she would go out and buy herself several dresses. She also sent herself flowers.

As seems to be the case with the masters, Dr. Ross found that a common reward used by her maintainers was clothing. She also found that getting rid of clothes that were too large was "an almost universal behavior. It was as if the commitment was being made to never again gain the weight." Master Maxine D. advises, "Give your old clothes away. If you keep them, you are saying to yourself, 'I plan to gain again.'" When Don M. reached his weight goal, he rewarded himself with new all-cotton sweaters—27 of them! "It reminds me of accomplishing my goal, so I don't overeat."

Don also developed a reward system for himself *as* he was losing weight. "It used to be that I'd lose 10 pounds and reward myself with homemade ice cream or a hot fudge sundae. I was sabotaging my own efforts. Then I'd be off the diet. But when I started Optifast, my wife said, 'Don't reward yourself with food.' She planted the seed, and it sprouted into music, my one vice. For each 10-pound loss, I bought myself a compact disk or a tape."

Similarly, when Donna C. was losing her 108 pounds, if she went down a size, she might buy herself new clothing, "not a hot fudge sundae." When getting together with a friend, she might suggest going for a walk or to a movie. Vicki B. also gave herself new treats as she was losing. "At a certain point, I planned a professional [beauty] makeover; at another point, I got my nails done—I have ever since. Now, I try to base my rewards less on pounds lost and more on my level of exercise and keeping my fat intake down. I might treat myself to a massage, a hairstyle or new perfume."

Irene S. says that when she first started losing weight (she also gave up alcohol at the same time), she went through a period of feeling, "This is no fun." Then she decided, "I have to face things with a clearer head. Now, I will take a nap, a bubble bath, do a facial mask, listen to a relaxation tape or elevate my legs and read. I may take a whole day and pamper myself, do whatever I want to do."

She periodically rewards herself by looking at three photos of herself: before, during and after her 77-pound loss. She admits, "I have to constantly remind myself of my success." Similarly, Peppi S. keeps a picture from when she was heavy and glances at it when she feels dissatisfied with her body. "I need to accept that there is always room for improvement, but I've come a long way."

Taking Care of Your Own Needs

Drs. Colvin and Olson found that their female success stories had become "selfish," meaning they had learned to act in their own self-interest. (The psychologists also state that most men in their study didn't see this issue "as a big deal.")

A number of masters confirmed the psychologists' findings:

• Jennifer P. told me, "It's important for me to know my own needs, wants and desires in addition to helping others. But when I help others, it's a choice. I try to be human, not perfect."

• Vicki B.: Her philosophy is, "You can't fill others' needs unless your own are met. Like a lot of women, I spent a lot of time doing things for everyone else and feeling put upon and hating it. I started taking care of my own needs. When I started running, my 5-year-old son wanted to come with me. I felt bad, but I knew if he did, it would have thrown off my plan for myself." It was hard, but Vicki had to say no.

- Mary Ann K.: Shortly before her decision to lose weight, her father died. "I was always taking care of him, always taking care of others." Then she read a book about codependency. "I learned I had been a second-class family member. It took about six months to say, 'Hey, I'm as important as everyone else.' If you're not number one physically and mentally, you're not good for anyone else."

- Irene S.: As she approached readiness to lose weight, she said to herself, "I am important, so why aren't I doing something about it?" She added, "I needed to be selfish and prioritize. I think a lot of fat people don't give themselves time and attention because they don't feel good about themselves."

- Charlotte O.: She still feels her children come first. "But," she stated, "instead of it being the kids, my husband, the dog, then me— I've moved myself up to second."

- Ann F.: One of her top priorities is to take good physical care of herself. "I have to exercise, eat well and sleep. I can give more to others when I'm less worried about what I'm not doing. Today, [before work] it took me 20 minutes to put together my breakfast and lunch. I have no qualms about it."

Changing Relationships

W HEN YOU START TO FEEL BETTER ABOUT YOURSELF, cultivate new interests, get involved in a career or other outside activities, take care of your own needs more, become more active and look better because of your weight loss, these changes can affect your relationships. *For some masters, the impact was painful, but apparently best for them in the long run.* Susan C., the master profiled in Chapter IV, stated that when she lost her weight, she also lost her first husband. "My husband had been happy with me the way I was. But when I lost weight, I wanted to go dancing, go to parties, wear nice clothes. Men started looking at me. I got a sports car. My head started spinning. I went out a lot with friends and did things I'd never done before. My husband and I grew apart, and the marriage ended."

Jeffrey B. thinks, too, that his weight loss of 55 pounds had something to do with his marital split. "I started to fool around. I never had the confidence to do that before." About a year after Charlotte O. lost 96 pounds, her then-husband told her he would have left her if she hadn't lost weight. She decided, " 'If that's all there is [to our marriage] . . .' so I went out and got a job. I changed everything. He couldn't understand the changes. We drifted apart, and about two to three years later, we got a divorce." Finally, Thalia P. stated that the changes she had to make to keep her weight off led to her recent separation from her husband. "I am sad about this, but ultimately I'm becoming more and more myself and not living by someone else's rules."

The conclusion to be drawn is not that losing weight and losing your spouse go hand in hand. Rather, it's important to realize that all change entails risk.

There are masters who note positive changes in relationships since their weight loss. Lorene N. and her husband decided to work through their marital problems by getting counseling. Vicki B. found, "The sparkle came back into my marriage. My husband started sending me flowers. He wanted to show me off." Irene S. notes that, when she first started losing, her husband would encourage her to eat fattening things. "When he really noticed the changes, he got kind of ugly. I think he thought I had a boyfriend. Then he started walking with me. Now, he's proud of me and tries to emulate me. Our relationship is better." Mary Ann K.'s husband also became her partner in exercise. "At my halfway point, he decided to lose 40 pounds." Now, they work out at a gym together.

Some people noted positive changes in relationships outside of their marriages. Jennifer P. states, "People treat you differently. I feel that, jobwise, people see me as a more disciplined, professional person." As for friendships, she adds, "When I was in college, I used to pick a friend and hide behind her. Now I have a greater variety of friends. Having more self-esteem because of the weight loss has allowed me to branch out more." Vicki B. finds that she, too, has more friends since her weight loss. "It's not because people didn't like me, but because I have the confidence to make friends. It has opened up avenues because I feel good about myself."

When people lose weight, another part of changing relationships can be others' reactions to the "new you." Some of the people in Dr. Ross's study found that certain of their friends were supportive until their success became obvious. Then they became jealous and almost mean. "It took adjustment and sometimes loss of a friendship before the issue was resolved." Master Liz D. found after she first lost her 55 pounds, "I really got tired of everybody noticing and talking about it, seemingly constantly. I just wanted to be normal, to be just an average person instead of having to talk about it to everyone. I guess I was putting so much pressure on myself to succeed that I felt anyone who talked about my weight loss was just adding pressure. But now I have come to enjoy talking about it and try to encourage others who are dealing with weight."

You Are Much More Than Your Weight

REACHING YOUR GOAL WEIGHT isn't all there is to life. Jennifer P., for instance, sometimes thinks she could stand to lose another 10 pounds. So she talks to herself, saying, "Life is not a beauty contest. Who cares if I weigh 130 or 140? I'm fine the way I am, and it isn't worth giving up other things to focus on that."

Likewise, Connie M. feels that it's important to enjoy life and not worry about being a size 10. "I'm satisfied with myself at a size 12. Life's too short to struggle with your weight. Goal weight is important, but not to the extent that it's the most important thing in your life. The emphasis is on the thin body, but let's be healthy and happy too." Similarly, Dr. Joyce Nash states, "Life is not about weight control. When you find yourself at the pearly gates, God forbid that you should say to St. Peter when he asks what you did with your life, 'I watched my weight.'"

It may help to deemphasize the importance of appearance, as you find other sources of satisfaction. Consider the things happy people have in common, according to psychologists John Foreyt and G. Ken Goodrick: they are active and busy, spend more time socializing, are organized, are productive at meaningful work, are realistic in their goals, have close relationships and focus on the positive. Nowhere do you see mention of appearance. Placing too much value on attractiveness thwarts personal development and can prevent you from feeling good about yourself and going out and getting more out of life. As master Ann B. states, "Part of my feeling good is that I'm not caught up in how society says you have to look."

Paradoxically, this acceptance that life is about more than weight control and appearance leads to weight loss—at least for some people. Kelly S. states that her motivation to lose weight once and for all came when she realized that her "entire life and self-worth" were tied up in her weight. "Very draining and unempowering," she says. Likewise, Vicki B. attributes her success to being able to look beyond her appearance. "There's so much more to life than weight!" She says this acceptance enabled her to lose 40 pounds, which she's kept off for 12 years—minus the periods when she had her five children.

If you stop allowing your weight to get in the way of a more fulfilling life, as well as feeling good about yourself, the need to use food to enrich your existence will diminish. Then you can get on with more important aspects of life, which make it worthwhile to maintain whatever weight you lose.

X

Don't Go It Alone

N OW THAT YOU'VE ACCEPTED RESPONSIBILITY for your weight, you should be able to go it alone. Right? Not necessarily. The prospect of taking the reins, making exercise a way of life and getting more out of life may seem like overwhelming proposi- tions. *The good news is: you don't have to go it alone.* Many masters turn to others for support, some on a regular basis, others as needed.

Weight-control experts have determined that support from family and friends is associated with long-term success at weight control. On the other hand, lack of encouragement and interpersonal conflict can lead to relapse. So how can you use support from others to work for you? Whom should you turn to—a professional, a group or an indi- vidual who's close to you? How can you deal with people who are un- supportive of your weight-control efforts? Examples from the masters will show that you can find strength from others in your effort to take personal control of your weight.

Muriel and Jordan F.'s Stories

T HEY LOST WEIGHT TOGETHER, they keep it off together. Combined, they've lost more than 100 pounds and have main- tained that loss for 3 years. I knew Muriel and Jordan F. would have a lot to say about "Don't Go It Alone" when she wrote me, "My husband and I did our program together, and we support each other strongly." He told me, "We do it together; I have to watch her, and she watches me." Yet they don't have a watchdog relationship: they maintain a strong sense of independence along with the sharing that characterizes their lives together.

After a lifetime of struggling with weight, it took both of them until they were in their fifties to finally find success. About four years ago, Muriel was inspired by Oprah Winfrey's weight loss, so she decided to try Health Management Resources' liquid diet. Jordan joined the program, too, but only to support Muriel. "I didn't think it would be successful beyond the diet. It was just another attempt. I figured we'd lose and regain the weight." Muriel did the liquid "fast" for 16 weeks and went from a weight of 207 to 150 pounds. (She's 5'5" tall.) Jordan could only take the fast for about two weeks. "It bothered me. So they told me to add a 4-ounce potato to the liquid meals each day. That worked for me." Within 12 weeks, Jordan dropped from 242 pounds to 205. (His height is 6'2".)

What led Muriel and Jordan to this point? Muriel's battle with weight began when she was a teenager. At the age of 19, when she was about 30 pounds overweight, her doctor gave her diet pills. But she never lost much weight, and her pharmacist eventually refused to refill the prescription. As she got older and had two children, her weight steadily increased and tended to stay around 185—that is, when she wasn't trying some new weight-loss scheme. "I tried every one of them—TOPS, Weight Watchers, Overeaters Anonymous, Weight Loss Clinic and Diet Workshop." With most programs, she had very little success.

When I asked her what she thought was the main cause of her weight problem, she responded, "Being home with my kids, not working, boredom, not thinking about what I ate and watching TV." She added that socializing played a role as well. "Any time we got together with friends, food was involved. We would play cards, but the snacks were very important."

Muriel went back to work in the 1970s, when her children were teenagers. Around 1980, she had her greatest success until that time with Diet Center; she lost 60 pounds, but slowly regained the weight.

Then, four years ago, several important events came together. Muriel was working as the administrator of a synagogue when a rabbi, who was also a health-conscious friend, said to her, "Muriel, please, for your own sake do something about your weight." She felt that his comment came from caring, not meanness. At the same time, it really sunk in that her mother had died when she was 65. Muriel was 50 at the time, and she realized that she was "getting older and wanted to live longer. I knew I had to do something."

In retrospect, Muriel now sees as well that her father's death had an impact on her readiness to lose weight. I asked her if it had been difficult to lose weight during that stressful time. "I loved my dad, but there are certain things from childhood that I don't forget," she replied. "When he died, I was finally free. He always wanted me to be a blond: I was the fat blond. Now, I'm the slim brunette." Today, Muriel can see what her weight may have been doing for her. "My father wasn't pleased about my weight. I may have kept it on in anger. It was the only way I could show my disapproval of him. As long as he was around, I had one thing over him: the weight. When my father died, I grew up."

When did Jordan's weight problem start? "I was always overweight, always the biggest baby, always fat. My parents were both heavy." Jordan's father owned a bakery, and pastry and baked goods were always in the home. "If we were good, pastry was the reward." Jordan also recalls "coming home from school, throwing a steak under the broiler, eating it as a snack, then eating dinner shortly thereafter. There was always lots of food around, and I always indulged in it." By the time he graduated from high school, he weighed 262 pounds.

Like Muriel, Jordan's first serious attempt at weight loss involved diet pills, when he was in his late twenties. "I lost 40 or 50 pounds but gained it back when I went off the pills." From there he "tried the gamut": Weight Loss Clinic, Diet Workshop and Weight Watchers, to name a few. But the most he would lose was about 20 pounds.

Jordan doesn't recall any critical event or change in motivation that led to his readiness to lose even more weight four years ago. He merely did it for Muriel. The difference for him from all the other times was "education from a dietitian." Specifically, he related to HMR's intense education about calorie intake and expenditure. "I learned that if I exercised to this level and ate this food, I should lose weight. I believed it because they proved it to me. I'm an engineer, and I identified with the facts and figures. It was purely educational." As an example, Jordan remembers the time the dietitian demonstrated how the calories can add up in a typical tuna sandwich: "She showed us the tuna, the bread and all the mayonnaise." Muriel concurs, "The key was working with a registered dietitian. The most important things we learned were about fat, calories and portions. We just never knew about it." And of course, the support from each other played an important role.

Neither Muriel nor Jordan had a difficult time making the transition from the liquid diet to "real" food, primarily because they stuck with the HMR program and learned to retrain their eating habits. Muriel states, "We were weaned onto good foods, so there was no problem." For Jordan, the transition to low-fat "real" foods was exciting but somewhat scary. "But I continued to lose weight, so I was encouraged." Muriel and Jordan stayed in HMR's maintenance group and saw the dietitian regularly for about a year. Had they not had this follow-up, they both feel they probably would have gained the weight back. Muriel states, "The learning process continued that year."

What about now? Jordan has elected not to continue with any support system other than Muriel but admits he could use help since his weight is up some, in part because he hasn't been able to exercise. Muriel has found it difficult to exercise as well. They both have long commutes and are in the process of moving but plan to get back into exercise when they relocate. Jordan admits, "It makes me feel good, and it's good for me."

Muriel now goes to a Jenny Craig facility, which she decided to join the summer of her second year of maintenance after she regained 18 pounds. That was when she discovered she is not the type of person who can "have a little. I love sweets. If I have one little piece, the next time it's bigger." She also attributes the weight rebound to giving in to friends who wanted to go to restaurants with poor food choices. "I realized I couldn't make everyone else happy. I had to either back off or stand my ground." She stood her ground, and friends now "ask her permission" before selecting restaurants.

She chose Jenny Craig because it was local, and she found it to be a good program. Although she does not consider herself a group person, she enjoyed the classes. Muriel continues to go back once a month to weigh in. That way, if she ever gains weight, she says she can go back to the program at no charge.

Currently Muriel weighs 152, down 55 pounds from her all-time high. At a weight of 196, Jordan is 69 pounds shy of his maximum weight. They both feel it was critical that they achieved their success together. Says Jordan, "I probably wouldn't have done it without her." Although they go their separate ways during the day, their maintenance eating patterns are similar: three low-fat meals a day with several snacks in between. (Muriel can tell you exactly when she eats them.) Unlike Muriel, Jordan allows himself occasional treats like a piece of pizza, a drink or candy. Most evenings they both treat themselves to a "measured" cup of ice milk.

When it comes to planning and cooking meals, they work as a team. Jordan states, "We both work, so it's unfair for me to come home and say, 'Make me supper.' So we share the responsibility. We plan ahead and make sure someone has purchased the food for supper." Muriel adds, "He loves to cook, and I like to clean up." Jordan has become "a fanatic about oil and butter and the way they're used in food." Yet he has learned creative alternative ways to make food tasty. For instance, he talked about making broccoli with peppers, scallions, lemon juice and a little Parmesan cheese.

It's quite clear that the main source of support for Muriel and Jordan is each other. She maintains, "We talk about what we're doing all the time. We catch each other. One of us might say, 'I think you're losing it.' It's not critical or mean, just caring."

Support for the Support Theory

L IKE MURIEL AND JORDAN, a number of masters told me they find
support for their maintenance efforts from significant people in
their lives—be it spouses, friends, relatives, counselors or groups.

◆ Michael and Cindy F. are another couple who control their
weight together. Combined, they've lost 288 pounds, and each has
kept weight off for at least 7 years. In addition to their joint efforts,
both say that one of their keys to success is continued involvement
with Weight Watchers.

◆ Linda Sue S. (78 pounds, 6 years) continues to see her counselor
at Diet Center if she gains some weight.

◆ Mary B. (90 pounds, 11½ years) goes to a weekly Take Off
Pounds Sensibly (TOPS) meeting.

◆ Cindy B. (38 pounds, 3 years) goes to weigh in once a month at
Weight Watchers.

◆ Bob W. (250 pounds, 21 years) initially lost weight by going to
Weight Watchers but now goes to Overeaters Anonymous for support.

◆ Steve S. (210 pounds, 13 years) has gone back to the HMR program (where he lost his weight) four times in the last 13 years for
"professional coaching" when he began to gain.

◆ Mary Ann K. (84 pounds, 3 years) returns to Jenny Craig classes
when "I feel like I'm slipping."

◆ Connye Z. (34 pounds, 5½ years) gets support from her husband.
"To this day, he still comments on my size, like 'Let me see those
skinny legs!'" Connye also goes to Weight Watchers once a month.

◆ Jim J. (181 pounds, 5 years) goes to a weekly class with fellow
long-term maintainers and talks on the phone with a professional
weight-control counselor once a week. He also finds support from his
wife, who makes an effort to cook low-fat foods.

A number of studies involving individuals who were enrolled in
research-based weight-loss programs lend strong credence to the notion that getting support is important for maintenance, at least for
certain people. Some of the most important work was conducted by
Michael G. Perri, PhD., currently at the University of Florida, and co-

workers. They completed a series of studies suggesting that support—from therapists or peers—is associated with the ability to maintain weight loss. All people in their studies were mildly to moderately obese when first treated with a comprehensive behavioral program that included a 1,000-to-1,500-calorie diet, behavior-modification techniques and positive-thinking strategies. Afterward, some of the patients received no further treatment. Others were assigned to various combinations of maintenance strategies, including the following: an aerobic exercise program; relapse-prevention training; ongoing therapist contact by mail and telephone; and peer support groups that met regularly to monitor weight, praise and encourage each other and to use problem-solving strategies. (The therapists in most of these studies were either psychologists or graduate psychology students.)

The studies consistently indicated that people who received therapist and/or peer support kept off more weight than did those without such support. Moreover, people who took part in multiple maintenance strategies tended to do better than did those who simply went through the behavioral program or who were involved in one maintenance strategy. For instance, one of Dr. Perri's studies revealed that the group that received three different maintenance strategies, as opposed to one or two, was the only group that showed significant *additional* weight loss during the 18-month follow-up period. People in this group maintained almost all of their initial weight loss. Dr. Perri and his co-workers concluded that the combination of therapist contact, frequent exercise and peer support holds promise for improving weight maintenance.

Another study, published in the *British Medical Journal*, involved 53 obese women who started out at an average weight of 245 pounds. They participated in an intensive weight-loss regime followed by a four-year maintenance program that included weekly sessions, therapist contacts by phone and mail and "refresher" courses when they experienced relapses. Six years after this aggressive program, the women reported that, on average, they had kept off almost two-thirds of their peak weight losses.

What conclusions should you draw from these studies? First, support has something to do with maintenance. Second, multifaceted approaches to maintenance are best. In other words, finding support alone may not sustain weight loss. But when support is coupled with such keys to success as exercise, problem-solving and facing the food facts, the prospect of losing weight and keeping it off is enhanced.

Support can also come from a commercial weight-loss group such as Weight Watchers or a self-help group like TOPS or Overeaters Anonymous. One study revealed that Weight Watchers members who continued to attend meetings in the same location and with the same leader after reaching their goal weights were more likely to keep their weight off than were members who did not.

Finally, support can come from family and friends. Robert Jeffery and colleagues at the University of Minnesota studied a group of overweight men who had taken part in a 15-week behavior-modification program. The men were later contacted to see what factors had contributed to successful maintenance. One factor was support of family and friends. (Support was defined as family cooperation in weight-loss efforts or as having friends who had changed eating or exercise behavior in response to the study participants' involvement in the weight-loss program.) Two years after the initial program, men who reported high family cooperation kept off about 21 pounds, yet those with low cooperation from families kept off an average of about 6 pounds. The men who reported that friends had changed their diets kept 19 pounds off; those who reported no changes on the part of friends had only maintained about a 10-pound loss. This study also found that men who used a variety of different techniques to keep their weight off were the most successful.

What Can a Support System Do for You?

WHETHER YOU ELECT TO SEEK THE HELP of a professional counselor, formal group, friend or family member, having a support person or persons can do a lot to keep you at your new weight. What can you get from others?

◆ **Advice and new ideas.** Sometimes it helps to have input—say, when you're having a rough time with food intake, struggling with a personal problem that makes you want to overeat, slacking off on exercise or anticipating a social situation. Jim J. admits that, in the past, he'd use any excuse to "blow it all off. I would gain 5, then 10 pounds and throw up my hands. Now, if I gain 5 pounds, the group helps head me off. It talks openly and helps you come up with a plan." He particularly benefits from the last 15 minutes of his weekly maintenance group when members pair off to come up with a plan or "tricks" for the week ahead. "Sometimes, it helps to hear someone say, 'Why don't you try this again?' The broader your repertoire of tricks, the better you are."

* **Empathy, encouragement and commendation.** After having kept off 71 pounds for 4 years, Mary S. has found, "The general public doesn't want to hear about my problems or my diet. My family is tired of hearing about it." But when she goes to her maintenance group, she can "let my hair down."

* **Education.** As Muriel and Jordan stated, the knowledge they gained from a dietitian about calories, fat and energy expenditure was invaluable. Likewise, Connye Z. gained new ideas from Weight Watchers, "like steaming vegetables." She added, "I really internalized which foods were better for me or lower in calories. I changed my eating habits, and I haven't changed them back."

* **Assurance that you are not alone.** Nick R., who once weighed 288 pounds and now holds his own at 210 (he's 6'2" tall), finds that going to OA allows sharing of common experiences, "like when I used to eat on my way home, but didn't tell my wife, then I'd eat dinner. [At OA] when you see the nods, you know they understand, so you don't feel like you're so different."

* **Help with getting your problems in perspective.** After Jim J. took a recent 3-week vacation from work and his maintenance group, he worried that he had regained weight and became "a little panicky. After all the years of being heavy, I thought, 'Maybe I really am slipping.' " But talking with his counselor and returning to group meetings helped him get things in perspective and reassured him.

* **Heightened accountability to yourself.** Connye Z. has been at her goal of 118 pounds for nearly 6 years, yet she goes to Weight Watchers once a month to weigh in and sometimes stays for the meetings. "They record your weight in a book that you keep. It motivates me to see the stability once a month."

◆ **Constructive criticism from others.** Muriel and Jordan "catch" each other in a caring way. Jim V. gets feedback from his dietitian who, as noted in Chapter VII, reminds him of all his hard work and how far he's come. Steve S. makes the following analogy: "Just as any professional athlete needs a coach, sometimes you need someone with an objective eye outside of you."

◆ **Reminders of where you've come from and what you need to do to stay there.** Joy B., who's kept off 35 pounds for more than 4 years, finds, "I just slide a bit, get lazy or space out every once in a while and find that I've put on 3 to 5 pounds without even knowing it. If I do gain a few pounds, I find going back to Weight Watchers meetings really helps me. It reminds me of why I want to be a certain weight [115; she's 5'1"], and the process of going 'on-program' makes me recheck portion sizes and reeducate myself."

use support only for crisis intervention—if, for instance, they've been maintaining their weight for years and suddenly gain 5 or 10 pounds. Master Ed G., for example, has kept off at least 30 pounds for 17 years. When his weight creeps up, he returns to Weight Watchers. "I've gone back twice now; I need to do it again." (At a height of 5'10", he's up about 10 pounds above his desired weight of 170.)

Many people, like Muriel and Jordan, need more support in the beginning, within the first year or two of reaching their goal weights. Franca Alphin, R.D., nutrition director at Duke University's Diet and Fitness Center (a residential weight-loss facility), notes that a number of their successful patients come back for a "refresher" three to four times the first year. Within a few years, they return just once a year.

The trick is to not let your weight get out of hand before you take action. And having some place to turn, particularly right after you've reached your goal, may be critical to your success. *Like many people, you've probably had some success with weight loss but very little with weight maintenance, and it's critical to get support before matters feel out of control.*

It's not always easy to seek help when you've gained, admits Teresa M., who has gone through HMR's "restart" program twice, after she gained back some weight. "I felt like a failure, but I wanted to be thin more than anything. They made me see the positive." After initially losing about 60 pounds, she's never crept back up to her all-time high of 196, but she has regained as much as 30 pounds. Unlike her first attempt with HMR, however, she currently goes to weekly classes with fellow maintainers. (She's now down to 140.)

Time and time again, I had patients who would stop coming for appointments when they regained some weight. Some would refuse to come in until they were "doing better." *They didn't realize that they needed help most when they were struggling.* As Syracuse University's Thomas Wadden points out, avoiding help when you're having a hard time with your food intake is analogous to avoiding your physician when you have the flu!

The masters, on the other hand, recognize when they need outside aid. Paul A., for example, found his weight creeping up when he stopped his involvement with Weight Watchers. "I realized it was because I didn't have my support group, and that within a year, I'd be back up 60 pounds." Paul returned to Weight Watchers and is now one of their leaders. Likewise, Peppi S. lost 65 pounds in 1986, which she maintained until 1½ years later when she had a debilitating back injury. She regained about 40 pounds, but went back to Nutri/System to lose the extra weight and now maintains at about 138, down 62 pounds from her all-time high.

What Are Some Warning Signs That You Need Support?

◆ You are 5 to 10 pounds over your goal weight and cannot seem to lose it. Says Ed G., who goes back to Weight Watchers, "Every once in a while, I think I can do it on my own, but I don't."

◆ Your "thin" clothes are getting tight, and you find yourself buying new, bigger clothes. Teresa M. told me, "When my clothes didn't fit, I knew I had to do something, or I'd be right back where I started."

◆ You find the "tricks" that used to help you control your weight are no longer effective. Muriel F. knows she needs help when "I find myself falling off, eating high-fat foods."

◆ You find yourself turning to food to handle stress or problems. When Jim V. finds himself eating without thinking when he's under pressure, he visits his dietitian.

◆ Your mental attitude has changed. Jordan F. realizes he has a problem when he finds himself not being as careful with food, succumbing to pressure to eat in social situations.

◆ You find yourself getting lazy. Mary Ann K. says she goes back to Jenny Craig when she starts buying high-fat foods again—like ice cream instead of yogurt—and when she slacks off on exercise.

◆ You are feeling somewhat hopeless about your weight, wondering if the effort is worth it, or you feel out of control. After losing more than 25 pounds with TOPS, Maxine D. found herself regaining when she no longer had transportation to get to meetings. (She does not drive.) "I was actually only 5 pounds over, but out of control." Then her husband agreed to take her each week and wait for her. Now, she faithfully attends meetings and has kept off 38 pounds for 9 years.

Finding Support That's Right for You

T HE MOST EFFECTIVE WAY to head off trouble is to have a support
system in place before the "warning signs" hit, as does Muriel F.,
who maintains her relationship with Jenny Craig so she can return
if she needs to. If you're a private person, you may prefer to get support from an individual counselor, close friend or family member. If,
however, you're more of a social, self-disclosing, outgoing person, a
group situation may be more to your liking. Here are some factors to
consider when making your selection:

◆ **Individual counseling.** If you're a loner, you may feel more comfortable finding a support person with expertise in weight control: a
psychologist, physician, registered dietitian, social worker or trained
employee of a weight-loss organization. (This is for counseling for
weight-related issues, not for psychological problems.) You may simply want to make a few visits to get to know each other, then go back
on an "as-needed" basis. Or you may start out with more frequent visits, then taper off. For the first several years after she lost her 50-plus
pounds, Susan D. saw a dietitian "religiously" every week. "I'm the
type of person who needs to be monitored. If helps me to focus."
Now, she's on her own but plans to join the YMCA and possibly go
back to a dietitian.

You can also get one-on-one support from a peer at a group like
Overeaters Anonymous. Attendees are encouraged to form a relationship with another OA member whom they call a "sponsor." These
people are not trained weight-control counselors; they're fellow group
members who are experienced with the OA program. Some masters
find great support from their sponsors. Nick R. says of his, "That person understands me. With a sponsor, you can also share personal stuff
that you couldn't share at a meeting." In return, if you become a sponsor, as Bob says, "you have to live it. It's an incentive to be honest. It
makes you appreciate what you have and where you've been."

◆ **Group support.** Many people like groups because they find it
helpful to be with others who have the same problem. "We're in it together," says Jim J. of his group of fellow maintainers. Connye Z.,

who lost 34 pounds with the help of Weight Watchers, found, "To hear people say that they had a similar success or similar problem was encouraging—to know they had gone through it too. They're encouraging. Once I gained 2 pounds, and they said, 'Oh, you're still way under your goal.' "

Another advantage of groups is the motivation you can get from being around others who have found success. When Nick R. first went to OA and saw thin people there, it gave him hope. "I saw people who were losing weight, and their lives were getting better." After having kept off 78 pounds for 5 years, Nick points out that there can also be great satisfaction in helping someone else.

Groups can also provide a way to "get more out of life." Maxine D., for instance, says she has "an enlarged social life with all the TOPS family." Mary S. says of her maintenance group, "We shared hints. We discussed upcoming events and how to cope." Finally, some maintainers, like Paul A., choose to lead weight-control groups because, "For me, it isn't enough to go to meetings. I need to stand before the group. It's a watchdog for me; I can't be in front of the group and not keep my weight down."

If you go the group route, it pays to shop around. Muriel F. found self-help groups to be discouraging because of members who could eat more than she, yet still lose weight. Yet she liked the professionally run group at HMR because, "It was only learning. There were no comparisons of weight gain or loss."

Shopping around entails checking out umbrella groups, as well as individual chapters. For example, don't rule out TOPS, OA or Weight Watchers on the basis of one meeting and one group. If you investigate several different meetings or chapters, you may find that you like the personality of one group or leader better than another. The size of the group may enter into your decision: some individual groups of any one organization are larger than others. (TOPS and OA are self-help groups, while Weight Watchers meetings have a leader who lost weight on the program. Another option chosen by certain masters is a weight-loss group run by a local hospital.)

Instead of attending a formal weight-loss group, you may want to start one of your own. It could be a group of friends, or you could start a low-fat cooking class. Another possibility would be to approach a local dietitian or psychologist to lead a group of fellow maintainers. (Of course, you'd have to pay him or her.) It's probably wise for the group to set up certain ground rules for attendance and for calling each other between meetings or if someone doesn't show up. The group could also have a particular focus, such as a helpful weight-loss book or a weekly predetermined topic.

• **Support from family and friends.** Many maintainers get their support from an individual. Like Muriel and Jordan F., Cindy and Michael F. attribute much of their success to their "team approach." Cindy states, "We plan meals and work together to keep our motivation high." Connye Z.'s husband is willing to eat low-fat cooking and keep tempting foods out of the house. She says of her husband, "Since he won't cook, he eats whatever I prepare. None of this preparing two different meals. We do not keep candy and potato chips in the house. He did not try to sabotage my efforts by cooking or offering foods I needed to stay away from."

Mary Ann K. involves her whole family in the process of maintenance. Not only do she and her husband help each other in the kitchen, they share their knowledge about low-fat cooking with their kids. She exclaims, "All four of us support each other!"

Rosemary O. turns to her sister. Nearly six years ago, they joined a weight-loss program at a medical center, and they continue to work on maintenance as a team. "We live together, work together, play together, walk together. We talk about it. I ask [my sister] to keep reminding me how to eat. It's a togetherness issue."

Interestingly, studies on the effectiveness of involving spouses in weight-control efforts have yielded conflicting results, probably because some people are better off with group support, while others prefer to go it alone, and still others simply have unsupportive spouses. In the Kaiser Permanente study comparing maintainers with regainers, more than half of both groups of women reported their husbands were not supportive. Another study showed that more than 40 percent of the participants identified family members as both the most and least helpful people in their weight-management efforts.

If you decide you would like to enlist an individual for support, you have to pick the right person and train that person about how to be supportive. How can you get what you need? As trite as it may sound, you have to communicate. As a case in point, Jordan F. talked about how, when he was on the liquid diet, he had to travel with superiors who were into wining and dining. "I was afraid to go, so I talked with my boss, who talked with his boss. They were very supportive and told me to do whatever I needed to do. There was no ridicule."

What Should You Look for in a Support Person?

* Someone with whom you feel comfortable talking about your weight and problems having to do with your weight.
* Someone who compliments you, for instance, when you do something well or look nice.
* Someone who reassures you when things are not going your way.
* Someone who, in a pinch, would help you—say, with childcare or transportation.
* Someone who is honest with you in a nice way and will give you feedback.
* Someone who is available to you most of the time.
* Someone to whom you can talk even when you are not doing well with weight control.
* Someone who offers good advice and helps you through crises.
* Someone who shares feelings and problems.
* Someone who supports your taking responsibility for your weight problem.

What Don't You Want in a Support Person?

* Someone who hassles you or makes too many demands on you.
* Someone who doesn't understand having a weight problem.
* Someone who offers you food or pushes it on you when it's clear you are watching your weight.
* Someone who says critical things about you and your weight or about overweight people.
* Someone who is jealous of you or competitive with you.

◆ Someone who is self-righteous and/or who thinks he or she has all the answers.

◆ Someone who is also struggling with weight and who encourages you to indulge with him or her.

◆ Someone who offers simplistic advice like, "Just eat less," "Push yourself away from the table" or "Simply cut your portions in half."

◆ Someone who makes you feel as if you're constantly being watched.

To sum up, if you choose not to go it alone, you have to find the support system that works for you. If, like Paul A., your spouse is not supportive enough, you may want to turn to a group or professional. He told me, "My wife doesn't have a weight problem. After I lost weight, I felt like I needed support, so I became a Weight Watchers leader." Some people combine support systems. At various times, Muriel F. has had all three: professional, group and family. But like Muriel, you may find that what is right for you at one time doesn't suit you at another, so you need to switch support systems. For example, if you lost weight through a group program, the group may suit you just fine for a while. But with time, you may tire of sitting in the same room with the same people, or you may find you don't want to be with folks at earlier stages of weight control. At that point, you could hook up with a professional for "as-needed" support.

Dealing With Nonsupport

T HE WORD "SABOTAGE" FREQUENTLY CREEPS UP among weight-control experts. You have control over sabotage and can often put a stop to it.

A common form of sabotage described by many masters is performed at the hands of the "food pusher," someone who tries to force food upon you. Jim J. says he encounters this all the time. "I might be sipping Perrier at a bar, and someone will say, 'Are you going to be on a diet your whole life?' " Jim may tell him, "I'd rather save my calories for something later." He adds, "You have to speak your mind and be up-front about what you need." Likewise, Muriel F., who has found that she "can't eat just one" of certain foods, deals with food pushers by firmly letting them know, "This is not what I care to do or want to do." (She admits that sometimes she will take the unwanted item "to get the person off my back." But she leaves the food on her plate.)

The importance of these skills is reinforced by preliminary results from a study of 224 women and men who completed the Nutri/System Weight Loss Program. Yale University researchers studied these people to determine what strategies they used to maintain weight 2 years after they finished the program. Individuals who said others tried to interfere with their efforts to keep weight off—for instance, by encouraging them to eat high-calorie foods—were less successful in maintaining their weight losses than were those who reported no interference.

However, another critical determinant of success was the way people handled interference. Researcher Michaela Kiernan, M.S., reported that even in the face of interference, people maintained their weight loss as well as those who had no interference if they took two steps: 1) they refused to give in, and 2) they explicitly said, "No."

Mary S. has learned to be assertive in order to keep off her 71 pounds. She is a school secretary who finds that co-workers often bring "their excess fatty food to work." They tend to place it by the office coffee pot, which is near her desk. "I asked them to move it elsewhere. Once I got a little too excited and told them, 'I'm allergic to fat; I break out!' "

Another form of sabotage can occur within your social circle, particularly if it tends to be food-centered. Note how Muriel F. "stood her ground" in order to get her friends to go to more healthful restaurants. As in her case, you don't have cut yourself off from your friends: just communicate and make compromises with them.

Certain cultural philosophies about how you should eat or how thin you should be can interfere with your weight-loss efforts. Rosemary O., for instance, is of Lebanese/Italian heritage, cultures that tend to place high value on the connection between food and affection. Not surprisingly, her mother is a "food pusher" and an "exceptionally fine cook and baker." When Rosemary refuses food or leaves something on her plate at the end of a meal, her mother takes it personally. How does Rosemary respond? "I am just very firm. I tell her,

'If you ask me again, I'll just have to keep saying no.'" She adds, "It is still hard for me; it leads to confrontation."

Sometimes sabotage comes from within, from our "shoulds" about food and relationships. Don M. states, "I wanted to be loved, and food equaled love. I couldn't say no when something was given to me."

Jennifer P. sometimes has to deal with her overweight sister who feels it is an affront to a host or hostess not to eat everything offered. "Somehow, to my sister, it's saying 'I'm important and you're not,'" observes Jennifer. If you suspect a loved one is threatened by your weight loss—for example, your husband because you look more attractive at your new weight—talk with him about what he's feeling and offer reassurance.

Whatever the sabotaging situation, psychologist Joyce Nash advises that you give the saboteur a coherent message. In *Now That You've Lost It*, she warns, "Avoid saying no with your voice, but yes with your eyes." She also suggests making it clear in your tone of voice and body posture that you really mean what you say.

Let the person know you appreciate the offer, but be direct and open, firmly stating what your decision is. In the face of a persistent saboteur, tell him or her to stop asking you, then change the subject.

A Word About Not Going It Alone for Exercise

SUPPORT CAN ALSO BE IMPORTANT for making exercise a part of your life. One study showed that the dropout rate from an exercise program was three times higher when spouses were negative or indifferent to the program compared with when spouses were supportive. A number of masters mentioned that they exercise with a spouse, relative or friend. As Mary Ann K. says of her exercise partnership with her husband, "There are days he doesn't want to exercise, but I'm going, so he does, too, and vice versa. We don't want to disappoint each other."

Certainly the popularity of group exercise programs attests to our dependence on others for support and motivation. There is evidence that beginning exercisers tend to prefer working out with others. Some studies suggest that people who exercise in groups are more likely to stick with it. If you do join an exercise group, try to stay with it long enough to form some relationships, for a number of studies indicate that finding friendships within programs motivates people to continue.

Maintaining Your Independence

NONE OF THIS IS TO SAY that if you do choose to go it alone for overall weight control or exercise, you're doomed to remain heavy. In fact, strong independence characterizes many masters. Bear in mind that if you do choose to use a support system, weight control is ultimately up to you and is in your power. Consider Mary Ann K., who has family support, who enjoyed weight-loss classes at a commercial organization and who still goes back if she feels like she's slipping. Ultimately, however, "the support comes from inside myself. I don't look to the outside."

Muriel and Jordan F. seem to have struck a balance between self-reliance and support from others. As Jordan states, "We don't sit and watch each other all day. I know it has to come from me."

EPILOGUE

IT *can* BE DONE. People can—and do—become thin for life. Admittedly, when I began the research for this book, I had doubts. Would I find a significant number of masters at weight control? Would there be similarities in their strategies to keep off weight? After locating 160 masters and spending over a year getting to know them, I am convinced more than ever that despite the "failure talk" about the odds against losing weight and keeping it off, plenty of people manage to do so—far more than we've been led to believe.

There are striking common threads in how the masters have found success:

- **To lose weight once and for all, the masters accepted that no one could do it for them.** They realized that they must lose weight for themselves—not for their spouses, parents or anyone else. Although they have assumed ultimate responsibility for their weight, the masters know when to seek support from others—whether from friends, family, groups or professionals.

- **The masters give themselves permission to be imperfect.** That is, they accept themselves—bodily flaws and all—many at a higher weight than the so-called "ideal." They allow themselves treat foods that others might view as "forbidden." As part of the process, they talk to themselves positively, pick themselves up when they fall short of their goals and focus on triumphs rather than on shortcomings.

- **The masters have changed their attitudes about weight control.** They've stopped viewing the strategies to *lose* weight as separate from those used to *maintain* weight. For example, the vast majority make exercise a way of life but not in a fanatic manner. And most adopt and enjoy new, low-fat eating habits.

- **The masters view what they do to control their weight as lifelong change.** They accept that they cannot return to their old ways, but they neither regret their choices nor feel sorry for themselves. They understand that weight maintenance takes effort and determination. Yet the masters make it clear than any hardships associated with maintenance are far less troublesome than the difficulties endured when they were overweight.

- **The masters immediately deal with small weight gains before**

the extra pounds seem insurmountable. They set upper weight limits that trigger action until they reestablish a comfortable weight.

• **The masters stop using food as a shield from problems and learn to handle life's ups and downs more effectively.** They develop confidence in themselves—either before they lose weight or as they are losing—and they extend that confidence to other areas of their lives so they can be proud of more than just being thinner.

• **The masters believe in themselves.** Somewhere along the way, they started to have faith in their own ability to conquer their weight problems. They stopped seeing themselves as failures who had repeatedly lost and regained and began to view themselves as people who could take control and be successful.

By way of example from the masters at weight control, you, too, can start to believe in your own ability to conquer your weight problem, be it large or small. Give yourself time and realize that your new behaviors and attitudes will take practice and continued attention. After all, if you were treated for high blood pressure or diabetes for just three months, would you expect to see beneficial effects three years later? For that to happen, you would have to continue to follow a special diet, take medication and/or exercise in order to stay well. Likewise with weight control, you must keep taking action if you want to become a master.

Finally, look beyond the weight-loss phase and accept that the real challenge is *maintenance.* If your mind is made up that you want to make permanent changes in order to lose weight and keep it off, you're off to a great start. Then, if you practice the keys to success, you'll come to find, as most masters have, that your old way of life is no longer an option. As they reveal, the pay-off is well worth it. Shirley C., who has kept off 26 pounds for 12½ years, exclaims, "No one takes me for 69, and I *feel* 15 years younger." Connye Z., master of a 34-pound loss for 5½ years, says, "I don't feel I'm a better, smarter or more capable person than before. But I feel I look better, and that's important to *me.*" Finally, Michael F. sums up his 7 years of living at 160 pounds lighter: "I enjoy my life 100 percent more now."

Who would ever want to go back?

Recipes From the Masters

S OME OF THE FOLLOWING RECIPES stem from the masters' own "from-scratch" creations; others are the masters' adaptations of high-fat recipes. You'll find most of them simple to make from readily available ingredients. The recipes are clustered into three groups: "Soups, Salads and Accompaniments," "Main Dishes—Light to Hearty" and "Satisfying Sweets."

Each recipe contains nutrition information per serving for calories, fat, cholesterol, sodium, protein and carbohydrate. The recipes were analyzed by nutritionist Mary Jane Laus with the Massachusetts Nutrient Data Bank at the University of Massachusetts, Amherst.

The emphasis in these recipes is on lowering fat and calories, but not on lowering sodium. If you are on a low-sodium or other special diet, you may want to make some additional modifications, according to your physician's and/or dietitian's advice. Sodium values of commercial tomato products are particularly high. Homemade versions can be much lower in sodium.

Note that when an ingredient option is listed for a recipe—for instance, "jam or preserves"—the first ingredient was used to calculate nutritional data. Optional ingredients in recipes are not included in the analyses. If a range is given for an ingredient amount, the average was analyzed. Nutritional data for recipes are approximate.

A few words about specific foods:

• When eggs are used in a recipe, they are always large.

• A number of masters submitted recipes with ground turkey, which can be deceptively high in fat. In recipes calling for it, we purchased skinless turkey breast and had it ground at the supermarket. The taste was much preferred to that of regular ground turkey.

• Nonstick cooking spray, such as Pam, is used in many recipes and is not noted in the ingredient lists for recipes.

• When low-fat cheese is used in a recipe, it should contain no more than 5 grams of fat per ounce. (For the nutritional analyses, low-fat cheeses with 5 grams of fat per ounce were used.)

• Salad dressing should have no more than 25 calories per tablespoon.

• Hamburger for these recipes should be at least 85 percent lean.

Soups, Salads & Accompaniments

Thick and Hearty Bean Soup

Jordan F.

IT WAS LOVE AT FIRST TASTE with this satisfying soup, which makes plenty for leftovers. Says Jordan F., "This freezes well in individual servings. Take a serving of soup, a piece of bread and fruit for an excellent lunch."

1	pound mixture assorted dried beans
1	large carrot, sliced (1 cup)
1	large onion, chopped (about 1 cup)
1	cup sliced celery (about 2 stalks)
1	28-ounce can whole, peeled tomatoes, chopped (save juice)
1	tablespoon minced garlic
4	teaspoons chicken bouillon granules
3	quarts water
½	teaspoon dried basil
½	teaspoon dried oregano
¾	teaspoon ground cumin
1	6-ounce can tomato paste
	Tabasco sauce to taste (optional)

1. Soak beans overnight in enough water to cover and drain. Place in a large soup kettle.

2. Add carrots, onion, celery, tomatoes and their juice, garlic, bouillon granules, water, basil, oregano and cumin. Bring to a boil.

Reduce heat and simmer for about 2 hours.

3. Stir in tomato paste and cook for ½ hour longer. Season with Tabasco, if using.

Makes about 14 servings.

PER SERVING: CALORIES: 147; FAT: NEGLIGIBLE; CHOLESTEROL: 0 MG.; SODIUM: 450 MG.; PROTEIN: 9 G.; CARBOHYDRATE: 28 G.

Sweet and Sour Cabbage Soup

Don Mauer

DON SAYS, "When icy Chicago winds are really roaring, this soup can truly warm me up from the inside out." The recipe makes a large quantity and keeps well.

2	quarts defatted chicken broth
1	pound skinless, boneless turkey breast, cut into ½-inch cubes (about 3 cups)
1½	pounds green cabbage, coarsely chopped (6-7 cups)
2	medium-size ripe tomatoes, peeled and chopped (about 2 cups)
1	medium-size onion, chopped (about ⅔ cup)
1	small green bell pepper, finely diced (about ¾ cup)
1	large stalk celery, strings removed, thinly sliced (about ¾ cup)
1	large carrot, scraped and thinly sliced (about ¾ cup)
⅓	cup tomato paste
1¼	cups catsup
¼	cup light brown sugar
⅓	cup freshly squeezed lemon juice (about 1½ lemons)
1	teaspoon salt
½	teaspoon freshly ground black pepper

1. Place chicken broth in a large soup kettle over medium-high heat. Add cubed turkey and bring to a boil. Lower heat and simmer, skimming from time to time, for about 30 minutes.

2. Add cabbage, tomatoes, onion, green pepper, celery and carrot.

Stir in tomato paste, catsup, brown sugar, lemon juice, salt and black pepper. Cover and simmer gently for 1½ hours.

Makes about 14 servings.

PER SERVING: CALORIES: 101; FAT: 1 G.; CHOLESTEROL: 20 MG.; SODIUM: 729 MG.; PROTEIN: 12 G ; CARBOHYDRATE: 11 G.

Summer Garden Gazpacho

Karen S.

A GREAT WAY TO USE UP your end-of-summer garden overflow. Thick but light-tasting, this soup is great as an appetizer or a meal in itself when served with bread and low-fat cheese.

Hint: It's easiest to chop the first three ingredients in a food processor.

2½	cups diced fresh tomatoes (about 1 pound)
1½	cups finely chopped green bell pepper (1 large)
¾	cup finely chopped onion (1 medium-large)
3	small cloves garlic, minced
2	tablespoons snipped chives
1	teaspoon paprika
1	teaspoon salt
½	teaspoon sugar
	Freshly ground black pepper to taste
2	cups tomato or V-8 juice
1	medium-size cucumber, peeled, cut lengthwise, seeded and shredded with a grater (about 1 cup)
	Juice from ½ fresh lemon (about 2½ tablespoons)
	Tabasco sauce or horseradish to taste (optional)

1. In a large bowl, combine tomatoes, green pepper, onion, garlic, chives, paprika, salt, sugar and black pepper.

2. Stir in remaining ingredients. (If too chunky, process briefly in food processor.) Cover and chill at least 2 hours.

Serves 6 as an appetizer.

PER SERVING: CALORIES: 53; FAT: NEGLIGIBLE; CHOLESTEROL: 0 MG.; SODIUM: 656 MG.; PROTEIN: 12 G.; CARBOHYDRATE: 12 G.

Snow Peas and Carrots

Pat Baird

TURN PEAS AND CARROTS INTO A SIDE DISH festive enough for a holiday meal. The microwave brings out the natural flavors of the vegetables, so no one will notice that there is less butter than would normally be used. (Adapted from *Quick Harvest: A Vegetarian's Guide to Microwave Cooking* [Prentice Hall Press, 1991] by Pat Baird.)

1	medium onion, thinly sliced
4	teaspoons olive oil or butter
2	medium carrots, peeled and cut into 2-x-¼-inch strips
½	pound snow peas, strings removed
3	tablespoons chopped fresh dill or 2 teaspoons dried
	Salt and freshly ground black pepper to taste

1. In a 2-quart microwavable casserole or oval dish, combine onion and oil or butter, stirring well to coat. Microwave on high for 1 minute.

2. Stir in carrots; cover tightly with lid or vented plastic wrap. Microwave on high for 2 minutes.

3. Stir in snow peas and dill. Re-cover and microwave on high for 6 to 8 minutes, or until vegetables are tender-crisp. Let stand, covered, for 3 minutes. Add salt and pepper.

Makes 4 servings.

PER SERVING: CALORIES: 86; FAT: 5 G.; CHOLESTEROL: 0 MG.; SODIUM: 22 MG.; PROTEIN: 2 G.; CARBOHYDRATE: 9 G.

Weequahic Slaw

Karen S.

PRONOUNCED "WEEK-WAKE," this salad is a nice, light switch from traditional mayonnaise-laden coleslaw. It was inspired by a more oily version served at Karen's childhood country club. It keeps for days in the refrigerator.

1   16-ounce package coleslaw mix (about 7-8 cups shredded cabbage and carrots)
1   small onion, chopped (about ⅓ cup)
1   medium-size green pepper, diced (about 1 cup)
1   medium-size cucumber, peeled and thinly sliced (about 2 heaping cups)

Dressing

3-4   tablespoons apple-cider vinegar
3   tablespoons vegetable oil
1   tablespoon sugar
1   teaspoon salt

1. Mix vegetables in a large bowl.
2. In a small bowl, whisk together the dressing ingredients.
3. Toss dressing and vegetables together. Cover tightly. Refrigerate for at least 1 hour. (The mixture "shrinks" as it sits.)

Serves 6 generously.

PER SERVING: CALORIES: 107; FAT: 7 G.; CHOLESTEROL: 0 MG.; SODIUM: 375 MG.; PROTEIN: 2 G.; CARBOHYDRATE: 11 G.

Sensibly Thin Vegetable Salad

Sam Eukel

FOR A CHANGE OF PACE, this light, crunchy and attractive salad is a great alternative to a traditional tossed salad. It's also a good company salad because it's made hours in advance. (This recipe is adapted from one in *Sensibly Thin Low-Fat Living and Cooking* by Sam Eukel.)

3	cups broccoli florets (bite-size pieces)
3	cups cauliflower florets
1	cup sliced celery
½	cup pitted black olives (about 18 medium), sliced
1	16-ounce can button mushrooms, drained
1	18-ounce can sliced water chestnuts, drained
¾	cup fat-free Italian salad dressing

Combine all ingredients in a large bowl. Stir or cover and gently shake several times to coat vegetables. Chill for at least several hours before serving.

Serves 8.

PER SERVING: CALORIES: 59; FAT: 1 G.; CHOLESTEROL: 0 MG.; SODIUM: 451 MG.; PROTEIN: 3 G.; CARBOHYDRATE: 12 G.

New-Fashioned Creamy-Style Potato Salad

Don Mauer

THIS IS SO GOOD it's hard to believe it's no-fat. The red skins add color, and the celery gives it plenty of crunch. It makes a large batch—great picnic fare. This recipe is adapted from one first published in Don's Chicago-area *Daily Herald* column.

3	pounds medium-size red-skinned potatoes
4	stalks celery, diced (about 1¼ cups)
1	medium-size onion, chopped fine (about ⅔ cup)
1½	cups fat-free mayonnaise
1	tablespoon Dijon-style mustard
2	tablespoons chopped fresh parsley
1	teaspoon salt
	Generous grating black pepper
3	hard-cooked egg whites, chopped (optional)

1. Scrub potatoes under cold water. Bring a large pot of water to a boil; cook potatoes in it for 25 minutes. Drain, cool and refrigerate.

2. After potatoes are cold, coarsely chop them with skins still on. Place in a large bowl along with celery and onion.

3. In a small bowl, whisk together mayonnaise, mustard, parsley, salt and pepper.

4. Pour dressing over potato mixture and toss gently to combine. Cover and refrigerate.

Serves 10.

PER SERVING: CALORIES: 135; FAT: 0 G.; CHOLESTEROL: 0 MG.; SODIUM: 553 MG.; PROTEIN: 3 G.; CARBOHYDRATE: 32 G.

Pasta Salad

Kelly S.

THIS HEARTY, HEALTHFUL PASTA SALAD is a breeze to prepare. Make it in a large bowl, cover, and it keeps for days.

1	12-ounce package pasta (such as rotini, small or medium shells, spirelli or fusilli), cooked according to package directions and drained
4	cups frozen-vegetable mixture (such as cauliflower, broccoli and carrots)
1½	cups drained, canned kidney beans or chickpeas
¾	cup low-fat or fat-free liquid salad dressing
1	tablespoon Dijon-style mustard
	Generous grating black pepper

1. Combine pasta, vegetable mixture and kidney beans or chickpeas in a large bowl.

2. Mix together salad dressing and mustard in a small bowl.

3. Toss dressing with pasta mixture gently to combine. Refrigerate overnight, or until vegetables are thawed. Stir again before serving.

Serves 8.

PER SERVING: CALORIES: 244; FAT: 3 G.; CHOLESTEROL: 1 MG.; SODIUM: 392 MG.; PROTEIN: 9 G.; CARBOHYDRATE: 45 G.

Yellow Squash Custard

Bonnie R.

A TASTY AND FILLING RENDITION of an otherwise plain vegetable, this casserole can be served as a side dish with a light meal or as a main course with a large salad and bread.

7	medium-size or 12 small yellow summer squash (about 1½ pounds), sliced ¼ inch thick
1	medium-size onion, sliced
1	10¾-ounce can reduced-fat, reduced-sodium cream soup concentrate (any flavor)
1	egg plus 2 egg whites, beaten
1	cup unseasoned bread crumbs plus 2 tablespoons for topping
¼	pound grated reduced-fat Colby, mild Cheddar or Monterey Jack cheese (about 1 cup), lightly packed

1. Preheat oven to 350 degrees F. Steam squash and onion until very tender, about 20 minutes. Place in a large bowl and mash with a fork or potato masher.

2. With a wire whisk, mix soup and beaten eggs into squash mixture. Add 1 cup bread crumbs and mix well.

3. Coat an 8-x-8-inch baking pan with nonstick cooking spray. Spoon in squash mixture. Bake for 25 minutes. Sprinkle cheese evenly across top, then remaining 2 tablespoons bread crumbs. Bake for another 5 to 10 minutes, or until firm in the middle and piping hot.

Serves 6 as a side dish; 4 as a main course.

PER SIDE-DISH SERVING: CALORIES: 212; FAT: 6 G.; CHOLESTEROL: 50 MG.; SODIUM: 525 MG.; PROTEIN: 12 G.; CARBOHYDRATE: 27 G.

Creamy Leek Dip

Joanna M.

JOANNA ADAPTED THIS from a recipe given to her by a former exercise teacher. Even nondieters enjoy it.

2	cups 1% fat or nonfat small-curd cottage cheese
¼	cup skim milk
1	packet Knorr's leek soup mix
1	cup fresh parsley sprigs

1. In a food processor fitted with the metal blade, combine cottage cheese, skim milk and leek soup mix until smooth.

2. Add parsley and process until it is finely chopped. Place in a medium bowl and refrigerate for at least 2 hours. Serve with raw vegetables.

Makes about 2½ cups or 10 servings.

PER SERVING: CALORIES: 65; FAT: 1 G.; CHOLESTEROL: 3 MG.; SODIUM: 588 MG.; PROTEIN: 7 G.; CARBOHYDRATE: 6 G.

Rosy Red Beet Dip

Pat Baird

THIS LOW-CALORIE AND ALMOST FAT-FREE DIP has a stunning look that brightens any hors d'oeuvre tray. Use the microwave to cook the beets for about 10 minutes; then serve the dip in the center of steamed vegetables like broccoli, mushrooms and green and yellow squash. (Adapted from *Quick Harvest: A Vegetarian's Guide to Microwave Cooking* [Prentice Hall Press, 1991] by Pat Baird.)

4	medium beets, scrubbed, stems and roots trimmed
¾	cup nonfat ricotta cheese
2	tablespoons apple-cider vinegar or rice vinegar
2	tablespoons minced scallions
1	teaspoon Dijon-style mustard
½	teaspoon dried basil
½	teaspoon dried tarragon
	Salt to taste

1. Place beets in a shallow 1-quart microwavable casserole dish. Cover tightly with a lid or vented plastic wrap. Microwave on high for 10 to 12 minutes, or until beets are tender. Let stand, covered, for 3 minutes.

2. Drain and cool beets. Slip off skins under cold running water. Cut beets into 1-inch chunks.

3. In the workbowl of a food processor, process beets and remaining ingredients until mixture is smooth, stopping occasionally to scrape down the sides of the bowl. Add salt.

Makes about 2 cups or 8 servings.

PER SERVING: CALORIES: 25; FAT: NEGLIGIBLE; CHOLESTEROL: 1 MG.; SODIUM: 30 MG.; PROTEIN: 3 G.; CARBOHYDRATE: 3 G.

Buttermilk Salad Dressing

Don Mauer

MOST COMMERCIAL SALAD DRESSINGS, especially buttermilk-based dressings, are stratospherically high in fat, with as much as 90 percent of their calories from fat. This recipe has practically no calories from fat. The dressing is not only good for green salads but makes a delicious dip for raw vegetables, baked tortilla chips and nonfat potato chips. You can double it to make enough to last a week or more, since its flavor only improves over time. (Adapted from a recipe in *Lean and Lovin' It!—A Lean Cook's Book* by Don Mauer, published by Don Mauer and Associates, 1993.)

1	cup buttermilk
1	cup nonfat sour cream
¼	cup nonfat mayonnaise
1	tablespoon grated Parmesan cheese
2	small cloves garlic, minced
1	tablespoon minced fresh parsley
1	teaspoon grated onion
½	teaspoon freshly ground white pepper
¼	teaspoon dry mustard
¼	teaspoon salt

1. In a nonaluminum mixing bowl, combine all ingredients. Whisk together until completely combined.

2. Cover and chill.

Makes approximately 1¾ cups.

PER 2-TABLESPOON SERVING: CALORIES: 30; FAT: NEGLIGIBLE; CHOLESTEROL: 1 MG.; SODIUM: 126 MG.; PROTEIN: 2 G.; CARBOHYDRATE: 5 G.

Donny's Zippy Tartar Sauce

Don Mauer

"REGULAR TARTAR SAUCE IS DANGEROUS STUFF for people like me, " says master Don Mauer. "It's virtually all mayonnaise, which means something close to a whopping 99 percent of the calories come from fat. Yikes!" This is a fiery and virtually fat-free version. (Adapted from a recipe in *Lean and Lovin' It!—A Lean Cook's Book* by Don Mauer, published by Don Mauer and Associates, 1993.)

1¾	cups nonfat mayonnaise
2	tablespoons Dijon-style mustard
1	teaspoon Worcestershire sauce
½	teaspoon reduced-sodium soy sauce
¼	cup finely chopped fresh parsley leaves
2	tablespoons chopped fresh dill
2	tablespoons finely chopped dill pickle or dill-pickle relish
1	tablespoon chopped scallion, white part only
1	tablespoon drained capers
½	teaspoon cayenne pepper
½-1	teaspoon Tabasco sauce to taste

1. Place all ingredients in the bowl of a food processor fitted with the plastic blade.

2. Pulse several times, or until mixture is well combined. Place in a bowl or jar, cover and refrigerate for a few hours to allow the flavors to blend.

Makes approximately 2 cups.

PER 2-TABLESPOON SERVING: CALORIES: 17; FAT: NEGLIGIBLE; CHOLESTEROL: 0 MG.; SODIUM: 278 MG.; PROTEIN: NEGLIGIBLE; CARBOHYDRATE: 5 G.

Blueberry Yogurt Muffins

Don Mauer

ALTHOUGH LOW IN FAT, these muffins literally burst with the fresh flavor of blueberries. If you don't have a nonstick muffin pan, use a standard metal one sprayed with nonstick cooking spray. (Adapted from a recipe in *Lean and Lovin' It!—A Lean Cook's Book* by Don Mauer, published by Don Mauer and Associates, 1993.)

2	cups all-purpose flour
1	tablespoon baking powder
½	teaspoon salt
1	cup fresh blueberries, rinsed and picked over, plus 12 whole berries for garnish (frozen may be substituted)
4	egg whites, at room temperature
1½	cups plain nonfat yogurt, at room temperature
½	cup granulated sugar plus 3 teaspoons for sprinkling over tops
1	teaspoon vanilla

1. Preheat oven to 400 degrees F.

2. Sift together flour, baking powder and salt. Add blueberries to sifted dry ingredients. Stir lightly to coat. Set aside.

3. Place egg whites in the bowl of an electric mixer. Beat them at high speed until they hold soft peaks. Add yogurt, ½ cup sugar and vanilla. Mix for 30 to 45 seconds until combined. Add liquid mixture to dry ingredients and fold together just until flour is moistened. Batter should not be smooth. Do not overmix.

4. In a nonstick 12-cup muffin pan, divide batter evenly between the cups. Place 1 blueberry in the center of each muffin. Sprinkle ¼ teaspoon sugar evenly over each muffin. Bake for 20 minutes, or until tops are golden. Remove from the tins immediately and allow to cool. **Makes 12 muffins.**

PER MUFFIN: CALORIES: 137; FAT: NEGLIGIBLE; CHOLESTEROL: 0 MG.; SODIUM: 245 MG.; PROTEIN: 5 G.; CARBOHYDRATE: 29 G.

Zucchini Bread

Don Mauer

DON MAUER TRANSFORMED this zucchini bread from one containing as much fat as he normally allows himself for six days into an almost fat-free version. It also makes a delightful dessert when topped with a scoop of nonfat pineapple sorbet.

3	cups all-purpose flour
2	teaspoons baking soda
1½	teaspoons ground cinnamon
1	teaspoon salt
¾	teaspoon nutmeg, preferably freshly grated
¼	teaspoon baking powder
2	cups granulated sugar
1	cup unsweetened applesauce
1	egg plus 4 egg whites
2	teaspoons vanilla
2	cups shredded zucchini
1	8-ounce can crushed pineapple, well drained
1	cup chopped pitted dates
1	cup Grape-Nuts cereal

1. Preheat oven to 350 degrees F.

2. Sift together twice: flour, baking soda, cinnamon, salt, nutmeg and baking powder. Set aside.

3. In the large bowl of an electric mixer, beat sugar, applesauce, egg, egg whites and vanilla until sugar has dissolved. At low speed, add flour mixture and mix until dry ingredients are just moistened. (Batter will appear lumpy.) By hand, fold in zucchini, pineapple and dates.

4. Lightly spray the bottom and sides of two 9-x-5-inch loaf pans with nonstick cooking spray. Divide batter equally between the loaf pans. Sprinkle Grape-Nuts over the top of batter.

5. Bake 1 hour, or until a toothpick inserted in the center comes out clean. Remove the pans from the oven and set on a cooling rack. Cool 5 minutes, remove from pans and place on rack to cool completely.

Makes 2 loaves or 16 servings.
PER SERVING: CALORIES: 265; FAT: NEGLIGIBLE; CHOLESTEROL: 13 MG.; SODIUM:
367 MG.; PROTEIN: 5 G.; CARBOHYDRATE: 61 G.

Mexican Corn Bread

Bonnie R.

BONNIE'S SIMPLE ADAPTATIONS have turned a high-fat recipe into one that's
much lower in fat and calories. This corn bread can serve as a side dish or as
a light meal with low-fat sour cream or salsa on the side.

2	cups cornmeal
1½	cups skim milk
4	egg whites
1	15-to-17-ounce can cream-style corn
1	4-ounce can chopped mild green chilies
1	teaspoon baking soda
1	teaspoon salt
¾	pound extra-lean hamburger
1	medium-size onion, chopped (about ⅔ cup)
1½	cups grated low-fat Monterey Jack cheese (about 6 ounces)

1. Preheat oven to 350 degrees F. In a large bowl, mix cornmeal,
milk, egg whites, corn, chilies, baking soda and salt. Set batter aside.

2. Coat a large nonstick skillet with nonstick cooking spray. Brown hamburger over medium-high heat. Drain, blot with a paper towel and set aside.

3. Coat a 9-x-13-inch baking dish with nonstick cooking spray.
Pour half the batter into the dish.

4. Evenly sprinkle onion, cooked hamburger and grated cheese over
batter. Pour remaining batter over all and spread to cover filling. Bake
for 40 to 50 minutes, or until corn bread is done. (It will be firm to
the touch in the center and a toothpick should come out clean.)
Serves 10.
PER SERVING: CALORIES: 261; FAT: 7 G.; CHOLESTEROL: 31 MG.; SODIUM: 740 MG.;
PROTEIN: 16 G.; CARBOHYDRATE: 34 G.

Main Dishes : Light to Hearty

Egg and Potato Frittata for One
Jordan F.

THIS IS A TASTY, quick one-dish meal. Enjoy it for breakfast, lunch or supper. To further lower cholesterol, replace the whole eggs with a cholesterol-free egg substitute.

1 medium-size potato (about 6 ounces, preferably red or yellow fin variety), partially cooked by boiling or microwaving (it should still be quite firm)
1 medium-size onion, chopped (about ⅔ cup)
¼ cup defatted chicken broth
2 eggs, beaten
1 tablespoon grated Parmesan cheese
   Salt and freshly ground black pepper to taste

1. Dice the cooked potato, with skin, into ½-inch pieces. Set aside.
2. Coat a large nonstick skillet with nonstick cooking spray. Over medium heat, sauté onion in chicken broth until translucent.
3. Add chopped potato, cover, reduce heat and simmer until pieces are tender.
4. Pour eggs over vegetables and cook like a large pancake.
5. When eggs are firm, slide onto serving plate. Top with cheese and add salt and pepper. (For a kick, Jordan adds a little crushed red pepper.)
Serves 1.
PER SERVING: CALORIES: 338; FAT: 12 G.; CHOLESTEROL: 429 MG.; SODIUM: 705 MG.; PROTEIN: 19 G.; CARBOHYDRATE: 39 G.

Chicken Curried-Rice Salad

Mindy B.

PERFECT FOR LUNCH OR SUPPER, served on a bed of greens. Also delicious as an accompaniment to fresh cut-up fruits.

3	cups cooked white rice (let cool 15-20 minutes)
¾	pound raw chicken breast, cooked, cubed (1½ cups cooked)
⅓	cup currants
1	teaspoon curry powder
½	teaspoon onion powder
¼	teaspoon salt
⅓	cup slivered almonds
½	cup fat-free mayonnaise
½	cup nonfat plain yogurt
1	tablespoon olive oil
1	tablespoon freshly squeezed lime juice

1. Preheat oven to 350 degrees F. In a large bowl, combine rice, chicken, currants, curry, onion powder and salt. Refrigerate for about 30 minutes.

2. Meanwhile, toast almonds in the preheated oven for about 8 minutes, or until lightly browned. Stir into rice mixture. Combine mayonnaise, yogurt, olive oil and lime juice. Gently combine with chilled rice mixture. Refrigerate for several hours or overnight before serving.

Serves 4.

PER SERVING: CALORIES: 402; FAT: 10 G.; CHOLESTEROL: 52 MG.; SODIUM: 444 MG.; PROTEIN: 26 G.; CARBOHYDRATE: 51 G.

Cold Chicken and Pasta Salad

Don Mauer

THIS FOOLPROOF SUMMERTIME LUNCHEON is delicious served in the hollow of a cantaloupe or on lettuce.

3	cups defatted chicken broth
3	5-ounce skinless, boneless chicken breasts
5	ounces shell-shaped pasta (2 cups)
1	cup nonfat mayonnaise
½	teaspoon Dijon-style mustard
½	teaspoon celery salt
½	teaspoon freshly ground black pepper
2	ribs celery, cut crosswise into ⅛-inch slices
1	cup baby peas, cooked briefly, drained and cooled
1	cup seedless red grapes, washed, dried and sliced in half

1. In a medium saucepan, bring chicken broth to a simmer and add chicken breasts. Return to a simmer and cook for 20 minutes. Remove breasts, drain and chill. Save broth for another use.

2. Cook pasta according to package directions, drain and rinse under cold water. Set aside.

3. In a medium nonaluminum mixing bowl, whisk together mayonnaise, mustard, celery salt and pepper. Cut chicken breasts into bite-size pieces and add to the mixing bowl, along with pasta, celery, peas and grapes. Toss to combine. Cover and refrigerate.

Makes about 5 to 6 cups; serves 8.

PER SERVING: CALORIES: 173; FAT: 2 G.; CHOLESTEROL: 33 MG.; SODIUM: 535 MG.; PROTEIN: 16 G.; CARBOHYDRATE: 24 G.

Italian-Style Stuffed Zucchini

Carole C.

THIS MAKES A SUPER DINNER: it tastes as if it were prepared with high-fat Italian sausage. It is pretty enough to serve to company.

2	zucchini (8-to-9-inch)
⅓	cup chopped scallions or shallots
1	clove garlic, minced
2	cups finely chopped fresh mushrooms
½	pound extra-lean ground beef or ground turkey breast
¾	cup 1% fat cottage cheese
1	tablespoon grated Parmesan cheese
1	teaspoon dried basil
½	teaspoon dried oregano
	Generous grating black pepper
⅓	cup grated part-skim mozzarella cheese

1. Preheat broiler. Pierce whole zucchini several times and cook in the microwave, for 4 to 7 minutes on high. Or steam them whole for about 10 minutes on medium-high heat. (Zucchini should still be somewhat firm.) Set aside.

2. Coat a large nonstick skillet with nonstick cooking spray. Over medium-high heat, brown scallions or shallots, garlic, mushrooms and ground beef or turkey.

3. While meat is cooking, make "boats" out of zucchini by cutting them in half and scooping out the soft centers into a small bowl. (Be sure to leave some of the zucchini flesh next to the skin so that they are sturdy enough for stuffing.) Drain and gently squeeze liquid from zucchini insides. Add drained zucchini to meat mixture. Simmer until liquid evaporates.

4. Add cottage cheese, Parmesan, basil, oregano and pepper to meat mixture and stir until cheese is melted.

5. Stuff zucchini boats with meat-cheese mixture. (Use a slotted spoon so any extra juice drips off.) Evenly distribute mozzarella cheese over tops of boats. Place under broiler until cheese is melted and lightly

browned. (You can also bake these for 20 to 25 minutes at 350 degrees F if you want the zucchini softer.)

Serves 4.

PER SERVING: CALORIES: 199; FAT: 9 G.; CHOLESTEROL: 43 MG.; SODIUM: 277 MG.; PROTEIN: 20 G.; CARBOHYDRATE: 11 G.

Note: Zucchini boats can be made ahead and refrigerated. (Reserve mozzarella.) Preheat oven to 350 degrees F. Cover lightly with foil and bake for 30 to 40 minutes, or until centers are piping hot. Remove from oven and preheat broiler. Remove foil. Add mozzarella, return zucchini boats to oven and broil for 5 minutes, or until lightly browned.

Doug's Tuna-Noodle Casserole

Doug S.

A LOW-FAT TAKE-OFF on what we call in Minnesota "hot dish." A hot dish is basically any casserole, in this case, tuna-noodle.

1	can reduced-sodium, reduced-fat cream of mushroom soup concentrate
⅓	cup skim milk
1	cup spiral macaroni (rotini), cooked for the minimum amount of time according to package directions and drained
1	9-ounce package frozen French-cut green beans, cooked according to package directions and drained well (don't overcook)
2	4-ounce cans sliced mushrooms, drained well
1	6⅛-ounce can water-packed white tuna, drained and flaked
1	small onion, finely chopped (about ⅓ cup)
¾	cup crispy chow-mein noodles

1. Preheat oven to 350 degrees F. In a large bowl, whisk together soup and milk.

2. Add all other ingredients, except chow-mein noodles; combine.

3. Coat a small casserole dish with nonstick cooking spray. Bake, covered, for 35 to 40 minutes, or until bubbly. Uncover. If there is

excess liquid around edges, carefully drain. Top with chow-mein noodles, and continue baking another 15 minutes.
Serves 4.
PER SERVING: CALORIES: 277; FAT: 6 G.; CHOLESTEROL: 22 MG.; SODIUM: 688 MG.;
PROTEIN: 19 G.; CARBOHYDRATE: 38 G.

Enchilada Casserole

Mindy B.

THIS FILLING ONE-DISH MEAL is a hit with kids and adults alike. If desired, top with salsa and nonfat sour cream or plain yogurt.

½	pound ground turkey breast
1	medium-size onion, chopped (about ⅔ cup)
3	cups salsa or picante sauce
1	16-ounce package flour tortillas
1½	cups 1% fat cottage cheese mixed with 1 egg and 1 egg white
1	16-ounce can pinto beans, drained and rinsed
1	16-ounce can or one 9-to-10-ounce box frozen, thawed corn
1	4-ounce can chopped mild green chilies
1	cup grated low-fat Cheddar cheese (about ¼ pound)

1. Preheat oven to 350 degrees F. Spray a large nonstick skillet with nonstick cooking spray. Cook turkey and onion over medium-high heat, mashing with a fork to break up lumps, until turkey is browned. Add salsa or picante sauce and mix. Set aside.

2. Coat a 9-x-13-inch baking dish with nonstick cooking spray. Cover bottom and sides of dish with half the tortillas. (If necessary, cut them to fit and overlap them slightly.)

3. Spread half the turkey mixture over tortillas. Then top with layer of remaining tortillas.

4. Evenly spread cottage cheese-egg mixture over tortillas. Then top with a layer of each of the following: beans, corn and chilies.

5. Top with remaining turkey mixture, distributing it evenly.

Sprinkle with grated cheese. Bake 1 hour, or until piping hot in the center. (Lightly cover with foil for first ½ hour, making a tent so it doesn't stick to cheese. Remove foil for second ½ hour.)
Serves 8 generously.

PER SERVING: CALORIES: 429; FAT: 9 G.; CHOLESTEROL: 56 MG.; SODIUM: 1,592 MG.; PROTEIN: 27 G.; CARBOHYDRATE: 63 G.

Mallory's Lean Delight

Don Mauer

THIS RECIPE "comes from old family friends who shared the original high-fat version with my family more than 30 years ago." Don's version is filling, yet light on the fat.

1	large onion, chopped (about 1 cup)
1½	pounds ground turkey breast
1	15-to-16-ounce can tomato sauce
20	medium-size pitted black olives, drained and sliced
1	16-ounce can cream-style corn
1	tablespoon chili powder
½	teaspoon salt
1	8-ounce package elbow macaroni, cooked according to package directions and drained
1	cup unseasoned bread crumbs

1. Preheat oven to 350 degrees F. Coat a large nonstick saucepan with nonstick cooking spray. Over medium-high heat, sauté onion for about 2 minutes. Add ground turkey and sauté until no longer pink.

2. Stir in tomato sauce, olives, corn, chili powder and salt. Bring to a simmer and remove from heat.

3. Coat a 9-x-13-inch casserole with nonstick cooking spray. Evenly distribute macaroni across bottom. Top with turkey mixture. Sprinkle bread crumbs over top. Bake for about 45 minutes, or until piping hot. **Makes 8 large servings.**

PER SERVING: CALORIES: 333; FAT: 3 G.; CHOLESTEROL: 57 MG.; SODIUM: 862 MG.; PROTEIN: 28 G.; CARBOHYDRATE: 49 G.

Chili-Cheese Casserole

Diane J.

A ZESTY COMBINATION of cheeses, bread, eggs and green chilies. For even more pizzazz, you could top each serving with a dollop of nonfat sour cream and salsa. Serve as a main dish with a shredded carrot salad and a steamed vegetable, such as broccoli.

¼	pound shredded low-fat Monterey Jack cheese (about 1 cup, lightly packed)
2	ounces shredded part-skim mozzarella cheese (about ¾ cup)
¼	cup chopped onion
¼	cup canned chopped mild green chilies
6	slices whole-wheat bread
2	tablespoons Dijon-style mustard
3	cups evaporated skim milk
4	eggs, lightly beaten
½	teaspoon salt
½	teaspoon freshly ground black pepper

1. Preheat oven to 350 degrees F. In a medium bowl, toss together cheeses, onion and chilies. Set aside.

2. Spread bread with mustard and cut into 1-inch squares. Coat a 1½-quart baking dish with nonstick cooking spray. Cover bottom with half the bread, then half the cheese mixture. Repeat.

3. With a wire whisk, lightly mix milk, eggs, salt and pepper. Pour over cheese and bread. Press bread lightly into liquid to moisten.

4. Put the baking dish into a larger pan and pour 1 inch of hot water into the large pan. Bake 45 to 50 minutes, or until a knife inserted in the center comes out clean.

Serves 6.

PER SERVING: CALORIES: 305; FAT: 10 G.; CHOLESTEROL: 162 MG.; SODIUM: 792 MG.; PROTEIN: 25 G.; CARBOHYDRATE: 30 G.

Vegetable Lasagna

Mindy B.

A MEAT-FREE RENDITION of the traditional version. Serve with Italian bread and a romaine lettuce salad.

1	12-ounce container 1% fat cottage cheese
1	cup part-skim ricotta cheese
1	10-ounce package frozen chopped spinach, cooked according to package directions, drained and squeezed lightly
1	26-ounce jar reduced-fat spaghetti sauce
8	lasagna noodles, cooked according to package directions and drained
2	cups zucchini (about ½ pound raw), cut in ¼-inch slices, lightly steamed for about 5 minutes and drained
1	16-ounce can Italian green beans, drained, or one 9-to-10-ounce package frozen, cooked and drained
½	pound grated part-skim mozzarella cheese (about 2 cups)

1. Preheat oven to 350 degrees F. In a medium bowl, combine cottage cheese, ricotta and spinach. Set aside.

2. Coat a 9-x-13-inch baking pan with nonstick cooking spray. Spread 1 cup spaghetti sauce on bottom of pan.

3. Top with a layer of 4 cooked noodles, then half the cottage cheese mixture. Spread evenly.

4. Top with a layer of each of the following: all the zucchini, 1 cup spaghetti sauce, all the green beans. Top with 4 more noodles.

5. Spread evenly with remaining cottage-cheese mixture. Top with remaining spaghetti sauce. Bake, lightly covered, for about 30 minutes. Sprinkle with mozzarella cheese and continue baking, uncovered, for another 15 to 20 minutes, or until piping hot in the center.
Serves 8.

PER SERVING: CALORIES: 269; FAT: 8 G.; CHOLESTEROL: 28 MG.; SODIUM: 761 MG.;
PROTEIN: 21 G.; CARBOHYDRATE: 30 G.

No-Stir Five-Minute Risotto With Salmon

Pat Baird

CLASSIC RISOTTOS normally require about 30 minutes of continual stirring and are often made with lots of oil and cheese. Cooking the rice in a pressure cooker reduces the preparation time to just 5 minutes. This recipe also whittles the oil down to just a tablespoon, yet the results are rich and creamy-tasting. This dish can also be made on the stovetop. (Adapted from *Quick Harvest: A Vegetarian's Guide to Microwave Cooking* [Prentice Hall Press, 1991], by Pat Baird.)

Hint: If you're using canned broth—and you can't find a low-sodium one—dilute it with half water so the risotto isn't too salty.

1	tablespoon extra-virgin olive oil
1	cup coarsely chopped onions
1½	cups Arborio or other short-grain rice
3½-4	cups defatted low-sodium vegetable or chicken broth
¼	cup chopped fresh Italian (flat-leaf) parsley
½	pound salmon fillet, cut in 1-inch pieces
⅓	cup grated Parmesan cheese
	Salt and freshly ground black pepper

Pressure-Cooker Method:

1. In a 6-quart pressure cooker, heat oil over medium heat; stir in onions and cook for 1 minute. Add rice, stirring thoroughly to coat with oil. Stir in 3½ cups broth and parsley.

2. Lock the lid in place and bring to high pressure over high heat. Lower the heat just enough to maintain high pressure; cook 5 minutes longer. Reduce pressure immediately and remove the lid, making sure to tilt the pot away from you to allow excess steam to escape. (The risotto may be quite soupy, but it will continue to absorb liquid. If the risotto is still undercooked and needs more liquid, on the other hand, add a bit more broth.)

3. Over low heat, stir in salmon, cheese, salt and pepper to taste. Cook for 1 minute, until salmon is opaque. Ladle into shallow soup bowls. Sprinkle with more pepper.

Stovetop Method:

In a large heavy skillet, heat oil and stir in onions. Cook for 1 minute. Add rice, stirring thoroughly to coat with oil. Stir in ½ cup of broth, and stir constantly until almost absorbed. Add remaining broth, ½ cup at a time, stirring constantly, until grains are cooked through but not mushy and mixture is soupy. Stir in salmon and cheese, and salt and pepper to taste and cook 1 minute longer. Serve as directed above.

Serves 4.

PER SERVING: CALORIES: 482; FAT: 12 G.; CHOLESTEROL: 42 MG.; SODIUM: 526 MG.; PROTEIN: 25 G.; CARBOHYDRATE: 64 G.

Tuna and Pasta for Two

Muriel F.

THIS RECIPE has a pleasant lemon-garlic taste. Serve with crusty bread and a large spinach salad.

2	teaspoons minced garlic
3	tablespoons defatted chicken broth
1	14.5-ounce can stewed tomatoes
3	tablespoons freshly squeezed lemon juice
½	teaspoon dried basil
½	teaspoon dried oregano
1	6⅛-ounce can water-packed white tuna, drained and flaked
1	cup elbow macaroni, cooked according to package directions and drained
4	teaspoons grated Parmesan cheese

1. In a large nonstick skillet, over medium-high heat, sauté garlic in chicken broth for a minute or two. (Don't brown.)

2. Add tomatoes, lemon juice, basil and oregano. Bring to a boil, then reduce heat and simmer, uncovered, for about 3 minutes.

3. Stir in tuna. Remove from heat and serve immediately over macaroni. Top with Parmesan cheese.

Serves 2 generously.

PER SERVING: CALORIES: 462; FAT: 5 G.; CHOLESTEROL: 39 MG.; SODIUM: 1,063 MG.; PROTEIN: 35 G.; CARBOHYDRATE: 70 G.

Quick and Spicy Scallops and Peppers
Don Mauer

NOT ONLY ARE SCALLOPS sweet and tasty morsels, but they are very low in fat. This is wonderful served over rice. (Adapted from a recipe in *Lean and Lovin' It!—A Lean Cook's Book* by Don Mauer, published by Don Mauer and Associates, 1993.)

2	teaspoons extra-virgin olive oil
1	green bell pepper, thinly sliced
1	yellow bell pepper, thinly sliced
1	red bell pepper, sliced thin
1	jalapeño pepper, seeded and thinly sliced
1	scallion, chopped
2	tablespoons dry white wine
2	tablespoons freshly squeezed lemon juice
2	tablespoons freshly squeezed lime juice
2	teaspoons Tabasco sauce
1	pound bay scallops, cleaned, rinsed and patted dry
1	tablespoon minced fresh basil leaves or 1 teaspoon dried
1	teaspoon salt

1. In a large nonstick skillet, heat olive oil over medium-high heat. Add peppers and scallion and cook, stirring, for 3 minutes.

2. Add wine, lemon juice, lime juice and Tabasco sauce and continue to cook for 1 minute.

3. Add scallops, basil and salt and stir to combine. Cover and cook 3 to 4 minutes over medium heat, or until scallops are cooked through.

Serves 4.

PER SERVING: CALORIES: 159; FAT: 3 G.; CHOLESTEROL: 38 MG.; SODIUM: 720 MG.; PROTEIN: 20 G.; CARBOHYDRATE: 11 G.

Fish With Summer Vegetables

Don Mauer

THE BEST TIME TO PREPARE this dish is during the summer months when small squash and plum tomatoes are easy to find at your local farmer's market. Serve with steamed baby peas.

3	teaspoons olive oil
2	cups thinly sliced onions
½	teaspoon salt
½	teaspoon freshly ground black pepper
2	pounds firm, white fish fillets (such as red snapper, black bass, halibut or cod), cut into four 8-ounce pieces
1	tablespoon chopped fresh basil (optional)
1	small yellow summer squash (¼ pound), thinly sliced crosswise
1	small zucchini (¼ pound), thinly sliced crosswise
	Juice of 1 lemon
2	ripe plum tomatoes, diced (canned may be substituted)
2	tablespoons chopped shallots

1. Preheat oven to 475 degrees F. Heat 2 teaspoons olive oil over medium heat in a nonstick skillet and add onions. Cook, stirring frequently, for 15 minutes or until lightly browned. Set aside.

2. Spray the bottom and sides of a casserole dish just large enough to hold 3 pieces of fish with nonstick cooking spray. Sprinkle the bottom with ¼ teaspoon salt and ¼ teaspoon pepper. Place fillets, skin-side down, in the bottom without overlapping them. Distribute basil and cooked onion evenly over fillets.

3. Place squash and zucchini in a medium nonaluminum mixing bowl. Add lemon juice, remaining 1 teaspoon olive oil, and remaining ¼ teaspoon salt and ¼ teaspoon pepper, tossing to combine.

4. Distribute squash mixture evenly over fillets. Pour remaining liquid from the bowl over fillets. Distribute tomatoes and shallots around, not over, fillets. Bake for 15 to 20 minutes, or until fish is just beginning to flake in the center.

5. To serve, slide spatula under each fillet and place on a serving plate; serve tomatoes and shallots on the side.

Serves 4 generously.

PER SERVING: CALORIES: 302; FAT: 7 G.; CHOLESTEROL: 83 MG.; SODIUM: 374 MG.; PROTEIN: 48 G.; CARBOHYDRATE: 11 G.

Summery Swordfish With Vegetables and Cilantro

Jordan F.

A COLORFUL, LIGHT WAY to serve any fish steak—be it swordfish, shark, halibut or fresh tuna. The lime juice and cilantro highlight the taste of the fish and vegetables.

¼	cup defatted chicken broth
1½	pounds swordfish steak, cut into 1-inch cubes
2	stalks celery, sliced ¼ inch thick on an angle
1	medium-size bell pepper (red, yellow or green), cut in thin strips
1	medium-size tomato, chopped (about 1 heaping cup, drained of excess juice)
2	tablespoons freshly squeezed lime juice
1	teaspoon salt
2	tablespoons dry white wine
2	tablespoons chopped fresh cilantro

1. In a large nonstick skillet, heat chicken broth to a boil over medium-high heat. Add swordfish and sauté for 2 to 3 minutes, turning several times. (Fish will not be done.) With a slotted spoon or spatula, gently remove fish to a plate and set aside.

2. Sauté celery and pepper in remaining broth for about 2 minutes. Drain excess liquid. Add tomato, lime juice and salt. Bring to a boil and cook for another minute or two. Stir in wine.

3. Quickly drain fish of any standing liquid and add fish to vegetable mixture. Cover and cook, stirring once or twice, for another 2 to 3 minutes, or until fish just starts to flake. Remove from the skillet,

using a slotted spoon or spatula, topping with some of the juices if desired. Sprinkle with cilantro and serve immediately.

Serves 4.

PER SERVING: CALORIES: 233; FAT: 7 G.; CHOLESTEROL: 66 MG.; SODIUM: 801 MG.; PROTEIN: 35 G.; CARBOHYDRATE: 5 G.

Pasta-Shrimp Primavera

Gail M.

THIS DISH GETS AN A+ for color and eye appeal. It is simple to prepare, too.

1	14½-ounce can chunky tomatoes
1	cup reduced-fat spaghetti sauce
2	cups broccoli florets
2	cups cauliflower florets
2	cups sliced carrots (about 3 large carrots)
1	medium-size red bell pepper, sliced
1	pound medium-size shrimp, shelled, deveined and steamed until done
1	12-ounce package linguine, cooked according to package directions and drained (cover to keep warm)
8	teaspoons grated Parmesan cheese

1. In a medium saucepan, combine tomatoes with spaghetti sauce. Cover and bring to boil, then reduce heat and simmer.

2. In a large pan, steam broccoli, cauliflower and carrots, covered, for 4 to 5 minutes. Add pepper and steam for another 3 to 4 minutes. (Vegetables should be tender-crisp, not soft.)

3. In a large bowl, combine vegetables, shrimp and linguine. Toss lightly. Divide mixture among four individual serving plates. Ladle on tomato mixture. Sprinkle each serving with 2 teaspoons Parmesan cheese.

Serves 4 generously.

PER SERVING: CALORIES: 538; FAT: 4 G.; CHOLESTEROL: 140 MG.; SODIUM: 903 MG.; PROTEIN: 33 G.; CARBOHYDRATE: 95 G.

Baked Chicken With Orange-Apricot Sauce

Karen S.

CHICKEN IS COMPLEMENTED by an apricot and bread-crumb coating. Serve with brown rice and a marinated green bean salad.

2	whole bone-in chicken breasts (about 2 pounds), split in half and skinned
⅔	cup nonfat Italian salad dressing
1	cup seasoned bread crumbs
½	cup orange juice
¼	cup apricot preserves

1. Marinate chicken in Italian dressing for at least 1 hour, turning occasionally.

2. When chicken is finished marinating, preheat oven to 350 degrees F. One by one, shake excess dressing from each chicken breast and dredge breasts in seasoned bread crumbs.

3. Place chicken on a baking sheet that has been sprayed with non-stick cooking spray. Bake for 40 to 45 minutes.

4. While chicken is cooking, in a blender, mix orange juice with apricot preserves until just blended.

5. Remove chicken from oven. Spoon half the orange-juice mixture over chicken. Return chicken to oven and continue baking for 10 minutes. Spoon remaining orange-juice mixture over chicken and bake about 10 minutes more, or until chicken is completely done—when the juices run clear and no pink remains.

Serves 4.

PER SERVING: CALORIES: 338; FAT: 5 G.; CHOLESTEROL: 92 MG.; SODIUM: 1,021 MG.; PROTEIN: 38 G.; CARBOHYDRATE: 35 G.

Sam's Ham

Sam Eukel

LIGHT, LEAN HAM with fruit and yams makes a colorful, complete meal when served with a salad like Weequahic Slaw (page 272). (This recipe is adapted from one in *Sensibly Thin Low-Fat Living and Cooking* by Sam Eukel.)

1	20-ounce can pineapple rings, in juice
1	15-to-16-ounce can halved pears, in juice
1	15-to-16-ounce can halved peaches, in juice
¼	teaspoon pumpkin-pie spice
¼	cup brown sugar
1	teaspoon dry mustard
2	pounds fully cooked ham, very lean
2	16-to-17-ounce cans unsweetened yams

1. Preheat oven to 350 degrees F. Set aside ½ cup pineapple juice. In a large bowl, combine all fruit, 1½ cups of remaining juice (any type) and pie spice. Set aside.

2. Combine reserved ½ cup pineapple juice, brown sugar and dry mustard. Place ham and yams in a large baking pan that has been coated with nonstick cooking spray. Pour pineapple-juice mixture over hams and yams. Bake, uncovered, for about 50 minutes, or until internal temperature registers 140 degrees, basting with juice several times while cooking.

3. While ham is cooking, gently stir spiced fruit several times. When ham is done, drain fruit and arrange around ham. Bake 15 minutes longer. Just before serving, "fan" ham by cutting 12 thin slices, but avoid cutting all the way through. Serve with some pan juices.

Serves 6.

PER SERVING: CALORIES: 434; FAT: 8 G.; CHOLESTEROL: 58 MG.; SODIUM: 2,017 MG.; PROTEIN: 32 G.; CARBOHYDRATE: 62 G.

Turkey Meat Loaf

Wendy M.

THIS HEARTY MEAT LOAF could easily pass for the hamburger version, were it not for its lighter color. It is great topped with grated horseradish and served with baked potatoes and low-fat coleslaw such as Weequahic Slaw (page 272) or Sensibly Thin Vegetable Salad (page 273).

1½	pounds ground turkey breast
½	cup Italian bread crumbs
½	cup uncooked oatmeal
½	cup catsup
½	cup skim milk
2	tablespoons soy sauce
1	large onion, chopped (about 1 cup)
1	egg
	Generous grating black pepper

1. Preheat oven to 350 degrees F. In a large bowl, thoroughly combine all ingredients.

2. Place mixture in a 9-x-5-inch loaf pan coated with nonstick cooking spray. Bake until internal temperature is at least 160 degrees, about 1¼ hours. (If you don't have a meat thermometer, toward the end of cooking time, cut a slit in the middle and cook until juices run clear—not pink— and meat has lost its pink or reddish color.
Serves 8.

PER SERVING: CALORIES: 180; FAT: 2 G.; CHOLESTEROL: 84 MG.; SODIUM: 686 MG.; PROTEIN: 25 G.; CARBOHYDRATE: 16 G.

Donny's Pita Pizza

Don Mauer

DON SAYS THAT THIS RECIPE was born three years ago, while he was in the process of losing weight. As a guest at a small party, he was served wedges of pita smeared with sauce and sprinkled with cheese. The next day, he started experimenting in his kitchen and came up with his own pita pizza. (Adapted from a recipe in *Lean and Lovin' It!—A Lean Cook's Book* by Don Mauer, published by Don Mauer and Associates, 1993.)

6	6-to-7-inch pita breads (about 12 ounces)
¾	cup (12 tablespoons) reduced-fat spaghetti sauce
6-8	fresh mushrooms, cleaned and thinly sliced
3	scallions, trimmed and chopped (including several inches of the green part)
1	medium-size green pepper, seeds and stem removed, chopped coarsely
½	pound Lean-Style Italian Sausage *(recipe follows)*, browned

in nonstick pan with ½ teaspoon olive oil and crumbled

½	pound part-skim mozzarella cheese, grated (about 2 cups)

1. Preheat oven to 425 degrees F. Place pita breads on baking sheets. Spread 2 tablespoons spaghetti sauce over the surface of each pita, almost to the edge.

2. Divide mushrooms, scallions, pepper and sausage among pitas. Top each with a sprinkling of mozzarella.

3. Bake for 12 to 16 minutes. Remove from oven and cut into fourths. Serve immediately.

Serves 4 as a dinner with a large salad; serves 10 to 12 as an appetizer.

PER DINNER SERVING: CALORIES: 482; FAT: 14 G.; CHOLESTEROL: 70 MG.; SODIUM: 1,082 MG.; PROTEIN: 36 G.; CARBOHYDRATE: 57 G.

Lean-Style Italian Sausage

Don Mauer

THIS REDUCED-FAT SAUSAGE is very tasty. Don "invented" it to satisfy his past passion for cheese-and-sausage pizza. (From *Lean and Lovin' It!—A Lean Cook's Book* by Don Mauer, published by Don Mauer and Associates, 1993.)

2	pounds pork tenderloin, trimmed of all fat
½	medium-size onion, minced
1	medium-size clove garlic, minced
1½	teaspoons salt
1	teaspoon whole fennel seed
1	teaspoon paprika
½	teaspoon freshly ground black pepper
½	small bay leaf, stem removed, crushed
	Pinch dried thyme
¼	cup dry red wine or defatted chicken stock

Optional for "hot" sausage:

½	teaspoon hot red-pepper flakes

1. Cut pork into 1-inch cubes and feed it through a meat grinder intermittently with onion and garlic. (Pork may also be ground in a food processor by carefully pulsing with the steel blade. Add onion and garlic when meat is almost ground.)

2. Place ground-pork mixture in a large nonaluminum mixing bowl. Add remaining ingredients except wine or chicken stock. Mix well. Add wine or chicken stock. Mix well but do not overmix or over-handle.

3. Sausage mixture may be divided into 8 equal patties and frozen. **Makes 8 four-to-five-ounce patties.**

PER UNCOOKED PATTY: CALORIES: 147; FAT: 4 G.; CHOLESTEROL: 74 MG.; SODIUM: 458 MG.; PROTEIN: 24 G.; CARBOHYDRATE: 1 G.

Dogs in a Blanket

Paul A.

PAUL SAYS HE ADAPTED this from a low-calorie pancake recipe. He adds, "My family couldn't believe that a low-cal lunch could actually taste like fast food." Serve with mustard and catsup.

4	reduced-fat hot dogs
1	cup plus 2 tablespoons all-purpose flour
1	teaspoon baking powder
½	teaspoon baking soda
1	tablespoon granulated sugar
¼	teaspoon salt
1	cup nonfat plain yogurt
¼	cup water
2	tablespoons plus 2 teaspoons reduced-calorie margarine, melted
2	eggs
1	teaspoon vanilla

1. Preheat oven to 350 degrees F. Boil hot dogs for about 5 minutes or until steaming hot. Set aside. In a large bowl, stir together flour, baking powder, baking soda, sugar and salt. Set aside.

2. In a medium bowl, whisk together yogurt, water, margarine, eggs and vanilla. Whisk this mixture into the dry ingredients just until smooth.

3. Pour half the batter over the bottom of a 1½-quart baking dish or an 8-x-8-inch pan that has been coated with nonstick cooking spray. Evenly distribute batter.

4. Evenly space cooked hot dogs on batter. Cover with remaining batter. Bake for 20 to 25 minutes, or until batter is firm.

Serves 4.

PER SERVING: CALORIES: 297; FAT: 10 G.; CHOLESTEROL: 134 MG.; SODIUM: 1,032 MG.; PROTEIN: 15 G.; CARBOHYDRATE: 35 G.

Satisfying Sweets

Angel Food Berry Trifle

Karen S.

TRULY PRETTY COMPANY FARE: no one will ever guess how easy it is to prepare. It is refreshing after any meal.

- 1   cup boiling water
- 1   0.6-ounce package sugar-free strawberry-flavored gelatin
- 1   pint low-fat strawberry frozen yogurt (2 cups)
- 1   16-ounce angel food cake, cut into ½-inch slices
- 2   cups sliced strawberries or whole small berries, such as blueberries (or 1 cup each)
- 1   cup reduced-calorie Cool Whip

1. In a medium bowl, add boiling water to gelatin. Stir until dissolved. Add frozen yogurt and stir until melted. Set aside.

2. Layer the following in a glass trifle bowl (or any large bowl): cake, gelatin mixture, berries. Repeat twice, eliminating fruit on the last layer. Chill for at least 3 to 4 hours, or until gelatin mixture is set. Serve each portion with 2 tablespoons Cool Whip.
Serves 8.

PER SERVING: CALORIES: 240; FAT: 4 G.; CHOLESTEROL: 1 MG.; SODIUM: 505 MG.; PROTEIN: 6 G.; CARBOHYDRATE: 46 G.

Diane's Berry-Jam Roll

Diane J.

SIMPLE AND ELEGANT, this dessert is easy to make and skimps on fat and calories.

	Parchment paper
3	eggs, separated
¼	cup granulated sugar
1	tablespoon cornstarch
1	teaspoon vanilla
½	cup part-skim ricotta cheese
⅓	cup strawberry or raspberry jam or preserves

1. Preheat oven to 375 degrees F. Dampen a 9-x-13-inch cake pan with a little water, then line with parchment paper, making sure the bottom of the pan is covered. Coat paper with nonstick cooking spray. Set aside.

2. In a medium bowl, with an electric mixer, beat egg whites until stiff but not dry. (Peaks should just fold over when beaters are removed.) Set aside.

3. In a large bowl, beat egg yolks until thick and light lemon-colored. Beat in sugar gradually. Continue to beat until thickened. Fold cornstarch and vanilla into egg yolks. (Smooth out any lumps of cornstarch.)

4. Carefully fold egg whites into yolk mixture, then pour batter into prepared pan. Smooth evenly with spatula to edge of pan. Bake for 8 to 10 minutes, or until cake springs back when gently pressed.

5. Turn pan upside down on a towel-covered cooling rack. Cake should come right out, with parchment on top of it. Peel off parchment, then carefully roll cake up in a clean dishtowel. Cool.

6. When cake is cool, unroll and spread lightly with ricotta cheese, then jam or preserves. Roll cake to enclose filling. Place on plate, seam-side down. Refrigerate for 1 to 2 hours, then serve right away. **Serves 4.**

PER SERVING: CALORIES: 222; FAT: 6 G.; CHOLESTEROL: 169 MG.; SODIUM: 97 MG.; PROTEIN: 8 G.; CARBOHYDRATE: 34 G.

Peach Cobbler

Sam Eukel

A LOW-FAT BUT FLAVORFUL version of an old favorite. It is especially good topped with a scoop of vanilla ice milk or frozen yogurt. (This recipe was adapted from one in *Sensibly Thin Low-Fat Living and Cooking* by Sam Eukel.)

2	16-ounce cans sliced peaches in juice
¼	cup packed brown sugar
1	tablespoon cornstarch
½	teaspoon ground cinnamon
¼	teaspoon ground nutmeg
1	cup unsifted all-purpose flour
1	tablespoon granulated sugar
2	teaspoons baking powder
¼	teaspoon salt
2	tablespoons margarine
½	cup skim milk

1. Preheat oven to 450 degrees F. Coat an 8-x-8-inch baking dish with nonstick cooking spray. Drain peaches, reserving ¾ cup juice. In a medium saucepan, combine brown sugar, cornstarch, cinnamon and nutmeg. Blend in reserved ¾ cup juice.

2. Bring mixture to a boil over medium-high heat, stirring constantly. Stir in peaches. Pour into the baking dish. Set aside.

3. In medium bowl, combine flour, sugar, baking powder and salt. Cut in margarine until mixture resembles coarse meal. Add milk. Stir to moisten. Drop by tablespoonfuls over fruit mixture. Bake for 15 minutes. Best if served warm.

Serves 6.

PER SERVING: CALORIES: 217; FAT: 4 G.; CHOLESTEROL: 0 MG.; SODIUM: 315 MG.; PROTEIN: 4 G.; CARBOHYDRATE: 43 G.

Apple Charlotte

Diane J.

THIS DESSERT is a cross between apple crisp and bread pudding.

3	slices whole-wheat bread
3	teaspoons diet margarine
3	medium-size apples (about 1⅓ pounds), such as Granny Smith, peeled and very thinly sliced (about 4 cups)
2	tablespoons orange-juice concentrate
1	tablespoon plus 1 teaspoon freshly squeezed lemon juice
¼	cup raisins
2	tablespoons light brown sugar
¼	teaspoon ground cinnamon

Topping

½	cup all-purpose flour
¼	cup light brown sugar
½	teaspoon ground cinnamon
3	tablespoons diet margarine

1. Preheat oven to 425 degrees F. Spread each slice of bread with 1 teaspoon margarine. Cut each slice into ½-inch cubes and set aside.

2. In a medium bowl, combine apple slices with orange juice, lemon juice, raisins, brown sugar and cinnamon. Add bread and toss to combine. Coat a 6-x-10-inch baking dish with nonstick cooking spray and evenly distribute apple-bread mixture in it.

3. *To prepare topping:* combine flour, brown sugar, cinnamon and margarine until crumbly.

4. Crumble topping over surface of apple mixture. Bake 30 to 40 minutes, or until apples are tender.

Serves 6.

PER SERVING: CALORIES: 231; FAT: 7G.; CHOLESTEROL: 0 MG.; SODIUM: 175 MG.; PROTEIN: 3 G.; CARBOHYDRATE: 42 G.

Fat-Free Chocolate Sauce

Diane J.

DIANE RECOMMENDS serving this sauce over fresh fruit, pudding, frozen yogurt, low-fat cheesecake or angel food cake.

¾   cup granulated sugar
¼   cup unsweetened cocoa
1   tablespoon plus 1 teaspoon cornstarch
½   cup evaporated skim milk
1   teaspoon vanilla

1. Mix dry ingredients in a small saucepan. Add milk slowly, stirring.
2. Cook over medium heat, stirring constantly until sauce is thickened. Cook for 2 minutes longer, continuing to stir. Remove from heat and add vanilla.

Makes about ¾ cup or 6 servings.

PER SERVING: CALORIES: 131; FAT: NEGLIGIBLE; CHOLESTEROL: 1 MG.; SODIUM: 26 MG.; PROTEIN: 2 G.; CARBOHYDRATE: 31 G.

Black Bottom Cupcakes

Don Mauer

THE ORIGINAL VERSION of this recipe contained ⅓ cup vegetable oil, a whole egg, 6 ounces chocolate chips and lots of pecans, according to Don Mauer. "Hating to give up this cupcake confection, I made several changes that retained the moisture and rich flavor but removed almost all the fat." (From *Lean and Lovin' It!—A Lean Cook's Book* by Don Mauer, published by Don Mauer and Associates, 1993.)

Chocolate Chip Filling
2   egg whites, at room temperature
8   ounces Healthy Choice fat-free cream cheese, at room
     temperature (Don finds this brand works best)
⅓   cup granulated sugar

½ teaspoon vanilla
1 ounce mini-morsel semisweet chocolate chips (scant ¼ cup)

Cupcake Batter

1½ cups all-purpose flour
¼ cup unsweetened cocoa
1 teaspoon baking soda
1 teaspoon baking powder
½ teaspoon salt
1 cup granulated sugar
1 cup water
½ cup nonfat plain yogurt
1 teaspoon vanilla

Foil cupcake cups
2 tablespoons finely chopped pecans

1. Preheat oven to 350 degrees F. *To prepare filling:* in a small bowl, with an electric mixer, beat egg whites until foamy. Blend in cream cheese, sugar and vanilla until smooth. Stir in chocolate chips. Set aside.

2. *To prepare batter:* into a large bowl, sift together flour, cocoa, baking soda, baking powder and salt. Set aside.

3. In another large bowl, with an electric mixer, combine sugar, water, yogurt and vanilla. Mix until smooth, about 1 minute. Add dry ingredients and mix at low speed until barely moistened. Do not over-mix.

4. Line cupcake pans with 20 foil cupcake cups. Spray lightly with nonstick cooking spray. Fill each cup about half-full with batter. Top each with 1 tablespoon filling. (Add any leftover filling to less-full cups.) Sprinkle each cupcake with pecans.

5. Bake for 25 to 28 minutes, or until tops spring back when gently pressed. Cool. (Cupcakes will sink a little after cooling.)

Makes 20 cupcakes.

PER CUPCAKE: CALORIES: 117; FAT: 1 G.; CHOLESTEROL: 2 MG.; SODIUM: 230 MG.; PROTEIN: 4 G.; CARBOHYDRATE: 23 G.

Too-Tasty-To-Be-No-Fat Chocolate Cake

Don Mauer

DON RECALLS, "Once low-fat was a permanent way of life for me, the search for great low- or no-fat chocolate treats began. This recipe is high on my favorite list." (From *Lean and Lovin' It!—A Lean Cook's Book* by Don Mauer, published by Don Mauer and Associates, 1993.)

Batter

⅓	cup plus 1 tablespoon unsweetened cocoa plus more for dusting pan
1	cup all-purpose flour
1	teaspoon baking powder
1	teaspoon baking soda
6	egg whites, at room temperature
1⅓	cups firmly packed dark brown sugar
1	cup nonfat plain yogurt
1	teaspoon vanilla

Topping

1	tablespoon unsweetened cocoa
1	tablespoon confectioners' sugar

1. Preheat oven to 350 degrees F. Assemble a 10-inch springform pan. Spray bottom and sides with nonstick cooking spray. Dust pan with cocoa; tap out excess.

2. *To prepare batter:* into a medium bowl, sift together cocoa, flour, baking powder and baking soda. Set aside.

3. In a large bowl, with an electric mixer, beat egg whites, brown sugar, yogurt and vanilla until blended, about 1 to 2 minutes on medium speed. Mix in dry ingredients by hand or on low mixer speed until just moistened. Do not overmix. (This is not a smooth batter.)

4. Pour batter into prepared pan and bake for about 35 minutes, or until a toothpick inserted in the center comes out clean. (If the pan is of different size, cooking time may vary.) Cool in the pan on a wire rack for 15 minutes. Then use a knife to loosen sides of cake from the

pan. Remove ring and cool completely on a rack. Serve cake on the metal bottom of the pan.

5. *To prpare topping:* in a small bowl, combine cocoa with confectioners' sugar. Place mixture in a small fine sieve and dust top of cake before serving.

Serves 10.

PER SERVING: CALORIES: 188; FAT: NEGLIGIBLE; CHOLESTEROL: 0 MG.; SODIUM: 231 MG.; PROTEIN: 5 G.; CARBOHYDRATE: 43 G.

Fruit-Filled Coffee Cake

Bonnie R.

WHEN I FIRST TASTED this wonderful-looking coffee cake, I couldn't believe that it had next to no fat in it. It's delicious, either for breakfast or as a dessert.

1	cup unsweetened applesauce
1	cup granulated sugar
1	egg plus 4 egg whites
3	cups all-purpose flour
1	tablespoon baking powder
2	teaspoons baking soda
1	cup fat-free sour cream
1	tablespoon vanilla
1	teaspoon almond extract
1	20-ounce can light pie filling (any flavor)
2	teaspoons ground cinnamon mixed with 2 tablespoons granulated sugar

1. Preheat oven to 350 degrees F. In a large bowl, mix applesauce and sugar with an electric mixer. Beat in egg and egg whites, one at a time.

2. In a separate bowl, sift flour, baking powder and baking soda. Beat these dry ingredients into applesauce mixture, alternating with sour cream. Add vanilla and almond extracts. Mix until combined, but don't overmix.

3. Spray a 12-cup Bundt pan with nonstick cooking spray, then lightly flour. Evenly distribute half the batter in pan.

4. Evenly distribute pie filling over batter. Top with remaining batter and sprinkle with cinnamon-sugar mixture. Bake for 50 to 60 minutes, or until a tester comes out clean. Let cool on a rack for 20 to 25 minutes before inverting and removing from pan. Cool completely on a rack. It keeps best in the refrigerator.

Serves 12.

PER SERVING: CALORIES: 271; FAT: NEGLIGIBLE; CHOLESTEROL: 18 MG.; SODIUM: 392 MG.; PROTEIN: 7 G.; CARBOHYDRATE: 59 G.

Banana Rum Crepes

Diane J.

BANANAS FOSTER IN A CREPE: a sensational low-fat dessert.

Crepes
1½	cups evaporated skim milk
1	cup all-purpose flour
1	egg plus 1 egg white
½	teaspoon finely grated lemon rind
2	tablespoons dark rum

Filling
¼	cup diet margarine
3	tablespoons light brown sugar
1	teaspoon finely grated lemon rind
½	teaspoon ground cinnamon
5-6	ripe bananas, peeled and sliced
¼	cup dark rum

Topping
¾	cup low-fat cottage cheese
3	tablespoons light brown sugar
1	teaspoon vanilla
½	teaspoon ground cinnamon

⅛   teaspoon ground nutmeg

1. *To make crepes:* combine all ingredients in a food processor and process until smooth. Let stand 1 hour. Heat a small nonstick pan coated with nonstick cooking spray and measure out enough batter to cover the base of the pan (about ¼ cup). Cook until small bubbles appear and surface is dull, then turn and cook other side for 1 minute. Transfer cooked crepe to a clean dishtowel and cover. Repeat with remaining batter, stacking cooked crepes on top of each other, keeping them covered with a towel.

2. *To make filling:* melt margarine in medium nonstick skillet. Add brown sugar, lemon rind and cinnamon. Stir until bubbling. Add bananas and toss lightly. Carefully averting face, add rum and ignite mixture; shake the pan gently until the flames die down, being careful not to spill mixture. When all flames are extinguished, divide banana mixture evenly among crepes, spooning mixture over one-fourth of crepe. Fold crepe in half over filling and in half again.

3. *To make topping:* combine all ingredients except nutmeg in blender and blend until smooth. Pour into a small serving bowl and dust with nutmeg.

4. Spoon warm or room-temperature topping over crepes.

Makes 12 crepes.

PER CREPE: CALORIES: 180; FAT: 4 G.; CHOLESTEROL: 20 MG.; SODIUM: 146 MG.; PROTEIN: 7 G.; CARBOHYDRATE: 29 G.

Berry-Cheese Torte

Diane J.

A CHEESECAKE-LIKE TORTE minus much of the fat and calories.
Topped with the sweetened berries, each bite melts in your mouth.

1	cup nonfat ricotta cheese
1	8-ounce package Neufchâtel cheese, at room temperature
3	eggs
½	cup plus 3 tablespoons granulated sugar
¼	cup cornstarch
1	teaspoon baking powder
1	teaspoon lemon rind
1	tablespoon freshly squeezed lemon juice
¼	cup jelly, jam or preserves (of a similar flavor to berries)
1½	cups blueberries, raspberries or sliced strawberries

1. Preheat oven to 350 degrees F. In a large bowl, with an electric
mixer, cream together ricotta cheese and Neufchâtel. Beat in eggs,
then sugar, until mixture is smooth.

2. In a small separate bowl, stir together cornstarch and baking
powder. Beat into cheese mixture along with lemon rind and lemon
juice.

3. Pour into a 9-to-10-inch springform pan, coated with nonstick
cooking spray. Bake about 45 minutes, or until firm in the middle.
Let cool for 10 to 15 minutes, loosen and remove sides of pan, then
refrigerate torte until chilled.

4. Shortly before serving, place jelly or preserves in a small
microwavable bowl and microwave for a short time, until melted, or
heat in a small saucepan over low heat. Pour over berries and stir gently. (With blueberries, you may need to add several teaspoons hot
water to thin jelly.) When jelly mixture is cool, top each serving of
torte with an equal amount of berry mixture.

Serves 8.

PER SERVING: CALORIES: 244; FAT: 9 G.; CHOLESTEROL: 103 MG.; SODIUM: 216 MG.;
PROTEIN: 9 G.; CARBOHYDRATE: 33 G.

The Jump-Start Diet

THE JUMP-START DIET IS ONE MEANS of getting started on the business of weight loss. It gives you a "jump start" because, in its early stages, it is quite aggressive so you lose some weight quickly and become motivated to proceed. Women may lose as many as 2 to 4 pounds the first week and 1 to 2 pounds a week thereafter; men may lose more. Part of that loss will be water. In addition, your rate of weight loss will be influenced by your age, the amount of exercise you engage in, your metabolic rate and the size of your body frame.

The calorie level for Week 1 is somewhat low. Thus I stress that Week 1 be followed for *no more than 7 days*. Still, provided that the guidelines below are followed, all stages of the Jump-Start Diet are designed to be safe for healthy people. The Jump-Start Diet is recommended for people who, like many of my former patients, do well on a fairly strict diet that initially limits choices and is easy to follow.

In accord with the masters who lost weight *their* way, the Jump-Start Diet soon becomes "customizable," so you can tailor it to meet your own needs and preferences.

If you've had it with diets, the Jump-Start Diet is not for you. This is particularly true if you struggle with a relatively small amount of weight—say, 10 to 20 pounds—or have a history of compulsive dieting or binge eating. In these cases, it's advisable to try one of the nondieting approaches to weight control, such as the 6-Week Nondieting Weight-Control Plan (page 109). Quite honestly, as a dietitian, I prefer that people lose weight by making an effort to increase exercise and cut back on fat intake. But some masters did find success with low-calorie diets, and you may find the Jump-Start Diet helpful to get you started. The important point is to realize that, in the long run, you have to come up with your own food plan for maintenance. Chapter IV offers guidelines for doing so.

Before starting this or any diet, be sure to get your physician's approval. If you currently have any medical problems and/or more than 20 pounds to lose, you should be monitored by your physician while on the diet. (Certain medication needs can change with weight loss.) If you feel weak or experience any physical changes while on the diet, such as constipation or diarrhea, stop the diet and consult your physician. (This diet is not meant for pregnant or breast-feeding women, children or teenagers or people with serious medical problems, such as diabetes.)

Approximate calorie levels for the Jump-Start Diet are as follows:

Week 1: women = 1,000 calories per day; men = 1,400 calories
Do not follow Week 1 for any longer than 7 days.
Week 2: women = 1,100 calories per day; men = 1,550 calories
Week 3: women = 1,200 calories per day; men = 1,600 calories
· (women and men add 300 optional calories per week from Special Foods)
Week 4: women = 1,250 calories per day; men = 1,700 calories (women and men add 500 optional calories per week from Special Foods)

If, at any time, you are uncomfortable or feel deprived with your calorie level, move to the next level of the diet (the level of the following week). It is important that you weigh or measure foods. Be sure to eat all recommended food servings from each food group. Foods may be distributed throughout the day as you please, but it is advised that you divide them among three meals or several meals and several snacks. (See sample meal plans starting on page 329.) *Be sure to increase your foods and calorie levels as recommended each week.* Once you complete Week 4, it would be wise to shift to a plan that focuses less on calorie counting and more on healthful, low-fat eating. Ultimately, most masters found it best to fill up on fruits, vegetables and grains, and cut back on fatty foods and flesh foods like red meat. Men in particular can cut back from 8 to 6 ounces of protein.

The logistics of the diet are quite simple:

◆ On Week 1, your choices are a limited selection of foods from various food groups. (Within any one food group, you can substitute foods in the portion size shown for each other.) Each day, you choose several small servings (6 to 8 ounces total) of protein foods, 4 to 5 servings of vegetables, 2 to 4 servings of complex-carbohydrate foods, 3 to 4 servings of fruit, 2 servings of milk products and up to several "extras," such as diet margarine or mayonnaise. (The number of servings depends on your gender.) Some serving sizes for fruits and vegetables used in the Jump-Start Diet differ from the "looser" serving sizes in the 6-Week Nondieting Weight-Control Plan. The purpose of the strict portion sizes is to ensure precise weekly caloric levels. For the same reason, a few vegetables appear on the list of complex-carbohydrate foods. Once you finish the Jump-Start Diet, however, you needn't be as rigid with fruit and vegetable serving sizes.

◆ On Week 2, for each day, you add a complex carbohydrate and an "extra," and the selection of foods on these lists expands so you have more options.

◆ On Week 3, for each day, you add an extra complex carbohydrate; the fruit list choices expand as well, and you get to add 3 weekly "treats" from the Special Foods Lists.

◆ On Week 4, for each day, women and men add yet another complex carbohydrate or an extra fruit, and there are more meat choices. In additional, you can add 5 Special Foods per week.

While you're on the diet . . .

◆ Take a daily multivitamin/mineral supplement.

◆ To meet the RDA for calcium, you may need to take a supplement containing about 600 milligrams of calcium for ages 19 to 24 and 200 milligrams for ages 25 plus.

◆ Be sure to drink at least 6 to 8 cups of noncaffeinated liquids each day. (Caffeinated beverages in moderation are fine, but they don't count to fulfill your fluid requirement because they act as diuretics.) It helps some people to curb their appetites if they drink a cup of water before each meal.

◆ Make a grocery list of foods you need to have on hand and stock up.

• Plan meals at least 1 day in advance.
• Read package labels to see if products you choose have the same calorie levels as those on various Jump-Start Diet lists.

WEEK 1

Choose foods from Lists 1-8 according to the amounts recommended for Women or Men. Any combination is acceptable.

LIST 1: PROTEIN FOODS
(average 50 calories per ounce)

Women: 6 ounces per day   **Men:** 8 ounces per day

1 ounce protein=   1 ounce skinless, boneless chicken or turkey meat (breast or leg)

1 ounce fish or shellfish, any type, fresh or frozen, unbreaded

1 ounce tuna, water-packed

1 ounce lean meat (beef eye of round, top round or tip round/pork tenderloin, boneless sirloin chop or boneless loin roast/veal chops or roast)

1 ounce low-fat luncheon meat (no more than 50 calories per ounce)

1 large egg (no more than 4 egg yolks per week)

3 egg whites

¼ cup no-cholesterol egg substitute

¼ cup cottage cheese or ricotta cheese (1% or nonfat)

½ cup cooked dry beans (also known as legumes: kidney beans, chickpeas, white beans, split or blackeyed peas, lentils or low-fat baked beans*)

*Dried beans contain about 80 to 100 calories per ½ cup cooked. But unlike most of the other protein foods, beans contain only a trace of fat, making them an excellent substitute for flesh foods. Most people will find ½ to 1 cup of beans—the protein equivalent of 1 to 2 ounces of meat—extremely filling.

Note: All meats, poultry and fish are weighed after cooking and are boneless and trimmed of all visible fat (4 ounces of raw meat will yield about 3 ounces of cooked meat). All foods are cooked without added fat by baking, roasting, steaming, grilling, broiling or pan-broiling in a nonstick pan with nonstick cooking spray.

LIST 2: VEGETABLE "A" LIST
(20 calories or less per serving)

Women: 2 to 3 servings per day   **Men:** 3 servings per day

1 serving =   1 cup raw or ½ cup cooked shredded cabbage (any
                      type, including Chinese)

                   1 cup celery

                   ½ large cucumber

                   2 cups shredded lettuce (any type, preferably dark green)

                   1 cup raw or ½ cup cooked, sliced mushrooms

                   1 green, red or yellow bell pepper

                   20 radishes

                   1½ cups raw or ½ cups cooked, chopped spinach

                   1 cup raw or ½ cup cooked bean sprouts

                   1 cup raw or ½ cup cooked, sliced zucchini

LIST 3: VEGETABLE "B" LIST
(approximately 25 calories per serving)

Women: 2 servings per day   **Men:** 2 servings per day

Vegetables may be fresh, frozen or canned (which are higher in sodium).
Do not use any added fats or sauces, other than allowed fats. Unless noted otherwise,
1 serving = 1 cup raw or ½ cup cooked of any of the following vegetables:

Artichoke *(½ medium)*	Cauliflower	Tomato juice or
Asparagus	Eggplant	vegetable-juice
Beans *(green, yellow,*	Okra	cocktail *(½ cup)*
Italian)	Onions	Tomato sauce *(⅓ cup)*
Beets	Pea pods	Reduced-fat spaghetti
Broccoli	Sauerkraut	sauce *(¼ cup)*
Brussels sprouts	Summer squash	Turnips
Carrots	Tomato *(1 large)*	Water chestnuts

LIST 4: COMPLEX-CARBOHYDRATE FOODS
(approximately 80 calories per serving)

Women: 2 servings per day   **Men:** 4 servings per day

1 serving=

- 1 slice (1 ounce) regular bread (preferably whole-grain)
- 2 slices diet or "lite" bread (no more than 40 calories per slice)
- ¾ cup flake-type cereal, preferably high-fiber
- 1½ cups puffed cereal
- ½ cup shredded wheat
- ½ cup cooked cereal (unsweetened)
- 1 small potato, baked, boiled or mashed
- ½ cup cooked pasta
- 2 rice cakes

LIST 5: FRUITS
(approximately 60 calories per serving)

Women: 3 servings per day   **Men:** 4 servings per day

1 serving=

- 1 apple, 2 inches across
- ½ banana (9-inch)
- cantaloupe, one-third of a 5-inch melon or 1 cup cubes
- ½ medium grapefruit
- 15 small grapes
- 1 orange (2½-inch)
- 1 peach or nectarine (2¾-inch)
- ½ large or 1 small pear
- ¾ cup raw pineapple or ⅓ cup canned (in its own juice)
- 1 cup raw, whole strawberries
- ½ cup juice: apple, grapefruit, orange or pineapple

LIST 6: MILK PRODUCTS
(approximately 100 calories per serving)

Women: 2 servings per day   **Men:** 2 servings per day

1 serving=   1 cup skim or 1% milk

½ cup evaporated skim milk (some people prefer this to
    skim milk in coffee)

1 cup nonfat plain yogurt or "lite" yogurt (no more than
    100 calories per cup)

1½-2 ounces reduced-fat cheese (no more than 50
    calories per ounce)

LIST 7: EXTRAS
(approximately 35-45 calories per serving)

Women: 1 serving per day   **Men:** 3 servings per day

1 serving=   1 tablespoon diet margarine

1 teaspoon regular margarine

1 tablespoon reduced-fat mayonnaise

5 tablespoons nonfat mayonnaise (free, up to
    2 tablespoons)

35-45 calories reduced-calorie liquid salad dressing
    (check label)

4 tablespoons nonfat liquid salad dressing (no more than
    10 calories per tablespoon; free, up to 2 tablespoons)

1 teaspoon vegetable or olive oil

LIST 8: FREE FOODS
Unlimited amounts allowed.

Beverages   water

sugar-free soft drinks

carbonated water

black coffee or tea

sugar-free drink mixes

bouillon or broth (preferably reduced-sodium), without fat

Flavoring agents   sugar substitutes (aspartame, saccharin)

low-calorie butter-flavoring products

lemon or lime juice

flavoring extracts (vanilla, almond, etc.)

herbs and spices

horseradish

marinades (not as a sauce—just to marinate protein foods)

salsa (up to ⅓ cup)

soy or Worcestershire sauce (high in sodium, but there are
  reduced-sodium soy sauces)

mustard

vinegar

garlic

Miscellaneous   nonstick cooking spray

sugar-free gelatin (no more than 1 envelope per day)

sugar-free gum (up to 5 sticks per day)

unsweetened pickles (high in sodium)

WEEK 2

**Now, the Jump-Start Diet becomes more customizable, with
choices in the Complex-Carbohydrate List and Extras List
expanding. Continue to eat recommended servings from
all food groups for Week 1, but add
1 additional Complex Carbohydrate per day
1 additional Extra per day**

ADDITIONAL COMPLEX CARBOHYDRATES
You may add the following choices to List 4, page 322.

1 serving =   ½ bagel (1 ounce)

½ English muffin

½ hamburger or hot dog roll (or 1 low-calorie roll—
  no more than 80 calories)

1 small pita bread (1 ounce)

1 slice raisin bread

1 pancake (4-to-5-inch)

1 frozen fat-free waffle

6-inch tortilla

3 graham cracker squares

¾ ounce matzoh

5 slices melba toast

24 oyster crackers

¾ ounce pretzels

6 Saltines

2-4 (¾ ounce) nonfat whole-wheat crackers

½ cup cooked white or brown rice

½ cup cooked bulgur

½ cup cooked grits

3 tablespoons wheat germ

½ cup corn

1 ear corn (6-inch)

½ cup lima beans

½ cup peas

1 cup winter squash

⅓ cup yam or sweet potato

ADDITIONAL EXTRAS

You may add the following choices to List 7, page 323.

1 serving =

⅛ medium avocado

10 small or 5 large olives

35-45 calories' worth low-fat or nonfat sour-cream substitute

35-45 calories' worth cream-cheese product (e.g., ½ ounce
Neufchâtel or 2 ounces fat-free cream-cheese product)

2 tablespoons reduced-calorie maple-flavored syrup

1 tablespoon jam, jelly or preserves

2 tablespoons grated Parmesan cheese

WEEK 3

Continue to eat all the foods from Weeks 1 and 2, but add:
1 additional Complex Carbohydrate per day

ADDITIONAL FRUITS
You may add the following choices to List 5, page 322.

1 serving =
- ½ cup applesauce (no sugar added)
- 4 apricots
- ¾ cup blackberries or blueberries
- 12 large cherries
- ⅛ medium or 1 cup cubed honeydew melon
- 1 large kiwi
- ½ small mango
- 1 cup papaya
- 2 plums (each 2-inch)
- 1 cup raspberries
- 2 tangerines
- 1¼ cups watermelon cubes
- dried fruit: 4 apple rings, 7 apricot halves, 2½ medium dates, 3 medium prunes, 2 tablespoons raisins

Optional (women and men): you may have 3 Special Foods this week (see below) or you may have an additional 300 calories' worth of foods from any of the Jump-Start food lists.

SPECIAL FOODS LISTS

On Weeks 3 and 4, you may have some Special Foods. The foods on these lists, in the amounts shown, have between 70 and 100 calories each. Check product labels to be certain of 100-calorie (or less) serving sizes. If desired, you may save up your weekly 300- or 500-calorie allotments of Special Foods and spend them in one or two sittings each week.

For Your Sweet Tooth
1 ounce jelly beans
1 ounce marshmallows

1 ounce Good n' Plenty

1 ounce candy corn

1 ounce licorice (any type)

1 ounce gum drops

3 Hershey's Kisses

3 Tootsie Roll Midgies

½ ounce sweet or semisweet chocolate chips

1 small (1¼-ounce) muffin

8 animal crackers

1-ounce slice fat-free pound cake

4 ounces reduced-calorie pudding

1 low-calorie popsicle or ice cream sandwich

6 ounces Italian ice

½ cup frozen nonfat dessert or ice milk

½ cup frozen nonfat yogurt

⅓ cup sherbet

1 Fig Newton

3 ginger snaps

5 vanilla wafers

1 reduced-calorie brownie

2 half-ounce chocolate chip cookies

1½ Nabisco Snackwell's Oatmeal-Raisin Cookies

2 Nabisco Snackwell's Devil's Food Cookie Cakes

2 Oreos

For Your Salty Tooth

10 Pringles Light Chips

12 Pretzel Chips

⅓ cup chow-mein noodles

3 cups light microwave popcorn

10 low-salt Wheat Thins

33 Pepperidge Farm Goldfish Tiny Crackers

27 Nabisco Snackwell's Cheese Crackers

18 regular cheese snack crackers

½ cup Ralston Traditional Chex Mix

Alcoholic Beverages
1 "lite" beer
1 shot hard liquor (80-proof)
4 ounces dry white or red wine

Note: Items on Special Foods lists are representative of products available at time of writing. You may substitute 100-calorie portions of similar foods.

WEEK 4

Continue to eat all foods from Weeks 1, 2 and 3, but add 1 additional Complex Carbohydrate OR 1 additional Fruit per day

ADDITIONAL PROTEIN FOODS
You may add the following choices to List 1, page 320.
Follow preparation guidelines from Week 1. (Since these foods tend to be higher in fat and/or sodium, it's wise to limit yourself to no more than several 2-to-3-ounce servings of them per week.)

1 ounce protein = 1 ounce sirloin steak
 1 ounce flank steak
 1 ounce beef tenderloin
 1 ounce extra-lean ground beef
 1 ounce lean ham
 1 ounce Canadian bacon
 1 ounce of reduced-fat hot dog (no more than 50 calories per ounce)
 2 medium sardines, canned in tomato sauce or mustard
 2 tablespoons peanut butter (100 calories per tablespoon— it's wise to limit yourself to no more than 4 tablespoons per week)

Optional (women and men): You may have 5 Special Foods this week, or you may have an additional 500 calories' worth of foods from any of the Jump-Start food lists.

Sample Meal Plans

WEEK 1
(example for 1 day)

	Food List
Breakfast	
¾ cup bran flakes	1 carbohydrate
1 cup skim milk	1 milk
½ banana, sliced	1 fruit
½ cup orange juice	1 fruit
Men: add 1 slice whole-wheat toast	1 carbohydrate
1 teaspoon margarine	1 extra
Lunch	
Sandwich:	
2 slices low-calorie bread	1 carbohydrate
3 ounces smoked turkey breast	3 protein
Dijon-style mustard to taste	free
½ sliced tomato	½ vegetable B
1 yellow or red bell pepper, cut in strips	1 vegetable A
Men: use regular bread	2 carbohydrate
increase turkey to 4 ounces	4 protein
add 2 tablespoons reduced-calorie dressing	1 extra
for dipping pepper	
Snack (anytime)	
½ cup plain yogurt mixed with	½ milk
½ cup strawberries, sliced,	½ fruit
and sugar-free sweetener	free

	Food List
Supper	
Baked cod with cheese and tomatoes:	
4 ounces uncooked cod	3 protein (when cooked)
1 ounce reduced-fat grated or sliced	½ milk
Swiss cheese	
½ tomato, sliced	½ vegetable B
2 cups shredded romaine lettuce	1 vegetable A
with 2 tablespoons reduced-calorie	1 extra
ranch dressing	
½ cup steamed spinach with lemon	1 vegetable A
juice and nutmeg	
½ cup steamed carrots	1 vegetable B
Men: increase cod to 5 ounces (raw)	4 protein (when cooked)

Dessert or Bedtime Snack

Women: 8 grapes	½ fruit
in sugar-free gelatin dessert	free
Men: 23 grapes	1½ fruit
in sugar-free gelatin dessert	free

WEEK 2

(example for 1 day)

Food List

Breakfast

½ English muffin topped with	1 carbohydrate
1 tablespoon strawberry jam	1 extra
1 poached egg	1 protein
½ medium grapefruit	1 fruit
Men: increase English muffin to 1 whole	2 carbohydrate
add 1 teaspoon margarine	1 extra

Lunch

Slim sub:

1 low-calorie hot dog roll	1 carbohydrate
1½ ounces low-fat cheese	1 milk
1 ounce low-fat luncheon meat	1 protein
½ sliced tomato	½ vegetable B
lettuce leaves	free
sprinkling of chopped onion	free
dill pickle chips	free

Crunchy salad:

⅓ cup celery, ¼ large cucumber (sliced), ⅓ cup bean sprouts	1 vegetable A
½ cup chickpeas	1 protein
tossed with 2 tablespoons low-calorie Italian salad dressing	1 extra
Men: use regular hot dog roll	2 carbohydrate
increase lunch meat to 3 ounces	3 protein
add 1 tablespoon reduced-fat mayonnaise to sub	1 extra

Food List

Snack (anytime)

Banana shake—whip in blender until smooth:

½ banana	1 fruit
1 cup skim or low-fat milk	1 milk
sugar-free sweetener to taste	free
½ teaspoon vanilla	free
several ice cubes	

Supper

Steak stir-fry:

4 ounces top round steak, cut in strips	3 protein (when cooked)
and sautéed with 1 crushed garlic clove	free
in 3 tablespoons defatted beef broth	free
When meat is almost done,	
add raw vegetables:	
1 cup Chinese cabbage	1 vegetable A
1 cup sliced mushrooms	1 vegetable A
1 cup broccoli florets	1 vegetable B
½ cup pea pods	½ vegetable B
Cover and steam until vegetables are	
tender-crisp—just a few minutes.	
Sprinkle with soy sauce to taste.	
½ cup cooked white or brown rice	1 carbohydrate

Bedtime snack or dessert

Women: 1 small pear	1 fruit
Men: 1 large pear	2 fruit

WEEK 3

(example for 1 day)

	Food List
Breakfast	
2 pancakes (4-to-5-inch) with	2 carbohydrate
2 tablespoons reduced-calorie	1 extra
maple syrup	
⅓ cantaloupe	1 fruit
1 cup skim milk	1 milk
Men: increase maple syrup to	2 extra
4 tablespoons	
add ½ cup egg substitute	2 protein
scrambled in nonstick pan	
Lunch	
Tuna sandwich:	
2 slices diet bread	2 carbohydrate
3 ounces water-packed tuna	3 protein
1 tablespoon reduced-calorie mayonnaise	1 extra
chopped celery and onion to taste	free
1 cup mixed raw carrot coins and	1 vegetable B
cauliflower florets dipped in	free
Dijon-style mustard	
1 tangerine	½ fruit
Men: use 2 slices regular bread	2 carbohydrate
increase mayonnaise to 2 tablespoons	2 extra
have 1 orange instead of tangerine	1 fruit
Snack (anytime)	
Crunchy cucumber hors d'oeuvres—serve one on top of the next:	
1 ounce low-fat Cheddar cheese, sliced thin	½ milk
½ cucumber, sliced	1 vegetable A
10 low-salt Wheat Thins	1 special food

	Food List

Supper

Chicken tortilla:

    4 ounces boneless, skinless chicken breast — 3 protein (when cooked)

        *Cut in strips, marinated in fat-free
Italian salad dressing and sautéed in
nonstick skillet with nonstick cooking spray
When chicken is done, add raw vegetables:*

    1 green bell pepper, cut in strips — 1 vegetable A

    1 cup sliced onion — 1 vegetable B

        *Cover and steam until vegetables are
done to your liking. Serve open-face on*

    1 tortilla with — 1 carbohydrate

    1 ounce shredded low-fat Monterey
      Jack cheese — ½ milk

    salsa to taste — free

1½ cups spinach salad with — 1 vegetable A

    2 tablespoons fat-free French dressing — free

Men: increase tortillas to 2 — 2 carbohydrate

Bedtime Snack or Dessert

Women: 18 bing cherries — 1½ fruit

Men: 24 bing cherries — 2 fruit

WEEK 4
(example for 1 day)

	Food List
Breakfast	
1 cup cooked oatmeal made with	2 carbohydrate
½ cup skim milk and	½ milk
1 tablespoon raisins	½ fruit
⅛ honeydew melon	1 fruit
Men: increase raisins to 2 tablespoons	1 fruit
Lunch	
2-ounce reduced-fat hot dog	2 protein
1 low-calorie hot dog roll with	1 carbohydrate
mustard	free
½ cup low-fat baked beans	1 protein
(no more than 1 gram of fat per ½ cup)	
1 cup raw, shredded cabbage mixed with	1 vegetable A
2 tablespoons reduced-calorie ranch dressing	1 extra
1 cup skim or low-fat milk	1 milk
Snack (anytime)	
Fruit kebabs—alternate on toothpicks:	
1 ounce reduced-fat Cheddar cheese,	½ milk
in small cubes	
8 grapes	½ fruit
1 nectarine, cubed	1 fruit
Men: increase grapes to 15	1 fruit

	Food List

Supper

4 ounces raw flank steak, marinated in teriyaki sauce, grilled or broiled, sliced thin	3 protein (when cooked)

Ratatouille:

Cut all vegetables in ½-inch-thick slices and marinate in fat-free Italian salad dressing.

1 cup zucchini	1 vegetable A
3 slices eggplant	½ vegetable B
1 large tomato	1 vegetable B
½ large onion	½ vegetable B

Broil or grill, then serve layered.

Pesto pasta:

1 cup cooked pasta spirals	2 carbohydrate
seasoned with basil and crushed garlic or garlic powder	free
2 cups shredded bibb or leaf lettuce with	1 vegetable A
2 tablespoons reduced-calorie blue-cheese dressing	1 extra

Men: increase flank steak to 6 ounces	5 protein
increase pasta to 1½ cups and add	3 carbohydrate
1 teaspoon olive oil	1 extra
add 5 large olives to salad	1 extra

Bedtime snack or dessert

1 low-calorie brownie	1 special food
½ cup vanilla ice milk	1 special food

SELECTED REFERENCES

Andersen, R. E. (1991). Helping clients begin an exercise program. *The Weight Control Digest*, 1(6), 91-93.

Bartlett, S. J. (1992). Helping your clients who binge. *The Weight Control Digest*, 2(2), 148-150.

Beliard, D., Kirschenbaum, D. S., & Fitzgibbon, M. L. (1992). Evaluation of an intensive weight control program using *a priori* criteria to determine outcome. *International Journal of Obesity*, 16, 505-517.

Blackburn, G. L., Wilson, G. T., Kanders, B. S., Stein, L. J., Lavin, P. T., Adler, J., & Brownell, K. D. (1989). Weight cycling: The experience of human dieters. *American Journal of Clinical Nutrition*, 49, 1105-1109.

Bray, G. A., York, B., & DeLany, J. (1992). A survey of the opinions of obesity experts on the causes and treatment of obesity. *American Journal of Clinical Nutrition*, 55, 151S-154S.

Brownell, K. D. (1990). Dieting readiness. *The Weight Control Digest*, 1(1), 1, 5-9.

Brownell, K. D. (1990). *The LEARN program for weight control.* Dallas: Brownell & Hager Publishing Company.

Brownell, K. D., & Jeffery, R. W. (1987). Improving long-term weight loss: Pushing the limits of treatment. *Behavior Therapy*, 18, 353-374.

Brownell, K. D., Marlatt, G. A., Lichtenstein, E., & Wilson, G. T. (1986). Understanding and preventing relapse. *American Psychologist*, 41(7), 765-782.

Brownell, K. D., & Rodin, J. (1990). *The weight maintenance survival guide.* Dallas: Brownell & Hager Publishing Company.

Brownell, K. D., & Wadden, T. A. (1991). The heterogeneity of obesity: Fitting treatments to individuals. *Behavior Therapy*, 22, 153-177.

Brownell, K. D., & Wadden, T. A. (1992). Etiology and treatment of obesity: Understanding a serious, prevalent, and refractory disorder. *Journal of Consulting and Clinical Psychology*, 60(4), 505-517.

Cash, T. F. (1992). Body images and body weight: What is there to gain or lose? *The Weight Control Digest*, 2(4), 169, 172-176.

Colvin, R. H., & Olson, S. C. (1983). A descriptive analysis of men and women who have lost significant weight and are highly successful at maintaining the loss. *Addictive Behaviors*, 8, 287-295.

Colvin, R. H., & Olson, S. C. (1984). Winners revisited: An 18-month follow-up of our successful weight losers. *Addictive Behaviors*, 9, 305-306.

Colvin, R. H., & Olson, S. C. (1989). *Keeping it off.* Arkansas City, KS: Gilliland.

Cornyn-Selby, A. P. (1989). *Alyce's fat chance.* Portland, OR: Beynch Press Publishing Co.

Duncan, K. H., Bacon, J. A., & Weinsier, R. L. (1983). The effects of high and low energy density diets on satiety, energy intake, and eating time of obese and nonobese subjects. *American Journal of Clinical Nutrition*, 37, 763-767.

Dwyer, J. T., & Lu, D. (1993). Popular diets for weight loss from nutritionally hazardous to healthful. In A. J. Stunkard & T. A. Wadden (Eds.), *Obesity: Theory and therapy* (2nd ed.) (pp. 231-252). New York: Raven Press, Ltd.

Ferguson, K. J., Brink, P. J., Wood, M., & Koop, P. M. (1992). Characteristics of successful dieters as measured by guided interview responses and restraint scale scores. *Journal of the American Dietetic Association*, 92(9), 1119-1121.

Fitzgibbon, M. L., & Kirschenbaum, D. S. (1992). Who succeeds in losing weight? In J. D. Fisher, J. Chinsky, Y. Klan, & A. Nadler (Eds.), *Initiating self-changes: Social psychological and clinical perspectives* (pp. 153-175). New York: Springer-Verlag.

Foreyt, J. P., & Goodrick, G. K. (1991). Choosing the right weight management program. *The Weight Control Digest*, 1(6), 81, 84-90.

Foreyt, J. P., & Goodrick, G. K. (1991). Factors common to successful therapy for the obese patient. *Medicine and Science in Sports and Exercise*, 23(3), 292-297.

Foreyt, J. P., & Goodrick, G. K. (1992). *Living without dieting.*

Houston: Harrison Publishing.

Foster, G. D. (1990). Causes of obesity: Genetics. *The Weight Control Digest,* 1(1), 11-12.

Foster, G. D. (1991). Causes of obesity: Resting metabolic rate. *The Weight Control Digest,* 1(3), 42-44.

Ganley, R. M. (1989). Emotion and eating in obesity: A review of the literature. *International Journal of Eating Disorders,* 8(3), 343-361.

Gavin, J. (1992). *The exercise habit.* Champaign, IL: Leisure Press.

Goodrick, G. K., & Foreyt, J. P. (1991). Why treatments for obesity don't last. *Journal of the American Dietetic Association,* 91(10), 1243-1247.

Grilo, C. M., & Brownell, K. D. (1993). Relapse: Why, how, and what to do about it. *The Weight Control Digest,* 3(1), 217, 220-224.

Grilo, C. M., Brownell, K. D., & Stunkard, A. J. (1993). The metabolic and psychological importance of exercise in weight control. In A. J. Stunkard & T. A. Wadden (Eds.), *Obesity: Theory and therapy* (2nd ed.) (pp. 253-273). New York: Raven Press, Ltd.

Grilo, C. M., Shiffman, S., & Wing, R. R. (1989). Relapse crises and coping among dieters. *Journal of Consulting and Clinical Psychology,* 57(4), 488-495.

Grilo, C. M., Wilfley, D. E., & Brownell, K. D. (1992). Physical activity and weight control: Why is the link so strong? *The Weight Control Digest,* 2(3), 153, 157-160.

Have you been doing the other kind of exercise? (1993, July). *Tufts University Diet & Nutrition Letter.* pp. 3-6.

Heppner, P. P. (1983). Strategies for facilitating client's personal problem solving. In P. A. Keller & L. G. Ritt (Eds.), *Innovations in clinical practice: A source book. Volume 2* (pp. 73-85). Sarasota, Florida: Professional Resource Exchange, Inc.

Home exercise equipment. (1992, December). *University of California at Berkeley Wellness Letter,* pp. 4-5.

Jeffery, R. W., Bjornson-Benson, W. M., Rosenthal, B. S., Lindquist, R. A., Kurth, C. L., & Johnson, S. L. (1984). Correlates of weight loss and its maintenance over two years of follow-up among middle-aged men. *Preventive Medicine*, 13, 155-168.

Kayman, S., Bruvold, W., & Stern, J. S. (1990). Maintenance and relapse after weight loss in women: Behavioral aspects. *The American Journal of Clinical Nutrition*, 52, 800-807.

Kendall, A., Levitsky, D. A., Strupp, B. J., & Lissner, L. (1991). Weight loss on a low-fat diet: Consequence of the imprecision of the control of food intake in humans. *The American Journal of Clinical Nutrition*, 53, 1124-1129.

Kirschenbaum, D. S., Fitzgibbon, M.L., Martino, S., Conviser, J. H., Rosendahl, E. H., & Laatsch, L. (1992). Stages of change in successful weight control: A clinically derived model. *Behavior Therapy*, 23, 623-635.

Kreitler, S., & Chemerinski, A. (1988). The cognitive orientation of obesity. *International Journal of Obesity*, 12, 403-415.

Lichtman, S. W., Pisarska, K., Berman, E. R., Pestone, M., Dowling, H., Offenbacher, E., Weisel, H., Heshka, S., Matthews, D. E., & Heymsfield, S. B. (1992) . Discrepancy between self-reported and actual caloric intake and exercise in obese subjects. *The New England Journal of Medicine*, 327(27), 1893-1898.

Losing weight: What works. What doesn't. (1993, June). *Consumer Reports*, pp. 347-359.

Mahoney, M. J., & Mahoney, K. (1976). *Permanent weight control: A total solution to the dieter's dilemma.* New York: W. W. Norton & Company.

Marcoux, B. C., Trenkner, L. L., & Rosenstock, I. M. (1990). Social networks and social support in weight loss. *Patient Education and Counseling*, 15, 229-238.

Martin, J. E., Dubbert, P. M., Katell, A. D., Thompson, J. K., Raczynski, J. R., Lake, M., Smith, P. O., Webster, J. S., Sikora, T., & Cohen, R. E. (1984). Behavioral control of exercise in sedentary adults: Studies 1 through 6. *Journal of Consulting and Clinical Psychology*, 52(5), 795-811.

Mason, E. E., & Doherty, C. (1993). Surgery. In A. J. Stunkard & T.

A. Wadden (Eds.), *Obesity: Theory and therapy* (2nd ed.) (pp. 313-325). New York: Raven Press, Ltd.

Myers, D.G. (1989). *Psychology*. New York: Worth Publishers, Inc.

Morton, C. J. (1988). Weight loss maintenance and relapse prevention. In R. T. Frankle & M. Yang (Eds.), *Obesity and weight control* (pp. 315-332). Rockville: Aspen Publishers, Inc.

Nash, J. D. (1992). *Now that you've lost it.* Palo Alto: Bull Publishing Co.

NIH Technology Assessment Conference Panel (1992). Methods for voluntary weight loss and control. *Annals of Internal Medicine*, 116(11), 942-949.

'No sweat' guide to designing a fitness plan. (1992, April). *Tufts University Diet & Nutrition Letter*, pp. 3-6.

O'Neil, P. M., & Jarrell, M. P. (1992). Psychological aspects of obesity and dieting. In T. A. Wadden & T. B. VanItallie (Eds.), *Treatment of the seriously obese patient* (pp. 252-270). New York: Guilford Publications, Inc.

Peele, S., & Brodsky, A. (1991). *The truth about addiction and recovery*. New York: Simon & Schuster.

Perri, M. G. (1992). Weight maintenance strategies: The process and the practice. *The Weight Control Digest*, 2(6), 201, 204-207.

Perri, M. G., & Nezu, A. M. (1993). Preventing relapse following treatment for obesity. In A. J. Stunkard & T. A. Wadden (Eds.), *Obesity: Theory and therapy* (2nd ed.) (pp. 287-299). New York: Raven Press, Ltd.

Perri, M. G., Sears, S. F., & Clark, J. E. (1993). Strategies for improving the maintenance of weight loss: Toward a continuous care model of obesity management. *Diabetes Care*, 16(1), 200-209.

Polivy, J., & Herman, C. P. (1983). *Breaking the diet habit*. New York: Basic Books, Inc.

Prewitt, T. E., Schmeisser, D., Bowen, P. E., Aye, P., Dolecek, T. E., Langenberg, P. Cole, T., & Brace, L. (1991). Changes in body weight, body composition, and energy intake in women fed high- and low-fat diets. *American Journal of Clinical Nutrition*, 54, 304-310.

Rand, C. S. W., & Macgregor, A. M. C. (1991). Successful weight loss following obesity surgery and the perceived liability of morbid obesity. *International Journal of Obesity*, 15, 577-579.

Ravussin, E., Lillioja, S., Knowler, W. C., Christin, L., Freymond, D., Abbott, W. G. H., Boyce, V., Howard, B. V., & Bogardus, C. (1988). Reduced rate of energy expenditure as a risk factor for body-weight gain. *The New England Journal of Medicine*, 318(8), 467-472.

Ravussin, E., & Swinburn, B. A. (1993). Energy metabolism. In A. J. Stunkard & T. A. Wadden (Eds.), *Obesity: Theory and therapy* (2nd ed.) (pp. 97-123). New York: Raven Press, Ltd.

The recommended quantity and quality of exercise for developing and maintaining cardiorespiratory and muscular fitness in healthy adults. (1990). *American College of Sports Medicine*, pp.3-5.

Ross, S. T. (1985). *The process of personal change: A case study of adults who have maintained weight loss.* Unpublished doctoral dissertation, Northern Illinois University.

Schachter, S. (1982, August). Don't sell habit-breakers short. *Psychology Today*, pp. 27-33.

Schachter, S. (1982). Recidivism and self-cure of smoking and obesity. *American Psychologist*, 37(4), 436-444.

Shapiro, L. J. & Associates (1992). "National study of Weight Watchers leaders." Chicago: Leo J. Shapiro and Associates.

Sheldahl, L. M. (1986). Special ergometric techniques and weight reduction. *Medicine and Science in Sports and Exercise*, 18(1), 25-30.

St. Jeor, S., & Dwyer, J. T. (1991). Optimal diet: Does it exist? *The Weight Control Digest*, 1(7), 97, 100-109.

Strecher, V. J., DeVellis, B. M., Becker, M. H., & Rosenstock, I. M. (1986). The role of self-efficacy in achieving health behavior change. *Health Education Quarterly*, 13(1), 73-92.

Strength training for everyone. (1991, November). *University of California at Berkeley Wellness Letter*, pp. 4-5.

Wadden, T. A., & Bell, S. T. (1990). Obesity. In A. S. Bellack, M.

Hersen & A. E. Kazdin (Eds.), *International handbook of behavior modification and therapy* (2nd ed.) (pp. 449-473). New York: Plenum Publishing Corporation.

Wadden, T. A., & Kuehnel, R. H. (1993). Very-low-calorie diets: Reappraisal and recommendations. *The Weight Control Digest*, 3(4), 265, 268-270.

Wadden, T. A., & Stunkard, A. J. (1988). Three year follow-up of the treatment of obesity by very-low-calorie diet, behavior therapy, and their combination. *Journal of Consulting and Clinical Psychology*, 56, 925-928.

Webster, J. D., & Garrow, J. S. (1989). Weight loss in 108 obese women on a diet supplying 800 kcal/d for 21 d. *American Journal of Clinical Nutrition*, 50, 41-45.

Wesley, S. M. (1992). *Overcoming an addiction*. El Sobrante, CA.

Willis, J. D., & Campbell, L. F. (1992). *Exercise psychology*. Champaign, IL: Human Kinetics Publishers.

Wing, R. R. (1992). Binge eating among the overweight population. *The Weight Control Digest*, 2(2), 137, 142-144.

Wing, R. R., & Jeffery, R. W. (1978). Successful losers: A descriptive analysis of the process of weight reduction. *Obesity/Bariatric Medicine*, 7(5), 190-191.

Wing, R. R. (1992). Weight cycling in humans: A review of the literature. *Annals of Behavioral Medicine*, 14(2), 113-119.

Wolfe, B. L. (1992). Long-term maintenance following attainment of goal weight: A preliminary investigation. *Addictive Behaviors*, 17, 469-477.

Wolfe, B. L., & Marlatt, G. A. (1992). Reframing relapse: From endpoint to turning point. *The Weight Control Digest*, 2(5), 185, 188-193.

GENERAL INDEX

Kaiser Permanente Medical
Center, 66, 96, 148, 178,
204-05, 236, 259
National Institutes of Health,
30-31
in *New England Journal of
Medicine*, 30, 101-02
by Schachter, Stanley, 23
University of Alabama, 94
University of Florida, 74, 250-51
University of Iowa, 25-26, 67,
207
University of Minnesota, 25, 252
University of Pennsylvania, 31,
78
by Wadden, Thomas, and Albert
Stunkard, 24
by Wadden, Thomas, and Robert
Kuehnel, 76
of weight cycling, 33
of weight training plus aerobic
exercise, 190
Yale University, 148, 196, 262
Stunkard, Albert J., 18, 24
Substitutions for high-fat foods,
116-18, 121-22
Sugar and other sweeteners, 110
Support
lack of, 261-63
systems, 250-64
Surgery to lose weight, 79-80
Swimming, 189-90
Take Off Pounds Sensibly (TOPS),
64, 258
Thin people, eating habits of, 96
Thought-stopping, 164
Time required to meet weight-loss
goals, 73-75
Trade-offs, food, 97-99
*Truth About Addiction and Recovery,
The*, 57-58, 161, 210
*Tufts University Diet & Nutrition
Letter*, 187, 188
University of Alabama study, 94
University of Florida studies, 74,
250-51
University of Iowa, 25-26, 67, 207

University of Minnesota studies, 25,
252
University of Pennsylvania studies,
31, 78
Vegetables, 114-15
Vertical banded gastroplasty, 79
Very-low-calorie diets (VLCDs),
75-76, 81
Wadden, Thomas, 24, 25, 27, 49, 51,
52, 76, 93, 136, 255
Waist-to-hip ratio, 53-54
Walking, 187-88
Warning signs, and need for support,
256
Water, minimum daily requirements
for, 77
Weight buffer zone, 139
Weight control. *See also* Diets;
Maintenance; Weight loss
exercise and, 20
plan, 6-week nondieting, 109-16
Weight Control Digest, 31, 68, 143,
219
Weight cycling, 33
Weight as a defense, 47-48
Weight gain(s)
genetic factors in, 29-32, 52
after loss, 22
reversing small, 136
Weight loss. *See also* Diets;
Maintenance
age as factor in, 21
approaches to, 21, 71-73
and attitude(s), 44-49
behavior modification for,
102-04
calories and, 77-79
eating habits for, 100-02
exercise and, 177-200
failure before success in, 19-20
fallacies about, 19-23
fat reduction and, 91-96, 106-08,
109-23
goals for, 22-23, 34, 51-53, 72
gradual, 50
health benefits of, 32, 51
honesty as factor in, 43

349

RECIPE INDEX